Studies in Social Ecology and Pathology
General Editor: NIGEL WALKER

The Wincroft Youth Project

Studies in Social Ecology and Pathology

The Wincroft Youth Project
A SOCIAL-WORK PROGRAMME IN A SLUM AREA

Cyril S. Smith

M. R. Farrant

H. J. Marchant

TAVISTOCK PUBLICATIONS

*First published in 1972
by Tavistock Publications Limited
11 New Fetter Lane, London EC 4
Typeset in Great Britain
in IBM Press Roman
by Santype Ltd. (Coldtype Division)
Salisbury, Wiltshire
Printed in Great Britain by
The Redwood Press, Trowbridge,
Wiltshire, England*

SBN 422 73760 7

Distributed in the USA by
HARPER & ROW PUBLISHERS, INC.
BARNES & NOBLE IMPORT DIVISION

Contents

Figures

Tables

Youth Development Trust Committee 1964-70

Preface

This book is an account of an attempt by social scientists and social workers to come to grips with one of the principal preoccupations of the present day: the challenge to law and order presented by the young. It gives reasonable ground for hope that the bold measures of penal reform in the last few years can, with proper resources, be made to work. It offers a detailed documentation of a pilot scheme that affords a basis for much wider development. The approach it describes may seem unorthodox by traditional standards of British social work practice, but it is worth remembering that within the space of fifteen years this approach became the model of American professional youth work.

Any book with three authors is bound to suffer from unevenness of style while also running the double dangers of repetition or omission. The structure of this book was planned by Dr Smith, the senior author, but work on the first drafts was shared among all three. Successive drafts were produced by individual authors but the final revised version was edited by Dr Smith. The manuscript was discussed at considerable length with the professional workers engaged in the Wincroft Project and their many useful suggestions have been incorporated in the script, as have a number of case studies that they prepared. Helpful comments were received also from Miss Muriel Brown, Bernard Davies, George Goetschius, John Leigh, Miss Joan Matthews, Professor John Mays, Dr Gordon Rose, Stanley Rowe, and John Wrigley.

A cooperative effort such as the Wincroft Project must depend upon the support and energy of a great many different people, and a general thank-you is made to the many hundreds of people who were directly or indirectly involved in the life of the project. First, thanks must be formally offered to the 156 workers, voluntary and professional, who gave their services so unstintingly. Second, recognition is due to those who provided the resources to do the work: the Youth Committee of the City of Manchester; the Department of Education and Science; the Home Office; and the Manchester and Salford Street Children's Mission. Their willingness to experiment shows courage and foresight. A great deal of help was also given to the research by the heads, staff, and pupils of the eight schools in the two areas studied. A considerable amount of information was provided by the police, the Probation Service, and the Careers Advisory Service of the City of Manchester, for which we are very grateful.

Mrs F. A. Martin, the Departmental Secretary, and Miss Alison Smith, also of the Department of Youth Work, will no doubt be glad to see the last of the many drafts they typed and corrected make its way to the publisher. We gave them many headaches, but in return they caused us none.

It is perhaps unnecessary to add that Wincroft is a fictitious name given to a real neighbourhood, and all names of young people are likewise fictitious. On occasion certain details in the case studies have been altered to preserve anonymity, but the general substance of the truth has been maintained.

C S S
M F
H M

PART ONE

The Project

1 · Overview of the project

Tom was 15 when he first met workers from the Wincroft Project. He had one friend, but spent most of his leisure time alone or with his older brother. Even at that age he drank heavily and his passion for gambling had already possessed him. He has, since leaving school, rarely worked and his only other interest is crime.

After his return to the neighbourhood from his first spell in a detention centre he was introduced to a voluntary worker with a considerable knowledge of dog-racing, and together they made many trips to the local dog tracks and elsewhere. He was extremely unreliable and failed to appear on 9 of the 26 occasions when they had expected to meet. But then Tom doesn't care for anyone. When he was in the remand centre with two other boys awaiting sentence, they were asked what they missed most. The other two said 'home' and 'mum'. Tom replied 'cigs'. It will become clear later in the book that nobody cared for Tom, and that is perhaps what the Wincroft Project was all about.

Tom was one of 54 young men whom a group of social workers wanted to keep out of trouble. Growing up on the streets of Wincroft, a slum area of a large Northern town, exposed them to extra temptations and yet they lacked, more than most young people, the support and supervision of their families in dealing with them. Always likely to end up in the courts, they were particularly vulnerable when they did. They had no 'connections' and knew nobody who could exercise influence on their behalf. They lived in mean houses, they have been made to attend barrack-like schools, they dressed poorly, and their lives were circumscribed by intellectual poverty.

The work of the project described in this book is exceptional, though 54 similar young men with identical problems could be found in every poor urban neighbourhood of Britain. The fact that the work is exceptional is an indictment of the ignorance and indifference of those with wealth and power, and the fact that it happened at all is a testimony to the skill and dedication of those who wanted to make it happen. If there is a success story to be read here it is emphatically not a typical success story of the Youth Service, though without funds provided by the local authority and the Department of Education and

Science little could have happened. It is a story that should illuminate what is *not* being done.

The Wincroft Project sprang from an awareness of the limitations of the Youth Service, and a desire to effect some change through it. These limitations were, in brief, that the service was failing to offer help to those most in need. The layman may find this somewhat difficult to understand, for it is a common view that the Youth Service is there to keep young people off the streets and out of trouble and the public has been led to expect this from the service by the appeals of voluntary youth organizations for help and money. The Albemarle Committee observed that 'the crime problem is very much a youth problem, a problem of that age group with which the Youth Service is particularly concerned and towards which the public rightly expects it to make some contribution' (Cmd. 929, 1960, p. 17). It is true that not all voluntary youth organizations have set out to help the underprivileged youngster, and of those that did not all have maintained this purpose resolutely throughout their history. The YMCA and the Boy Scouts generally serve a section of the population that is relatively law-abiding and prosperous, and only the Boys' Clubs, mixed youth clubs (often church-sponsored), and the Boys' Brigade have really reached into the poorest areas of our cities. Yet even within these organizations the methods are more geared to work inside buildings, into which young people are expected to come on the understanding that they will observe the already established rules and structure of the organization. They seldom reach out to the street corners, commercial cafés, and public houses where a great many youngsters congregate. [1]

Public opinion about the role of the Youth Service has also been shaped by the nature of the situations in which governments have been prepared to support it. Apart from the acceptance of the Albemarle Report, all the significant developments in state support for youth work have come in time of war, or during preparation for it. The setting-up of the Juvenile Organizations Committee in 1916 was a direct response to the increase in delinquency in the first world war. The Physical Training and Recreation Act of 1937 and the Social and Physical Training Grant Regulations of 1939 were both conceived under the threat of war. Still more important was the issue of Circular 1486 in 1939 calling the Youth Service into being with these words:

'In some parts of the country, clubs and other facilities for social and physical recreation are almost non-existent. War emphasises this defect in our social services; today the black-out, the strain of war and the disorganisation of family life have created conditions which constitute a serious menace to youth. The Government are determined to prevent the recurrence during this war of the social problems which arose during the last.'

The acceptance of the Albemarle Report in 1960 marked a considerable departure in the statutory provision for youth recreation, since it was the first time that war played no part in a government decision in this field, but there is no doubt that the steeply rising rates of delinquency in the late fifties were an important reason for setting up the Committee and for acting upon its report.

Despite the expectations of the public, the traditions of some voluntary organizations, and the pronouncements of the government, very little was being done to counter the rise in delinquency. In 1963 it was nearly three times its pre-war level and still rising. New forms of delinquency were emerging and some of the older and more uncivilized forms, such as violence, were growing in importance. Illegitimacy had markedly increased among adolescent girls. The social conditions that heighten the risks of deviation were becoming more widespread. Substantial numbers of youngsters were irregularly employed and increasing numbers were 'sleeping rough' away from their homes. To make matters worse, the traditional forms of treatment such as approved schools were showing much less successful rates than in the past, and the country was more willing to accept punitive methods of treatment such as the detention centre and the attendance centre. This climate in which the present project was conceived shaped its objectives.

But why should the control of delinquency be so important to those who wanted to reform the Youth Service, especially since it is unlikely that they wanted to protect the existing distribution of wealth? It was because of the link that still exists between poverty and delinquency, and the belief that an attack on delinquency meant an attack on its roots in poverty. This was the reasoning behind the poverty programme in the United States of America, which sprang from the efforts of the Kennedy Administration to prevent delinquency. [2] It will become clearer later in the book what the nature of that link between poverty and delinquency was, for it was by no means a simple one, but it is sufficient to explain here why the control of delinquency was always an explicit objective of the Wincroft Project.

It should not be assumed, however, that the control of delinquency was the primary objective of the project, for this was much more positive. The objectives were finally crystallized in a paper for discussion in November 1965, and the relevant section of that paper read:

(a) to work with young people in need of help, and assist them in finding a dynamic adjustment to society, and thereby among other things to control delinquency;

(b) to develop methods of working with difficult young people in an unstructured setting.

The crucial concept here was that of 'dynamic adjustment'. The project was to be concerned not merely with adjusting young people to their environment but also with helping them to change it. They were to be helped to become more conscious of the factors, both personal and social, which shaped their lives and the ways in which they could exert more control over their own destinies. If they became dissatisfied with the poor range of jobs available in the neighbourhood they could be helped to find better jobs elsewhere. If they saw how the social pressures of their peers were forcing them into delinquency and maladjustment they could be helped to develop a social life elsewhere. However, the fact that these objectives were to be achieved through the process of social work, and, in particular, through the use of social group work method, effectively though not intentionally excluded change through political or social action.

The specific conception of the Wincroft Project derived from at least three developments, to which something further has been added during the four years in which it was realized. It is the combination of these three developments that is perhaps the most distinctive feature of the project. First, it was influenced by the notion of the Teen Canteen which had operated at the Elephant and Castle in London from 1955 to 1962, and from this source came the idea that a commercial-type café should be used as the means of making contact with young people in the neighbourhood. [3] Second, it was influenced by the notion of detached youth work, which had been pioneered in New York by the Welfare Council and later by the New York City Youth Board, [4] from this source came the idea that the workers should go out from the café into the neighbourhood. The third influence was the notion of experiment used in the United States by the Cambridge—Somerville Youth Study in its attempt to control delinquency, and in Britain by the Bristol Social Project. [5] Before more is said about each of these three influences, mention must be made of the National Association of

Youth Clubs Project, written up by Mary Morse, and of the YWCA Project, reported by Goetschius and Tash. [6] Both these projects preceded the present one, but neither directly influenced its conception, since the published reports did not appear until 1965 and 1967 respectively, by which time the planning of the Wincroft Project had been completed. There was, however, a very useful exchange of expertise between fieldworkers in the course of the project.

In relation to the first development, one of the authors of this book (Dr C. S. Smith) had been closely involved in the setting-up of the Teen Canteen at the Elephant and Castle in 1955. This café had been planned to provide a bridge between the 'unattached' young people and local youth organizations, and it was hoped that once relations had been established with the customers they could be encouraged to become members of youth clubs. A second aim was that the café's existence would limit the conflict between such youths and the local adult population by reducing the number of points of contact between them and, therefore, the possibilities of friction. The café would provide a place where young people would be accepted, a place to call their own. However, the first objective came to nothing when it was realized that most of the customers had already been thrown out of youth clubs and would not be welcomed back; and, though the second objective had seemed more realistic, the one member of staff, the café manager, found that a lot of the aggression that would have been directed towards other adults now found its way to him. He had little opportunity for taking his work beyond the walls of the café, and it is hardly surprising that there were nine managers in the seven years of the Teen Canteen's existence. However, certain lessons could be drawn from this experience: first, this kind of work needed a team of social workers rather than a single worker; and, second, the premises should be abandoned if they begin to get in the way of the social work.

These conclusions tied in well with the development of detached youth work by American youth workers then beginning to be discussed in England. The pioneer work of the Welfare Council of New York City showed that it was possible to reach young people on the streets without providing any facility for them, and this relatively small-scale experiment became the prototype for the city-wide pattern of detached youth work provided by the New York City Youth Board at the end of the 1950s, in an attempt to control the waves of gang violence and racial conflict in that city. This work seemed to complement the experience of the Teen Canteen and to be worth attempting in England.

The third new development that seemed applicable was to build research into the work. It was too much to expect the social workers to do their own evaluation, for they did not have the time, the expertise, or the detachment. Far too many experiments have been tried and concluded without any comprehensive analysis and evaluation; the one exception at that time was the classic Cambridge–Somerville Youth Study. It has provided an example of a systematic attempt to experiment in the changing of delinquent attitudes, and it has also made its contribution to the growing interest in action research. From this new interest in Britain there stemmed the Bristol Social Project, in which the prevention of delinquency was a major objective.

The need for a new kind of project seemed clear, but there was to be a delay of two years between the conception of the idea in 1963 and its realization, and most of the delay came from finding the money to do the work. The most obvious source for funds was the Department of Education and Science (then the Ministry of Education), since a certain sum of money had been earmarked for experimental work in line with the recommendation of the Albemarle Committee. At that time the Ministry allocated grants on the recommendation of the Youth Service Development Council, but when the application for funds for the Wincroft Project was considered by the Council in April 1964 it was turned down and a recommendation made that it should be referred to the local authority for support. Discussions with members of the Youth Service Development Council revealed that the proposals had not been considered sufficiently experimental, because they seemed to repeat features of work that was already being grant-aided, and, furthermore, the Council considered that the local authority should finance the work since it was not of sufficient national significance. In late September the application was duly referred by the Ministry to the local authority, which then suggested that the Ministry and the local authority should finance the work jointly. The Ministry agreed to take it back to the Youth Service Development Council for consideration on this basis in December 1964. Meanwhile active lobbying by members of the Youth Development Trust, the project's sponsoring agency, was taking place in an effort to raise support in the Youth Service Development Council for the revised application, and also to encourage enough support within the local Youth Committee. At the December meeting of the Youth Service Development Council it was recommended that the project should be supported, and in May 1965 the Ministry gave formal notification to the Trust of its support. It was to provide a grant of £1,750 a year for three years on the understanding that the local authority, the City of Manchester, did the same. The grant was later increased to cover the extra costs of salary awards and a small sum was made available to assist in the writing-up of the report.

However, the application for support from the Ministry of Education ran into trouble on another score, and this cut across the whole conception of building research into the work. The Ministry made it clear that any grant that might be given could only be for experimental work with the 'unattached'; it could not be for delinquency prevention, even though delinquents might indeed be 'unattached'. Responsibility for delinquency lay clearly with the Home Office. The Home Office, on the other hand, had not yet provided funds for action-research projects, though it was willing to provide money to study them. [7] At one stage it looked as though there would be money available to study a project that could not get off the ground for lack of money. Eventually the money was forthcoming from the Ministry and the local authority, but though the word 'delinquency' appeared in the application it described the area not the work. The Home Office offered a grant of £9,340 over four years to study 'Group Work in a High Delinquency Area'.

Money was not the only difficulty in mounting the work. An earlier problem had been to bring a committee together to manage it. The experience of the Teen Canteen had shown that the work would become effective only if it was supported by an active management committee, for this would not only ensure that resources would be available for the workers to get on with their work, but would also give it direction and take responsibility for it. Professional youth workers and other members of the community were brought together to found the Youth Development Trust. More will be said later about the functioning of this committee.

When placed alongside the problems of finding money to mount the project and a committee to manage it, other problems seemed much more tractable. Fortunately, the difficulties of finding experienced and qualified staff to undertake this stressful work, difficulties which had dogged other projects, were solved one by one; first by the appointment of a project director, an outstanding and experienced youth worker, and, subsequently, in the recruitment of an able supporting team. Another potentially difficult decision about where to locate the programme of work was taken relatively quickly. Research that had been carried out on the ecological distribution of delinquency in the city, which was eventually published as a pamphlet by the Youth

Development Trust, [8] showed the familiar pattern of high rates of juvenile delinquency in the inner slum areas. Premises were examined in two of the six areas with the highest rates of delinquency, but eventually a suitable shop was obtained in 'Wincroft', the area with the seventh-highest delinquency rate in the city and only two miles from the city centre.

It may help the reader to have a bird's-eye view of the whole project over the four and a half years of its operation therefore the main events are summarized in six-month phases:

Phase one	October 1963—March 1964	Discussions and first steps; location of area, and opening of Bridge Café (February 1964).
Phase two	April 1964—September 1964	Appointment of first full-time worker (the project director).
Phase three	October 1964—March 1965	Bridge Café observations, and beginnings of relationships with users.
Phase four	April 1965—September 1965	Extensive identification; arrival of two full-time fieldworkers.
Phase five	October 1965—March 1966	Arrival of fourth member of professional team (the caseworker); closure of Bridge Café (January); selection of 54 participants.
Phase six	April 1966—September 1966	Re-establishment of contact with participants in neighbourhood and commercial settings; replacement fieldworker appointed.
Phase seven	October 1966—March 1967	Build-up of group work and casework to peak.

Phase eight	April 1967—September 1967	Major reassessment of needs and resources, and cut-back of fieldwork in some areas.
Phase nine	October 1967—March 1968	Preparation and implementation of plans for the termination of the work.
Phase ten	April 1968—September 1968	Transfer and referral of work where necessary; completion of fieldwork.

It is possible to look at the history of the project from at least three different perspectives: first, from that of the workers offering the service, which would include an account of the resources available to them; second, from that of the young people who made use of the services; and, third, by looking at the relationships between the workers and the young people and the way in which these changed over the period of the project. Each of these perspectives will receive much more detailed treatment in separate chapters later in this book. It is necessary to describe only the third perspective in this introduction.

The project was conceived as depending on social group work method and this conception was reflected in the basis on which the team of four professional workers was recruited. Three were group workers by training and experience and only one (and this a part-time appointment) was a caseworker. Although there was an important shift to work with individuals in the last year of the project, the overall balance of effort was in working with groups.

It took some considerable time for the workers to create the conditions in which group work method might be relevant. Contact had to be established before the workers could use any social-work techniques, and it was for this purpose that the Bridge Café was opened in the area by the Youth Development Trust in February 1964. [9] It had been a shop used for storage previously and now had to be converted for use as a café that could stand a good deal of wear and tear. The café was open five nights a week, and was staffed entirely by voluntary help until the project director arrived in September 1964. Thereafter he was always on duty when it was open until the full team of professional workers had arrived a year later. From then on one professional member of staff was always on duty, but the number of evenings the café was open dropped to three a week, and then to two.

It was closed in January 1966. It was not easy to develop working relationships with the customers in the Bridge Café. Nevertheless, by September 1965 the director reported that basic relationships had been established with 130 boys and 54 girls.

The café provided a basis of friendship for the subsequent development of the more professional relationships of group work and casework, and even before it closed in January 1966 there had been a considerable extension of work outside its walls. As early as the month of March 1965 there had been 22 *ad hoc* group meetings involving from one to nine persons. Activities had included indoor football, attendance at football matches, ice-skating, camping, and table tennis. The young people had visited workers' homes and had been with them to theatres and to the seaside. Apart from the useful opportunities for talking privately, these excursions also provided workers with group situations that were a necessary prelude to a more regular and intense commitment. Among other things, they gave the young people a chance to see what sort of individuals the workers were. In the year September 1964 to September 1965 there had been 150 activity sessions involving 70 boys and 20 girls, but it was not until the café closed that the full resources of the project could be brought to bear in a systematic manner upon the needs of the young people. Moreover, it had been decided to concentrate the work on a small number of boys who were maladjusted or likely to get into trouble. These 54 boys were to be known as 'participants' (see pp. 21 and 22). Some thought had to be given to the new approach that was required, and time was needed to re-establish contacts. Within six months after the closure, 40 of the 54 boys who had been selected as Participants were either still in contact or had been contacted again, for the most part in four commercial cafés in the neighbourhood. For some young people, however, who did not use such cafés, it was necessary to tread the streets of the area in the hope of meeting them, and in all cases except two contact was eventually renewed.

The new freedom of movement made it possible for the workers to enlarge the number of group activities, and to employ the skills of group work. They were able to provide the resources that the groups needed, whether it was a place to meet or equipment for their activity, or to enlarge the area of social life by taking them out of the neighbourhood. They were able to offer emotional support when the groups were experiencing internal conflict or were failing to adapt themselves effectively to their external environment. They were able to move the groups from irregular and infrequent social encounters to more sustained, more demanding, and more satisfying group memberships.

Whatever the method used, or the way of describing the work, it is clear that the level of effort fluctuated considerably over the life of the project. From the relatively puny efforts of a small group of voluntary workers in early 1964 through to the arrival of the first professional worker in the September of that year, with the continuing build-up of voluntary helpers and the arrival of the three supporting workers, the resources were continuing to grow. A peak of 680 contacts with the 54 participants was reached in the three-month period January–March 1968 compared with fewer than 250 in January–March 1966. There was an increase from 33 sessions with groups containing participants in the month of January 1966 to 101 sessions in the month of February 1967.

One feature of the changing character of the relationships was that they nearly all passed through a phase of exploitation of the worker before finding a more reciprocal basis. The worker had offered himself to be used by the young people and it was not unexpected that their ideas of what uses they could make of him differed from his ideas of what use he could be to them. They saw him as somebody who could be 'tapped' for a loan, or for a cigarette, or for a cup of tea, or a lift. He saw himself as somebody who could help them make more effective relationships in which they respected the other person and did not exploit him. Their immediate assessment of him was 'soft'. His problem was how to show understanding without being thought 'soft'. He had to be prepared to tolerate this behaviour, though on the assumption that it was only temporary, and in this he was helped by having a clearer idea of where this relationship ought to be going than the young people had.

Nevertheless, given that the workers could persist in their supportive and accepting attitudes, sooner or later these paid dividends. Even the 'hard men' warmed and responded. One important step forward was the willingness to take part in something different from the usual round of being out with the lads. It might be going to a bowling alley in a different neighbourhood, or to a pub in the country, but it represented a significant step away from the existing pattern of behaviour. Even more significant was that this isolated venture became established into a routine of regular excursions or meetings. With very few exceptions, a pattern of regular meetings was established with most boys, and the workers accompanied the groups on their outings.

Not only did the overall number of sessions increase, but they became more regular and more purposive. The football team functioned effectively over three seasons, three friends became a skilful 'pop' group, a collection of rootless individuals became a regular crowd meeting for a drink in the local public house and occasionally going elsewhere together. During this time they were learning how to live with each other and to cooperate for the good of the group. It often proved possible for them in the group setting to discuss their relationships to authority, to their boy- and girl-friends, and to work, and to share their hopes for, and fears of, the future. They were able to do this with an adult who had the ability to understand them and was willing to accept them as they were. In practice there were many setbacks: groups failed to cohere; friends fell out; emotion dominated reason; action preceded discussion; and many group meetings seemed to get nowhere except further into chaos. That this should have happened sometimes is perhaps not surprising since many of the workers were not always sure of how to do what they were doing because of the novelty of the approach.

Although the weight of the project's professional resources was thrown into group work, a considerable effort was made in working with individuals. In September 1967 there were actually 77 sessions with individual participants, and a further 23 with their families. Not all of this work would strictly qualify as casework, but a great deal of it was supportive, especially in relation to crises about jobs, shelter, and appearances in court. Some of it reached the stage where the young person was helped to become aware of his problems and enabled to find a solution for himself. Some of it seemed to yield no tangible results at all.

The fact that young people were able to come to the workers for help in crises indicated the trust and faith they had in them, but support given during the crisis often later carried the relationship forward to new levels. With some young people the particular crisis was one of a continuing series of interrelated crises: their failure to keep a job had brought them into conflict with their parents; their leaving home brought them into greater risks of delinquency. The profound disorganization of a few meant such great demands on the workers' time that the workers had consciously to delay further help in order to protect the interests of other young people.

Whatever the links of friendship forged during the four and a half years of the project, they were likely to come to an end when the project finished. The professional objective had been to encourage the young people to become self-sufficient and to stand on their own two feet. The workers were in any case much older and of different educational backgrounds, and it would have been surprising if personal friendships on a basis of complete equality could have emerged from these circumstances. Nevertheless, a few of the young people still correspond with the workers, and during the follow-up survey after the end of the project a number spoke spontaneously and warmly of the workers they had known to members of the interviewing team. The object of this Introduction has been to show what brought the Wincroft Project into being, and how this difficult and complex enterprise was realized over four and a half years. Starting from an awareness of how far short the social services fell from meeting the needs of certain young people, a systematic effort, informed by research, was made to reach out and satisfy those needs. As will become clear later in the book, a certain measure of success was achieved in the operation, and some lessons were learned that may be of general benefit to the social services. But before the project is described and analysed it is necessary to say something more about those who took part in it, both the boys in trouble and the social workers who wanted to keep them out of it.

(ii) THE PARTICIPANTS AND THEIR NEIGHBOURHOOD

It is not possible to understand the 54 boys and the problems of working with them without understanding the environment of which they were a part. They lived in a neighbourhood close to the centre of a large conurbation. Until the recent inroads of slum clearance, the neighbourhood had a relatively stable population, but in 1962 also had the seventh-highest rate of juvenile delinquency of the thirty-eight wards in the city. [10] Within this neighbourhood there were nearly four hundred young men in the same age-group, but none quite shared the reputation of the individuals numbered among the 54.

Manchester, their home town, is a large industrial city. Many more people work in Manchester than live there, for it is a regional administrative, shopping, and entertainment centre. Sources of employment are completely diversified. There was little unemployment among juveniles or adults, and most school-leavers were quickly absorbed into the labour market.

The present population within the conurbation of four and a half million is 625,250, but, as in many other large cities, it has been declining in recent years, as the residents have moved out to the suburbs or have been moved out to council housing estates. There has been some counter-movement into the city, especially of incomers from the traditional source of Ireland, and, to a much lesser extent, of black people from Commonwealth countries. There are marginally more young people aged 10 to 19 years old in this city – 15.4 per cent of the population – than nationally, where the figure is 14.9 per cent (1961).

Manchester presents many of the features of social disorganization associated with large towns, but on many criteria the social problems among young people are much greater than in comparable towns. A comparison of boys and girls appearing before the courts charged with offences in 1960 in six large towns showed that the rate for Manchester was substantially above the rates for the other five towns. [11] Moreover, this situation is not a new one, for Manchester was shown by previous surveys to have a high rate of delinquency in the 1930s. [12] The general pattern of delinquency is very similar to elsewhere in Great Britain, with larceny by far the most important kind of offence, but locally there is much less violence and rather more drunkenness. [13] Although still numerically insignificant, drug offences have risen considerably since 1964. Delinquency is still very much confined to the poorer areas of the town.

A high delinquency rate is not the only indication of social disorganization in Manchester. Illegitimacy is exceptionally high—14.19 per cent of all live births compared with the national figure of 7.66 per cent for 1965—although, as with other large towns, a substantial minority of these women, attracted by the anonymity of the city, have moved from elsewhere in order to conceal the birth of their children. [14] Not unrelated to this high rate of illegitimacy is the relatively high proportion of children taken into the care of the local authority; in 1965 8.1 per thousand under 18 at risk compared with 6.2 for all county boroughs. [15]

Manchester, as a large town, not only offers greater temptations to the young, it also offers greater opportunities. The variety of education provided is considerable and there is a strong tradition, going back to the days of Mechanics Institutes, of helping those who want to help themselves. Although the city has now embarked upon a system of comprehensive education, it has in the immediate past offered selective education to a relatively large proportion of the young; in 1966 to some 29.2 per cent of the 13-year-old pupils as against 23.6 per cent nationally. Technical school places, however, accounted for a large part of this difference, for 12.8 per cent of that age-group took them compared with only 2.6 per cent nationally. Relatively few young people in the city stay at school after the age of 16, about one in eight of those aged 17; and expenditure on further education is substantially lower than the average for county boroughs, £2,714 per 1,000 population as against £3,921 (1965-6). [16]

Wincroft, the neighbourhood of Manchester where the 54 boys lived, has some of the worst social conditions in the city, but it does not suffer from all the city's features of social disorganization. The population is extremely overcrowded, with relatively large families living in small terraced cottage houses built in the middle of the nineteenth century. The density of population in 1963 was not only the highest for any ward in the city but was three times the overall density in the town. [17] The birth rate is 40 per cent higher than in the city as a whole and, though there is a relatively high rate of infant mortality (some 20 per cent higher), the net effect is much larger families, and a young population (about one-third are under 21). The high birth rate is not to be explained in terms of religious affiliation since the Roman Catholics, unlike elsewhere in the city, were a relatively small minority. Migration has added little to the population and there are relatively few families of Irish origin and none that are black. There are still, however, traces of the displacement of European population that occurred in the last war, for example, Polish men who married and settled in the area. This picture of residential stability was confirmed by a survey of 13- and 14-year-olds in the local schools, most of whom were born locally and who, on average, have lived in their present homes for nine years.

Wincroft was built to house workers for the local engineering and textile factories, and for the colliery, and though coal and textiles are no longer important sources of employment, a great many men are still employed locally as manual workers. Since the neighbourhood is only two miles from the city centre, many men and women work in town, still in unskilled or semi-skilled employment but in a greater range of occupations. There is, and has been since the war, very little unemployment, but wages are not high. From a survey of local schools, to be discussed in detail later, it appeared that every family of the 13- and 14-year-olds questioned had a television set, one in every three possessed a car, two in five a refrigerator, and one in ten a telephone.

Many women had to work to ensure having these consumer goods, and sometimes, especially in the absence of a male wage-earner, even to keep the family together.

The boundaries of Wincroft as a neighbourhood are not immediately visible to the eye of the stranger. It is just one of those stretches of blackened terraced cottages which lie on either side of the main roads leading from the city centre. It has no obvious beginning and no obvious end, but on closer inspection it becomes clearer that there are physical features that serve to enhance the social separation of the neighbourhood. To the north and south two main roads spread out radially from the city centre, and immediately behind these roads are extensive industrial areas. In between these two roads lies Wincroft. The western edge of this rhomboid-shaped area is defined by a railway line, and the eastern edge by another main circular road. To the residents these physical features are less important than their common use of the amenities lying within the area – the corner shops, the bingo hall, the cinema, the numerous public houses, and the schools. Of great importance to residents is the network of kinship that spreads throughout the area as a result of the high frequency of local intermarriage and the pattern of settlement of young couples near their parents.

Within the neighbourhood the streets are laid out on a speculator's simple grid pattern, with row after row of terraced cottages, usually having two rooms up and two rooms down. Given the large families, it is not surprising that there is a great deal of overcrowding: the proportion of the population living at a density of 1.5 people per room is four times the average rate for the city. [18] This fact, combined with a style of family life centred on the kitchen, may help to explain why children and young people spend so much time on the streets and out of the home.

Wincroft is in some ways typical of the older working-class areas of Manchester. In common with them it has a high delinquency rate, which contributes to the high rate for the city, but the origins of delinquency in this neighbourhood are rather less related to the social disorganization that follows migration. The significance of this absence of population movement can be seen also in the statistics of illegitimacy, for the rate for Wincroft is only about one-half of that for the city.

It might be thought that with such a young population overcrowded schools were inevitable, and though this was true of the secondary schools in the early 1960s, because of the post-war population bulge, it was no longer true in 1964, 1965, and 1966, during which time many of the 54 participants were still at school. Most of them were educated in classes of fewer than thirty pupils. Part of the pressure had been taken off by movement of families out of the area, but also the area was relatively well served by schools that were usually up to their establishment of staff. All of the four secondary modern schools were small, with never more than 300 boys on their roll during the four years from 1963 to 1966. All have since been closed as a result of the comprehensive plan for education, and because of the antiquated nature of their buildings.

It has been emphasized earlier that Manchester had, before its reorganization of schools on 'comprehensive' lines, a relatively high proportion of its children in selective schooling (29.2 per cent). It is perhaps surprising in view of the slum character of Wincroft to learn that 27 per cent of the primary school population left to enter selective secondary education: 9 per cent to grammar schools and 18 per cent to technical schools, but it must be noted that this total figure seriously underrepresents grammar schools. Very few children of the participant group received selective schooling.

It is the attitudes of the children who went to the secondary modern schools in Wincroft that are most relevant here, for not only can it be assumed that those children who ended up in selective schools were likely to be relatively well disposed to education, but also they ceased to interact with the participant group. Other children in the schools the participants attended were likely to be an important influence upon them, and their attitudes to education were studied in two ways; first, by seeing how regularly they attended school and, second, by asking them questions about it. In all, 76 young males aged 13 and 14 completed questionnaires to provide us with more information on the social attitudes of young people of the area in which the project was conducted. More details are given in Chapter 5 (p. 188), but the overall picture of their attitudes to education can be summed up as follows: very few remain at school until after the statutory leaving age, but, with the exception of a minority (among whom those like the participants of the Wincroft Project are likely to be numbered) though they are not enthusiastic about education they are generally well disposed towards it. This attitude is reflected in their attitudes to work.

For most young people in the area the ideal on leaving school was to enter an apprenticeship, but less than half did so: in 1965-66 the proportion of school-leavers from the four schools entering 'good' apprenticeships was 47 per cent, a figure little different from the city average. [19] Eagerness to learn a trade was part of the general importance placed upon finding the right job and being willing to wait for rewards in the long term if they were able to find it. The schools survey respondents (see pp. 19 & 190) were given eight statements about the gratification they expected from work: four were in favour of immediate rewards and four in favour of deferred rewards; and 56 per cent of the respondents were, on balance, in favour of deferring gratification. Only one in ten was solely concerned with the immediate reward from the first choice of job. In Wincroft, fathers and sons usually avoid each other; the son keeps out of his father's way when he is at home (naturally a difficult matter in overcrowded homes) and he takes care to drink in a different public house from the one patronized by his father. His father is more likely to take an interest in him when he is doing something wrong than to encourage him in a positive way. One-third of the respondents in the schools survey claimed that they never went out with their parents, and only 14 per cent went out weekly with them. According to the children in the schools survey, fathers and mothers were equally likely to punish them if they had done something wrong, but day-to-day discipline was more likely to come from the mother, with the father being used as the ultimate threat by the mother.

More important than the influence of school, job, or home was the influence of a boy's friends. In the schools survey, 87 per cent considered it important to be 'straight with your friends' and 81 per cent considered it important not to split on your friends if you 'wanted to be liked by people of your own age'. How a boy chose to spend his leisure time and what kind of job he favoured were very likely to be influenced by his friends.

So far in this section of the chapter little has been said about the 54 participants who are the main concern of this book. The intention has been to describe the city and neighbourhood in which they lived, but in what ways did they resemble the youth of the neighbourhood? In their own age-group they accounted for about one-eighth of boys in the area, and about one-sixth of those who went to secondary modern schools. They were certainly different in at least one respect for either they had appeared before the court and been convicted on two or more charges, or they had been defined by their teachers as children who were maladjusted. Since other social attitudes, principally those towards family, school, and work, are likely to be associated with delinquency and maladjustment, it is likely that the 54 participants were not representative of the 76 boys tested in the schools survey but that they exhibited attitudes similar to those who disliked school, those who looked for immediate rewards in their choice of first jobs, and those who rated the peer group more important than parents or teachers.

Experimental social work programmes, especially those that are designated work with the 'unattached', rarely adopt any precise selection procedures in deciding with whom they are to work. Who actually gets the service very often depends on who asks (or shouts) for it when the workers are around. Seldom is an attempt made to differentiate in any way between the levels of need of different clients in order to decide where scarce resources should be allocated. For reasons of research and professional social work practice, the clients for the Wincroft Project were selected on explicit criteria of need. The research evaluation of the impact of the programme could be made only if there was a prior assessment of the behaviour and attitudes of the young people, and the social workers wanted to establish who was in greatest need and with whom they would be most effective.

It was clear, once the principle of selection had been adopted, that some decision would need to be made not only on which individuals should be included in the group but also on what the total number should be. In a discussion paper prepared prior to selection it was suggested that "the number of participants should not exceed 50 and should be all male. In order to have maximum effect over the life of the project it is recommended that no one over 16 should . . . become a . . . participant." Although the figure may seem unduly low for a team of four professional workers, it was kept in mind that each participant would be likely to involve other young people in the programme. The subsequent selection procedure led to a final list of 54 boys, and the average age at 1 January 1966 was 15 years 3 months.

Selection for the participant group was carried out throughout November and December 1965 in two ways. The workers compiled a list of boys in the appropriate age-group who seemed to them to be in need of further service. Almost all these boys had been observed at close quarters in the café at some point during the preceding twenty months. A second list was compiled by the research worker of boys living in Wincroft who had been before the courts and been convicted on two or more charges. Some names appeared on both lists and 71 boys were left as candidates for the programme. At this stage it was thought necessary to confirm the workers' judgements on the 'non-delinquent' boys by the judgements of the teachers who had known the boys at school. (About half were still at school and half had recently left.)

It was important from the research point of view to ensure that the teachers' judgements were made on some objective basis, and if possible to use a test that could be repeated at the end of the programme. After careful consideration, it was decided to use the only British test that had been developed with needs such as those of the Wincroft Project in mind: the Bristol Social Adjustment Guides. [20]

This Guide consists of a number of statements about the way a pupil behaves in the classroom situation, such as those about asking for the teacher's help:

> Always finding excuses for engaging teacher/seeks help only when necessary/seldom needs help/too shy to ask/not shy but never comes for help willingly/too apathetic to bother/sometimes very forward, sometimes sulky/depends on how he feels.

The teacher underlines the phrase that best fits the boy in question. When the guides are completed they produce, according to the author's scale, a score for maladjustment and for delinquency-proneness. In the author's words "they are a means of judging whether a child is suffering from emotional difficulties, such as might be the cause of failure in school work, or which might act as a warning sign of the possibility of delinquent breakdown". [21]

To apply the test to pupils the worker had to approach the schools in the area with a list of names. Unfortunately, 7 of the boys were not identified by the schools and another had been taught by masters who had subsequently left the school. Since some of these boys were known by the workers to present special risks, they were still included in the participant group, and a youth club version of the Bristol Guides was completed by them. The approach to the schools produced 49 completed guides, and this enabled the exclusion of 6 boys from the original list of 71 who had a maladjustment score of less than 6 or a delinquency-proneness score of less than 7. A further 11 were excluded either on grounds of age or because they had now moved a considerable distance from the area.

The 54 boys remaining in December 1965 who became the participants in the programme had qualified because of their delinquency and/or their maladjustment, and the final composition of the group looked like this: 18 'delinquents', that is, those with two or more convictions prior to 1966; 34 'maladjusted', that is, those who scored 6 or more in the Bristol Guides on delinquency-proneness and 6 or more on maladjustment (including 7 who reached this score on the youth club edition); and 2 who had scored 6 or more for delinquency-proneness on this same guide, but had not reached 6 on the index of maladjustment.

This was how the participants were chosen. Now it is necessary to continue to describe in what way they shared the social characteristics of Wincroft, particularly in their attitudes to school and education, to work, to their families, and to their age-mates.

Although more than a quarter of the boys in Wincroft received a selective education, only 2 of the 54 participants had attended technical schools, and none had attended a grammar school. Of the others, 38 had passed through the same school; 5 through another; 3 through yet another in the same neighbourhood; and 3 had attended Roman Catholic schools. The remaining 3 boys had attended a special school. Within secondary modern schools the boys were more likely to be found in the lower streams (30/44 of those known). All but two attended single-sex schools. Attitudes to school were fairly negative and resembled the negative attitudes of the 10 per cent picked up from the schools survey. This finding was evidenced in another way by the adverse judgements the teachers had made on some of the participants in the Bristol Social Adjustment Guides, and also by the fact that one-third had attendance rates lower than 80 per cent, although the average was much the same as for the area. Most had wanted to leave school at the earliest opportunity and only 5 (the 2 at the technical schools and the 3 at the special school who had to stay until they were 16) did not do so. A number did proceed to further education on leaving school, but within the following year almost all of them had given it up. In any case, they received little encouragement from the schools to continue beyond the school-leaving age, since none of the four schools had a fifth-year form.

To have been at the same school together, perhaps in the same class, was a very significant factor in the formation of friendships and the frequency of interaction in the leisure-time situation. The confrontation with authority in school and the response to it marked those who were acceptable in the cafés of the neighbourhood.

Almost all the participants were keen to leave school and start work though few had clear ideas about the work they were to do. Many of them relied upon their fathers or their male relatives to find their first job for them and sometimes in this way were influenced to choose a job with some further training. Many of the so-called apprenticeships, however, meant little more than being general dogsbody to a skilled man in a one- or two-man business. It was not long, for many of them, before they began changing jobs (one boy had as many as twenty-five jobs in his first two years of working life). Now they were no longer interested in work as a preferable alternative to school but work as a source of high wages. Throughout the last two and a half years of the project only 5 boys kept the same job; on average the whole group changed jobs at least five times; and 20 boys changed jobs on average at least every six months. It is likely that the attitudes to work of a substantial minority of the participants were not typical of youth in Wincroft, and among this minority were to be found the 'hard-core' delinquents.

The boys' attitudes to work were very often related to their attitudes to their fathers, and to the fathers' own performance at work. Three of the fathers suffered from crippling chronic illnesses and seldom worked, and another experienced long periods of unemployment for no apparent reason. On the other hand, some fathers could be exceptionally stern if sons lost their jobs, and mothers too would put considerable pressure upon a boy to work in order that he could 'pay his way'. Arguments over money when the boy was out of work were the most common issue in cases where boys left home.

Attitudes to parents and parental attitudes to sons varied enormously in the participant group. In nearly one-third of the families the boy was without one of his natural parents: 6 had only their mother; 4 only their father; and a further 5 lived in households where the male head was not their own father; one other child lived with his relatives (1 January 1966). In common with the neighbourhood pattern, relationships could not be described as close and much of a boy's leisure time was spent on the streets with little interest or supervision from the parents. Outside the house the boy would try to avoid his parents or friends of his parents who might observe his behaviour. Display of affection towards parents was rare; affection was much more likely to be expressed towards grandparents with whom many boys maintained regular contact, and some boys lived. Boys tended to be proud of their fathers, especially for their toughness, although they spoke bitterly when this was turned against them. The phrase 'he can do anything' was often used by the boys about their fathers, but in the workers judgement, at least 15 boys had weak, ineffective fathers. Their attitudes to their mothers varied considerably, but an exploiting attitude, of getting all they could from the 'old lady', was by no means rare. Its counterpart was the mothers' wish to indulge their children, even if this was sometimes erratic in its application. Certainly if they wanted anything, or were in any trouble, it would be to their mothers that the boys would turn first.

Siblings in Wincroft tended to avoid each other outside the house and the participants were no exception to this rule. Only 4 had no brothers or sisters, and 4 more had only sisters, but 22 had four or more siblings. Yet it was very seldom that brothers would associate in their leisure time, and workers in the Bridge Café were sometimes surprised to discover that two boys who had been coming regularly into the café, showing no signs of acknowledging each other, were in fact brothers. Within the participant groups there were three pairs of brothers. Of the 25 participants who had committed one offence by January 1966, 23 had brothers and 8 of these were delinquent.

Once they had left school the participants seldom interacted socially with adults outside the family responsible for their welfare. None had sustained membership of youth clubs, and adults who were their fellow workers almost never impinged on the social networks in which they passed their leisure time. Their parents seldom shared their free time out of the home. The few adults they did meet in the public houses and the commercial cafés were likely to exploit them—the publicans by serving them with alcohol while they were still well under the legal age, and some commercial café-owners by receiving stolen goods and paying little for them. Social segregation from the responsible adult world was accompanied by an increasing segregation from their more law-abiding peers, for whereas their age-mates began to expand their horizons on leaving school the delinquent social network remained neighbourhood-based.

Although the participants have already been referred to many times in the text as a group, it should be emphasized that they were not a natural group but rather a category of persons. While it is true that some of the participants had friends who were also defined as participants, many more had their friends outside the participant category. A considerable number, however, had no stable friendships at all. Perhaps one of the most surprising features was the absence or tenuousness of the adolescent friendships. Only one belonged to an organized gang, and, indeed, only one gang of five boys was encountered in the four and a half years' work in the neighbourhood.

This is not to say that their social life was completely without structure or that they were not subject to the pressures of their peers, but their social life is perhaps better described as being experienced within a loose social network centred on a number of public houses and cafés. This network had its heroes, its hierarchy, and its values. Not everybody could get into it and not everybody could get out of it once they were in. It rewarded certain behaviour and it punished other activities: those who best represented its struggle with the outside world were rewarded by becoming symbolic leaders; those who compromised its values were expelled.

The focal point of these networks was to be found in certain commercial cafés and public houses, and something further needs to be said about these. 'Caffs' are by no means a new institution in working-class neighbourhoods, but in February 1964 when the Bridge Café opened there was only one other in the locality open in the evenings. However, in the ensuing four years twenty-eight opened in Wincroft or within half a mile of its border, and seven of these were patronized frequently by participants. Most of the cafés had relatively brief lives. It is difficult to explain the increase in the number of cafés, but it is likely that it was linked to the boom in coffee bars in the city centre in 1963. Whatever the reasons for their growth, these cafés became the meeting-point for the dissident youth of the neighbourhood, establishing more effective channels of communication between them, strengthening their social ties, and reinforcing their common values. Very few girls used these cafés and then usually only those known as 'communials' (*sic*) because of their loose reputations.

One café in particular, Johnny's, was frequented by boys in the participant group, 32 of whom used it regularly. Three others were patronized by between 7 and 11 participants, and four, including Johnny's, were used by more than 12 boys. Many boys frequented more than one café: 30 went to between one and three, 10 to between four and six, 3 to seven or more, and only 9 did not frequent any at all. Seven participants were known to have lodged at cafés for various lengths of time when they had been in trouble at home.

Although these cafés did serve meals, very few of the boys ever made use of this service, but would sit for some hours over one cup of tea or stand playing the pin-tables. Unless it was payday there was very little money changing hands. It was therefore all the more noticeable when lads who had been out 'on a job' began to flash their money around. It might be wondered what economic incentive there was for adults to open and run these cafés. Five, including two of thoses most popular with participants, were owned by the same person, who rented them out. A friend of his controlled the supply of pin-tables. Three proprietors were known to have criminal records and these were among the owners of the seven cafés most popular with participants: one had appeared in court with two of the participants for receiving goods they had stolen; and a second also had a conviction for receiving stolen goods; the third actively encouraged boys to go on shoplifting expeditions and would occasionally accompany them. Another owner sent them out to rob gas meters. It is possible that most of these cafés could not have been economic propositions without deriving some benefit from the criminal activities of the boys who frequented them.

When the boys had money they were likely to be elsewhere: if they were old enough to pass muster they would be in the public houses. Six of the participants went drinking regularly when they were still only 15 years of age, and most of the 54 had become regular weekend drinkers by the age of 17. It is unlikely, however, that the publicans were as tolerant of criminal behaviour as were the café-owners, and certainly the teenagers were never as segregated from other age-groups or from the respectable local community when they were in public houses.

This description of the participants in their social context may have helped to explain why they were delinquent or maladjusted, and also to give some indication of the kinds of problem the project faced in trying to help them. The participants were by no means typical of the town in which they lived, nor even of the neighbourhood of Wincroft. Many did not share in the general prosperity of Manchester or the relative prosperity of Wincroft. Their education had failed to give them qualifications and their parents had failed to encourage a desire in them for education. They fell back on the pleasures of company in the cafés and public houses where they were accepted by adults who could find a use for them. It was at this late stage of their development that the project began its work and some description is now required of the people who accepted this challenge.

(iii) THE WORKERS AND THEIR RESOURCES

Over the four and a half years of its existence 156 adults worked on the Wincroft Project. What kind of people they were, and what ideas, skills, and resources they brought to the project must be indicated if the outcome described in this book is to be explicable. How did they go about their task of promoting 'dynamic adjustment' and controlling delinquency? It might be thought that they had to have, first, some idea of what caused delinquency and maladjustment if they were going to do something about it and, second, depending upon their view of causation, some strategy for reversing the effects of those causes. Unfortunately, as will be seen, social engineering has not yet developed that degree of sophistication and there was neither a theory, nor a theory of practice, to inform the workers in their efforts. To be sure, they made certain assumptions about behaviour and how to change it but these were never articulated into a coherent theory to be tested. In the event the workers played it by ear, following their intuition until they had some experience to build upon, or until they could interpret behaviour here in the light of past experience from different settings.

Maladjustment was seen in the project as an inability to function socially because of a failure to sustain social relationships, whether those relationships were with peers, parents, adults at work, or teachers. Most theories familiar to the workers by which they sought to account for maladjustment are of a psychological kind; they look for something in the individual which is missing or has gone wrong. For psychoanalysts it is a failure in the process of resolving the Oedipal conflict and of identifying with the parent of the same sex, or the absence of maternal care. [22] For behaviourists it is the absence of sufficient reinforcements towards adjustment. [23] The implication of such theories and the treatment derived from them is that it is the individual who has to be put right.

In practice, where the treatment of maladjusted adolescents in Britain does occur it is likely to be the work of psychiatrists, clinical psychologists, and psychiatric social workers, and to be heavily dependent upon ideas and techniques derived from psychoanalysis. The treatment will probably be individual, or sometimes group, psychotherapy aimed at increasing the patient's own understanding of his difficulties. Such ideas are part of the conventional wisdom of social work in Britain and as such were received by the project social workers in the course of their own training and taken for granted in their use of casework and group work with their clients. The value of a skilled diagnosis, especially with the more disturbed adolescent, was also accepted, but, as will be seen later, this was seldom available.

Much less conventional and much less psychologically conceived was the awareness of the project team of cultural deprivation as leading to hostile and uncooperative attitudes to strangers and an unwillingness to seek experience. They were aware that widening the range of people, places, and things experienced by participants would give rise to a need for growth in the use of language, conceptual thinking, and social skills.

Maladjustment was one specific concern of the Wincroft Project and delinquency was another. The two types of behaviour are of course not unrelated, and about one-half of the delinquent members of the participant group were also rated as maladusted by their teachers. Some delinquents have perfectly adequate social relationships with their friends and their families, but they refuse to obey the laws of society and only to that degree are they maladjusted. Others feel themselves unloved and unwanted and may commit crimes to draw attention to themselves. Delinquency has, however, increasingly been defined as a sociological problem whereas maladjustment remains largely the province of the psychologist.

In recent years the prevention of juvenile delinquency has received much more attention than the promotion of juvenile mental health, and one by-product of this interest has been the development of theories with a practical application. However, the application of these theories has not so far produced any significant reduction in delinquency. In any case most of this work is American and the relevance of these theories to Britain is limited by very real differences in social conditions. Nevertheless, since there is so little in the way of British or European criminological theory it is inevitable that we should try to explore the relevance of American theory.

Theorizing about delinquency and possible strategies for delinquency prevention in the Wincroft Project was a much more common occupation than theorizing about maladjustment and its causes, but it cannot truthfully be said that such theorizing had much effect on the way that the social workers went about their business. They saw delinquency in the way that they saw maladjustment: as the result of a failure in social relationships, usually with the mother or the father, and though the solution to the problem did not always lie in family casework the dimension of family relationships could not be ignored. The importance of the peer group to the individual boy and the bad effect it may have had on his behaviour were functions of the failure of the family to be effective.

Although theory had little effect on the strategies of the Wincroft Project it may be useful to describe the attempt to incorporate such thinking into the work. One of the authors (CSS) had set out a theoretical framework for the project in June 1965 derived from the theory formulated by A. K. Cohen, which suggested that delinquency was a response to status humiliation. [24] The working-class boy was thrust into a competitive system where he would be judged by middle-class standards of behaviour but where, because of his early socialization, he could never succeed. His response was to up-end the whole system of values and to give status to actions that were malicious, negativistic, and non-utilitarian. The delinquent gang provided the group by which these values were maintained. Nine courses of action were recommended to mitigate this status humiliation. Among these proposals some implied a community development approach, since it was recommended that an attempt be made to increase the number of positions in the community to which status was attached, and to increase access to these positions. Moreover, it was recommended that steps be taken to support respectable working-class culture and promote an ideology of equality. This approach was, however, never tried and the management committee allowed the project director to give central importance to group work and casework method.

Although theory as such did not guide the social workers' interpretation of their roles, the sociological thinking of Smith and Farrant was an ever-present influence. The regular meetings of the research group gave an opportunity to interpret the behaviour of young people in sociological terms and to illuminate the constraints on that behaviour for the workers. Moreover, one valuable line of thought did emerge which introduced a new concept to the workers and sensitized them to the pressures that were upon their clients: this was the concept of network. [25]

By November 1965 the research worker (MF) had begun to draw the attention of the team to the significance of the 'residual network'. He recommended that the task of the fieldworkers should be 'to lose the participant group into the existing community organization'. This would be achieved by helping the immature isolated boy sustain membership of small groups which would eventually be integrated into formal organizations. To do this it might be necessary to 'bolster up sagging community organizations or to create new ones'.

Much later in the project, in March 1967, a second theoretical paper was put to a meeting of the research group (which included the professional workers) and the notion of network was explored further. It was suggested that this notion might help to explain which boys in Wincroft were exposed to delinquent values and how boys from respectable homes could become delinquent. However, no recommendations were made for specific courses of action by the team.

The above discussion of the attempts to build a theoretical framework for the project reveals how limited those attempts were, but this is not surprising given the limited research resources available and the many pressing calls upon the research worker's time. His first priority had been to make it possible to begin the evaluation by establishing a control group; his second had been to establish a recording system that would enable that evaluation to be carried out. Theory-building had unfortunately to be seen as a luxury to be indulged when the other more immediate research tasks were under control.

Since no specific theory was to be tested there was no clear obligation upon the social workers to stick to one conception of their roles and, indeed, there was some difficulty in finding any clear role concept at all. It is this area of role definition that must now be considered. In the early stage of the project, Youth Development Trust members were very much involved in locating, opening, and staffing the coffee bar. But as the project developed the employing body devoted less time to the immediate problems of the fieldwork and concerned itself more with initiating new work and discussing broader policy issues. Although the day-to-day problems of the fieldwork came to be discussed by the staff team in their weekly meetings, individual Trust members continued to take a close interest in the fieldwork. The chairman acted as a focus of communication, linking the professional workers to the Trust, helping them to cope with problems and apply theoretical understanding to complex situations. The general areas of duty to be undertaken by each professional worker had been set out in the job specification, but a precise definition was dependent upon a close study of the needs of the work. This analysis had to take place before there could be any clarity about the specific roles to be filled by each worker.

The Trust Committee saw the task of the project director as including the day-to-day management of the coffee bar, which had already been opened in Wincroft, and the preparation of a scheme of work in readiness for the arrival of the other team members. In the first year the project director's role was to a large extent influenced by his position in the coffee bar. Here it became necessary for him to display some of the role attributes of a coffee bar manager as well as of a youth-worker. Both roles were essential, but it was important that neither should be at the expense of objective evaluation and thus of project development, the latter being the prime element of the director's task. He was only partially successful in avoiding this danger. The demands of coffee bar users, the stress of working in an alien and often hostile setting, the psychological need of the director to demonstrate his ability to work with groups and individuals, all tended to affect judgement and overall planning. His difficulties were increased by the delay in completing the full team of professional staff. Work generated in the first few months quickly escalated and the project director was forced to spend an excessive amount of time supporting volunteers, in direct contact with young people and helping to resolve recurring crises. Although largely unintended, this was beneficial, since the director's experience at ground level of the particular problems and conflicts of the work helped to remove any uncertainties that might have arisen amongst the other members of the professional team.

With the arrival of the other team members and the research worker the director's role was subject to a number of fairly rapid changes. At first more time was spent in planning, administering, and directing the work, the management of the coffee bar having been handed over to one of the other team members. He now spent more time in introducing and supporting voluntary workers, creating opportunities for groups to meet, and servicing groups. With the definition and selection of the participant group his role again changed. The coffee bar was closed in February 1966 and the director played a part in the team task of maintaining or re-establishing contact with the selected participants. As well as doing group work with specific participants in their natural groups, he continued his other tasks of directing team meetings, administration, and the recruitment, training, and support of volunteers. This further change, to some extent a reversal to the earlier pattern, was necessary not only to allow the director to maintain close contact with the fieldwork problems but also to maximize resources in the intensive fieldwork programme.

For the remaining two and a half years the project director's role continued to be that of group worker/administrator/planner, with the third aspect coming into greater prominence as time elapsed and especially in the final nine or so months of the project when the termination programme was being drawn up and implemented.

The roles of the other team members were shaped by the experience gained by the director in his previous twelve months' work. On their arrival in October 1965 the two group workers started out in the café.

It was felt that this would be a suitable position from which to gain initial contact with the adolescents, and become familiar with the neighbourhood. Also, connection with the café would give them an identity in the area. One worker took over the management of the Bridge Café for the final six months of its life, but latterly it was only open for three nights per week, thus giving him the opportunity to be seen in a group-work role elsewhere. After the closure of the Bridge Café this worker was involved exclusively with groups. Towards the end of the project he concentrated on the more difficult and disturbed adolescents, and was almost totally involved in work with young people in family, individual, and pair situations.

The second group worker, after a brief introduction through the coffee-bar-helper role, moved out to develop relationships with individuals and groups. She was exclusively concerned with group work during the ten months she was with the project. Her replacement was introduced at the outset to specific groups and from first contact in street situations operated as a group worker throughout the two years. Latterly more time was spent with specific individuals from groups with whom he was already working, but he was never in the position of having to work with an individual boy who was socially isolated.

The early fieldwork had revealed a number of highly disturbed adolescents. Originally it was intended to appoint a third detached worker primarily to operate with 'two or three small groups of difficult adolescents and [to deal] exclusively with their needs on group work principles'. But it was felt that the severity of the disturbance and isolation of the adolescents likely to be concerned would lead them to be more amenable to casework rather than group work, and thus the original idea was abandoned in favour of a casework appointment. The revised plan was for the group workers to be able to introduce to the caseworker particular individuals with whom he (or she as it turned out) would work exclusively, in cases where the client had no group affiliations, or as a supplement to ongoing group work experience. It proved difficult to recruit a caseworker and it was not until December 1965 that an appointment was made, some three months after the arrival of the other two workers. After a brief introduction period in the coffee bar, the caseworker began to develop work with certain individuals and with one group of young adolescents. Referral proved difficult, but the relatively small workload that had always been envisaged for the caseworker grew rapidly and soon exceeded the time available for it. Throughout the rest of the project it was a constant problem for the team to keep demands for the caseworker's attention within practicable bounds.

The roles of all workers changed over time, but that of the replacement worker was subject to the least change. This was due in large part to the fact that he did not join the project until after the participant group had been selected and was thus able to be directly introduced to a specific group workload. The absence of a period of general introduction to adolescents in the neighbourhood through the coffee bar meant that he did not come into contact with such a large number of other (non-participant) young people. Thus, unlike the other members of the team, he was able to keep extraneous demands on his time to a minimum.

From about the end of 1965, changes in the role-emphasis among workers came about increasingly as a result of conscious planning. Although individual staff members had a separate caseload and role, there was a considerable degree of flexibility. The total caseload of 54 Participants, and their associated natural groupings, plus the three other clients with whom the team had decided to continue work, was divided in late 1965 into four separate caseloads for each individual professional worker, mainly on the basis of who had the strongest relationship with the particular client concerned. A degree of reorganization was necessary on the departure of one worker and the arrival of another, and from time to time certain clients were moved from one worker's list to another.

There was considerable team involvement at the planning level and in introducing and training volunteers. There was also mutual assistance in periods of pressure from clients.

Predicting and controlling the amount of work for which any given staff member was responsible proved a recurring problem, and this effectively prevented any member from occupying a precisely defined and narrow role and, indeed, called for a certain degree of flexibility. However, the dominant emphasis in any worker's role was fairly clear at any point in the project.

The role of the research worker is dealt with in detail later in the book. His relationship to the fieldwork team changed only slightly and then only in the first few months. The original concept of his role had been one of separation and isolation from the fieldworkers, but this was quickly discarded as unrealistic both psychologically and practically and subsequently he was in frequent contact with them, attending and recording staff meetings, gathering additional information, and seeking clarification of points arising on fieldwork reports.

The project was fortunate in drawing together a team of people who did not feel the need to interpret their roles rigidly or in detail, and who were able to play their roles with the maximum degree of flexibility. They were able to adjust their roles to meet the needs of their clients in a way that made sense to them. Flexibility in the acting out of roles meant too that allowances could be made for future developments in relationships. The presentation of different aspects of total roles rarely hindered the work with young people, but in discussion with others professionally involved with young people it often gave rise to a number of difficulties. Teachers and social workers often demanded a defined and comprehensible description of the job and, in some cases, were unable or unwilling to understand the explanation given. This was in marked contrast to many of the clients who accepted with remarkable equanimity the ambiguous role and the change in function of a variety of workers.

In terms of acting out their more general roles many of the volunteers were required to exercise similar flexibility. Some were involved with disturbed clients during times of crisis and some were called upon to instruct in specific skills.

Compared with other detached youth-work projects the present programme made much greater use of voluntary workers. Voluntary effort accounted for just under half the total effort in the years 1966, 1967, and 1968. Prior to this the proportion was even higher and, indeed, the work was started in February 1964 by voluntary effort alone. Several Trust Committee members, assisted by students from Manchester University, had staffed the coffee bar that the Trust had opened in Wincroft. These early voluntary workers were instrumental in helping to demonstrate the existence of need in Wincroft and the feasibility of introducing workers into the area in an unorthodox manner. Without the pioneers of the early months of 1964 it is doubtful whether the work would have gone forward at all.

Between February 1964 and August 1968 a total of 151 adult volunteers took part, these were individuals offering a variety of skills and participating in the project for varying periods of time. Numbers at any one time varied from 20 to 40. Ages varied, ranging from 21 to 40 years old, with an average age of around 26 at the start of involvement with the project. Despite efforts at involving local people only one of these workers was resident in the area, by virtue of his profession as a priest. Most came from other residential areas of the city and were drawn from mainly middle-class backgrounds. Over 40 per cent were students. Further details are given in Appendix I.

Many of the volunteers were unhappy about moving out of the comparative safety and predictability of the coffee bar setting, yet once having been given support in the early stages of the move some soon proved able to assist in the work of re-establishing contact in the streets and generally operating without the background of the physical premises which many had thought indispensable. Volunteers worked, often alone, in all the premises operated by the Trust. As the project developed so did the possibilities of work for volunteers and, consequently, the scope and frequency of their contribution. In 1967 some volunteers joined with the professional workers in following up those participants who had moved to other areas, thus taking on the role of itinerant youth worker. By this date, too, many volunteers were solely responsible for much of the face-to-face work with 'their' group while the professional workers became more concerned with facilitating and servicing group meetings and working more intensively with more severely disturbed clients.

Many of the voluntary workers lacked any form of training in youth work and almost none had experience of this type of work. It was therefore incumbent upon the full-time workers to train the volunteers, but because of the pressures of a very full fieldwork programme this was extremely difficult to arrange. Up to the end of 1965 the project volunteers had little more than an opportunity to join in occasional discussions in which people compared their experiences in the café situation and gave their opinions on what action should or should not be taken. Those volunteers who were students on the University of Manchester Diploma in Youth Work Course received rather more systematic attention, as their fieldwork experience was related to their theoretical studies in weekly lectures and seminars. In this early stage when, it must be remembered, the professional workers also lacked specific expertise of detached youth work, all new voluntary workers served in the coffee bar. If they were fortunate they found an opportunity to talk about the evening's events before their next visit to the bar took place.

As the project developed in sophistication so did the training of volunteers. From October 1965, in order to help them to think more about their work, an information sheet was circulated about every six weeks. One of its subsidiary functions was to develop some kind of unity among a disparate number of adult helpers, few of whom knew each other well, and some not at all. Its main purpose was to make workers more observant and to think more about the young people they saw. It also encouraged volunteers to complete report forms following each visit to the coffee bar. Recording was an important part of each volunteer's contribution and, although primarily intended to assist the research and forward planning, contained a valuable self-training element.

All volunteers were invited to evening meetings, and meetings of this type were held every two months between September 1964 and August 1968. One-day conferences were held in 1966 and 1968 and two-day, residential, training weekends in 1966 and 1967. By the time the first training weekend was held the more experienced volunteers were involved in helping to train and support newcomers.

Following the closure of the coffee bar in January 1966 it became necessary to develop a system of assessing and introducing new voluntary workers. This led to the formation of a rudimentary training scheme. The project director met the new worker and, during an informal discussion, told him something about the work. This enabled some kind of assessment to be made and, following a discussion with the rest of the professional team, a suitable group or individual with whom the full-time workers were already involved was decided upon. Before introducing the new worker to the client or clients, he was taken on a visit to the neighbourhood by a professional worker. After this, a first meeting with the chosen group was attempted. If this was achieved, the new worker continued with the group in the company of the professional worker for a series of weeks. Finally, the professional worker withdrew leaving the new volunteer in regular contact with the adolescent group. The completion of report forms, personal and telephone contact with the professional worker, coupled with periodic team evaluations of progress, helped the volunteer to maintain commitment and increase his skill. All volunteers were urged to read relevant literature.

Very few volunteers had previous youth-work experience, although about one-quarter were in training for youth work. Only six potential volunteers were judged to be unsuitable for the work and were discouraged from starting and in addition three were eased out when they could not meet the required standard. Some of those without previous youth-work experience possessed specialist skills such as a knowledge of football or camping, but the majority did not and often found it hard to see what they had to offer. Yet sometimes this very lack of skill proved an asset when working with young people who were themselves conscious of their own lack of ability and low level of performance. More frequently what the volunteers had to offer was interest and concern demonstrated by their willingness to accept the young person without reference to his level of social development. Nevertheless, in the opinion of the professional team the more successful volunteers were those who had undergone some form of training in human relations; usually teachers (mostly in junior or primary schools) or social workers. Often a young person would come into contact with a number of volunteers during the project and there may well have been a cumulative as well as an individual effect in the contribution made by volunteers.

The focus of attention has up to now been on the human resources at the disposal of the project and certainly these were considered more important than buildings and equipment. The total cost to August 1968 was £20,226 of which some 78 per cent was paid out in salaries, and, by contrast, only 7 per cent went on buildings and equipment (excluding the research grant).

The policy on adequacy of premises was that they should be capable of flexible use, disposed of when no longer needed, and, most important of all, neither by reason of ownership or expense of furnishings should they put the worker in a position of having to consider the well-being of the property before that of the client. Three separate sets of premises, all situated in Wincroft, were hired for varying periods. The coffee bar, a converted shop, was leased for a period of twenty-three months, starting from February 1964. The office, also a lock-up shop, was opened in September 1965 and closed some two and a half years later in June 1968. The third, a house with a shop front, which was used for group meetings and named after its street number, was operated from October 1965 to April 1968. All these properties had a limited life and from 1964 were likely to be demolished in five to seven years as part of the comprehensive development plan for Wincroft. Total cost of renting and converting these premises was £1,168, 6 per cent of the total budget.

Although the workers were able to have some measure of control over premises by deciding when and whether to open them, once they had opened them they faced the inevitable problems of damage, both wilful and accidental, conflict over time of closure, possessiveness, and inter-group rivalry. This type of behaviour was, however, the exception rather than the rule and occurred mainly in the coffee bar and the house, but it served to underline the difficulties inherent in using premises for this type of work.

The functions of the Bridge Café for the workers (often clearer in retrospect than at the time) were seen first as a method of introduction of new workers to the potential clients. It provided a role identity for many of the workers to lean on and an unstructured situation where the behaviour of the 'customers' could be closely observed and their level of maladjustment assessed. The office served a number of separate functions and, apart from being the registered office of the Trust, was a place where professional workers could carry out some of the administrative tasks associated with the project—write reports and contact colleagues in other social-work agencies. It served as a place where clients could contact workers and the times of opening were displayed in the window. Later it came to be used as a place for group meetings.

Lack of suitable premises in Wincroft that could be hired on a nightly basis for small group meetings led to the decision to rent an old shop, and a number of groups used this building sometimes on the same evening. In Chapter 2 we shall say something more about the problems of planning the use of this building. Considerable damage was done to this property, although usually this happened in the absence of workers when young people, believed to be not associated with the project, broke in.

In addition to the above premises the Trust hired, or was loaned free of charge, a number of rooms on a one-night-per-week basis. Thus a gymnasium in a school was used for football training and a room in a church hall for table-tennis and weight-training.

Tenure of premises proved a valuable asset in an area almost devoid of places for small group meetings, but they did bring for the workers the added difficulties of control of behaviour as well as the time-consuming business of administration and maintenance. Without them, however, much of the group work, especially that done in the winter months, would not have been possible.

Transport was another valuable material resource of the project. Two the professional workers had their own cars, which were used extensively, and the Trust was fortunate to be given a minibus. Much time was saved by workers being able to move about the city fairly quickly and, especially when helping clients to find jobs, it saved many hours of frustrating travel on public transport. Many of the voluntary workers used their own cars in connection with the project and on a pure cost basis, in terms of worker efficiency, the money spent on transport (£921, 5 per cent of the budget) paid for itself by making available more time for face-to-face work with clients.

Cars and the minibus provided ideal settings for group work and casework which often occurred in the course of a journey to a specific activity or a lift home. In some instances a client was given the choice of companions and destination by the worker and the vehicle virtually became the premises for the group work. The availability of transport allowed many clients to visit places they could not otherwise easily have visited. In the development of the relationship with clients and in demonstrating the range of services being offered, transport often provided a readily available and easily visible tool. Thus requests were made for help with removal of furniture to new homes and for visits to friends and relatives in borstals and approved schools. Time spent on these journeys was often invaluable in the development and furtherance of relationships with clients and their families.

As with premises, using transport sometimes provided its own problems, especially where the vehicle in use was the worker's personal property, about which he was likely to have strong protective feelings. Demands for use of a vehicle sometimes could not be met, either because it was needed elsewhere or because the use for which it was wanted was felt to be outside the range of Trust services, and this could lead to resentment and damage to relationships. Certain of the more disturbed clients staged sit-ins, refusing to leave a vehicle, and a common practice for many clients was to shout obscene and derogatory remarks out of the windows. Since it was often difficult for the worker to keep his mind on the situation within the car and on the road at the same time, a second worker was sometimes included.

In terms of other material resources the Trust possessed very little. Workers, both voluntary and professional, often loaned their own property when equipment (sports equipment, for example) was required, but the Trust did possess sundry items—a set of weights, a sewing machine, some tools, a guitar, a set of football shirts, some camping equipment, and a number of boxed games and construction kits. From time to time minor items such as paint and playing cards were purchased. All served as the basis upon which a group-work session could be founded or helped establish the credentials of the Trust.

One essential resource for the workers was ready cash which could be used for day-to-day expenses, such as buying a round of drinks, tickets to theatres and cinemas, and meeting the costs of using their own transport. The total cost of this item was only £276 for all workers' expenses, both professional and voluntary (2 per cent of the total). Many workers deliberately did not claim the full amount they had spent in the course of the fieldwork and this acted as a hidden contribution to Trust funds. At the start of a relationship the willingness of the workers to provide more than their share might be necessary as the only way to gain acceptance, but it also was sometimes prolonged by the workers' insecurity in the situation. Occasionally money, or goods, were used as a direct and open subsidy to a specific client. This may have taken the form of a small amount for bus-fare home or for buying a meal, or loans might be given either to prevent a client being turned out of home or as rent for 'digs' or a flat. Constant attempts to borrow came from only a small number of clients and whenever possible the team would discuss the matter at some length in the weekly discussions before making the loan and the workers would try to get financial assistance from the statutory and voluntary agencies first.

It might be thought from this description of the workers and their resources that the project had more than many social workers would have in dealing with the needs of only 54 boys. To this it must be replied that of the total effort expended by the 156 workers in face-to-face encounters with young people in Wincroft only 30 per cent was with the 54 participants. Contact was made with some 600 young people in the four and a half years work. Also it must be remembered that nearly half the effort was accounted for by voluntary help. Perhaps a more realistic conclusion to draw from this description is how little the workers had at their disposal to deal with the accumulated problems of alienated youth in an industrial slum area. Certainly there was little experience to build upon and little guidance that could be expected from the application of social science. What perhaps compensated for these weaknesses, and what may not have come through in this description of the workers, is their commitment to the project. This will become clearer perhaps as they are seen in action later in the book.

This book has in mind a number of different readers: first, the expert whose field is touched upon by this work, whether criminologist, sociologist, psychologist, or psychiatrist; second, those who train social workers, teachers, and youth workers, and those who are being trained; third, the practitioners, and those who shape policy; and fourth, but not least important, leaders of local communities who might involve themselves in this work, even to the extent of mounting their own programmes. With such different levels of interest it has been important to bear in mind the need for readability, but also at the same time not to forget that the specialist will not be convinced, or at least challenged, unless the hard facts are also included, Chapters 5 and 6 are those to avoid if the reader is more interested in people than statistics.

For those who might like to know the outcome of the project it can be said briefly here that it was a modest success. The number of the participant (experimental) group who were convicted during the life of the project was significantly lower than the number of the control group also convicted. The estimated savings from this reduction of delinquency will be discussed in Chapter 7 (p. 255).

The book has been written in two distinct sections: the first part giving an account of the social-work programme and the second the details of the research evaluation. This layout should not be taken to indicate that research and action were rigidly separated in the life of the project for, in fact, the social work was enriched by a continuing feedback of research results as well as by the demands for clarity placed upon it by the research, and, on the other hand, the research was in turn nourished by the insightful observations of the social workers. The reason for separating the two is that among the readership there will be those who will be interested mainly in Part I, and those interested mainly in Part II.

The purpose of this introductory chapter was to give an overview of the whole project and to place it in a social context. The next two chapters describe and analyse the worker's and then the client's perspective to the programme of work and thus build upon the description given above of the people involved. These are followed by detailed case studies of how relationships between the workers and the participants changed, and what the outcome was in terms of better social adjustment and the prevention of delinquency (Chapter 4). The problems of terminating the project have been selected for special treatment because of their practical and ethical importance, and this concludes the description of the social-work programme. A statistical summary of the essential facts then follows.

In Part II of the book are two chapters concerned with research; the last Part discusses the implications of the project and makes certain recommendations. The two chapters on research (Chapters 5 and 6) are inevitably rather technical and therefore will be of less interest to the general reader than the specialist, but the important findings are summed up at the end of each chapter and repeated in the last chapter of the book.

NOTES AND REFERENCES

1 See Cyril S. Smith, The Youth Service and Delinquency Prevention, *Howard Journal of Penology and Crime Prevention* **12** (I), June 1966. Also see the recent report of the Youth Service Development Council, *Youth and Community Work in the 70s* (HMSO, London, 1969).

2 See Irving A. Spergel, *Community Problem-Solving* (University of Chicago Press, Chicago, 1969) for an account of the American delinquency prevention programmes. Also P. Marris and M. Rein, *Dilemmas of Social Reform* (Routledge and Kegan Paul, London, 1967).

3 A short report on this work was written for the Dulwich College Mission by Peter Massie, and is available from the Youth Service Information Centre, Leicester.

4 P. Crawford, D. Malamud, and J. Dumpson, *Working with Teenage Gangs* (Welfare Council of New York City, New York, 1950). A more up-to-date and comprehensive account of this work can be found in Irving A. Spergel, *Street Gang Work: Theory and Practice* (Addison-Wesley, Cambridge, Mass., 1966).

5 E. Powers and H. Witmer, *An Experiment in the Prevention of Delinquency: The Cambridge-Somerville Youth Study* (Columbia University Press, New York, 1951).
John Spencer, *Stress and Release in an Urban Estate* (Tavistock Publications, London, 1964).

6 Mary Morse, *The Unattached* (Penguin, Harmondsworth, 1965).
G. Goetschius and J. Tash, *Working with Unattached Youth* (Routledge and Kegan Paul, London, 1967).

7 This situation has now changed.

8 Youth Development Trust, *Juvenile Delinquency in Manchester: The Facts*. (Privately printed, 1965.) Out of print.

9 A full report on the café phase of the project can be made available by the authors to those professionally interested.

10 These, and subsequent statistics, may have changed since, but they are relevant to the period of operation of the project.

11 Youth Development Trust, 1965, op. cit.

12 M. Grunhut, *Juvenile Offenders before the Courts* (Oxford University Press, London, 1956).

13 There has since been a striking change for the worse in the late 60s in the recorded convictions for crimes of violence in Manchester.

14 Medical Officer of Health, the City of Manchester, *Report on the Health of the City of Manchester for 1965.*

15 The Institute of Municipal Treasurers and Accountants, *Children's Services Statistics: 1965-66.*

16 The Institute of Municipal Treasurers and Accountants, *Education Statistics: 1965-66.*

17 Medical Officer of Health, the City of Manchester, 1965, op. cit.

18 Ibid.

19 These figures were kindly supplied by the Chief Careers Advisory Officer for the City of Manchester.

20 D. H. Stott, *The Social Adjustment of Children* (University of London Press, London, 1958, 3rd edn. 1965). Manual to the Bristol Social Adjustment Guides.

21 Ibid.

22 See, for example, J. Bowlby, *Forty-Four Juvenile Thieves* (Baillière, Tindall, and Cox, London, 1946), and the more recent critical discussion by A. K. Cohen and J. F. Short in R. K. Merton and R. A. Nisbet (eds.), *Contemporary Social Problems* (Harcourt Brace and World, New York, 1966).

23 See A. Bandura, *Social Learning and Personality Development* (Holt Rinehart, and Winston, New York, 1963).

24 A. K. Cohen, *Delinquent Boys: The Culture of the Gang* (Free Press, New York, 1955).

25 See J. Clyde Mitchell (ed.), *Social Networks in Urban Situations* (Manchester University Press, Manchester, 1969), especially Chapter 1 'The concept and use of social networks'.

2 · The worker's perspective

The origins of the Wincroft Project have now been described. Next it is intended to show how those who took part in the project came together and interacted within the terms of a special kind of relationship – that of social worker and client. Although in conventional social-work terms the worker was by no means on familiar territory, he had the advantage of having specific aims and possessing the skills and resources to achieve his objectives. The client, on the other hand, was on his own home ground and was less committed to maintaining the relationship than was the worker.

It will have become clear that the workers had a definite brief from their employers. They were to help a specified list of young people reach some 'dynamic adjustment', and thereby to control their delinquency. It is true that the strategies of the programme were left open for the workers to decide, but even here they could take guidance from the professional practice of social work and, in particular, from that of social group work. The workers did not set themselves up as models for the young people to emulate, but there is no question that some identification with them did take place. One of the most difficult boys encountered in the whole project expressed a wish to become a 'youth worker'. Moreover, the workers often took the boys into strange territory where they relied upon the worker to know the correct way of behaving and followed his line. Nevertheless, the workers stuck determinedly to the professional principle of self-determination and saw their job as helping the young people fashion an identity for themselves. They might support them through a difficult patch in a style of behaviour which they personally found repugnant but this was always with an eye on the possible outcomes. They might accept permissively the free expression of hostility, but always with the assumption that it would be transitory. In the total encounter their job was to keep the options open and not to allow the young people to confirm their own self-fulfilling prejudices. For this reason the workers made a virtue of their own ambiguous role of detached youth workers. As will become clear later in this chapter, social-work practice was not always very helpful in the strange and novel situation of detached youth work, but it did at least specify certain procedures. It required

45

the workers to assess the needs of their clients, to plan a programme to help meet those needs, and to evaluate their actions to see if they were effective. It also recognized the therapeutic value of a permissive technique for certain young people and helped the workers accept an unusual amount of aggression from their clients.

Not only did the workers know what they were trying to do and, increasingly, how to do it, but they also knew why they had involved themselves in these relationships in the first place. Whereas it took the clients some time to discover that the workers were not running the Bridge Café for their own (or anybody else's) profit (which many of them believed despite the obvious evidence of very little being sold), the workers knew that for either professional or private reasons, they were committed to helping the customers.

One last point needs to be made before examining the worker's perspective in some detail — his awareness that his commitment was of a long-term finite nature. The professional workers knew when they were appointed in the autumn of 1965 that they would be working in the area for three years and they knew by the end of that year which young people they would need to sustain relationships with over that period.

In describing the worker's approach to his assignment there are dangers of presenting the work in too schematic a form. Although the work was tackled in a systematic fashion, it is tempting, especially in order to make it better understood by the layman, to portray it as more coherent than it was. The authors are conscious of this danger and at no point is it more relevant than when the operation of the principles and methods of work are described. Here the real-life situation rarely turns out like the text-book paradigm — assessment, planning, implementation, and evaluation. Sometimes the workers failed to assess the needs of young people; sometimes they failed to plan the course of the work with groups and individuals. Operating as they were in strange territory the workers had to act under the pressure of events without always understanding why, and indeed how, the work was carried through. But at all times they tried to apply a systematic process to the work of assessment and planning and, compared with many social-work and social education programmes, the project scored high on evaluation.

It is an unavoidable simplification to treat the 156 workers involved in the project as an individual entity, especially in the exercise of assessment and planning functions. The professional workers had each to make their own plans, and communicate them to volunteer workers operating with specific groups for which they were responsible, as well as to share in team discussions and joint decisions. Within the professional team the differences of skill, age, training, and experience all tended to colour assessment; variations in method and approach from worker to worker affected the way plans were put into operation; each worker's individual commitment inevitably affected his judgement on the success of his enterprise. In the field of work that the project had elected to develop the absence of close comparisons (at every stage of the process) made it difficult to separate objective fact from a deep belief in the value of the project. Negligent reporting, misinterpretation, and inaccurate worker observation sometimes served to complicate matters, and the commitment to using relatively untrained voluntary workers made further room for error in reporting and action. The need to respect an individual worker's motivation and skill, and the necessity of encouraging and supporting a worker's judgements when operating in very stressful situations, further hampered certain areas of planning and critical evaluation.

Some idea of how much thought the professional team gave to the procedures of social work is shown by the following retrospective analysis of subjects discussed at a typical weekly meeting of the professional team in December 1966. In this analysis an *assessment* is taken to include any report of information about a boy relevant to his needs, and any judgement made about the nature of his needs. Generally such assessments were made alongside *planning* to satisfy those needs, but this was by no means always so. *Evaluation* of the workers' effort includes the regular examination of frequency of contact with a boy as well as judgements about the effectiveness of the work carried out. The records that were subjected to analysis were often complicated and extensive documents, and frequently alluded (in a shorthand familiar only to the team) to events in the individual's or group's history. The extract set out below therefore requires a certain amount of explanatory material (inserted in parentheses). The use of italic face indicates in the first example assessment, in the second planning, and in the third evaluation. The reader should note the presence of indicators of all three procedures in each example.

Assessment

ROBERT. Workers had some contact with this boy, but he had always remained fairly remote from any relationship. Present concern precipitated by *the fact that he ran away to Sheffield last week*. Recovered by family and police action. We were told of departure by Freddie (his elder brother) who telephoned a worker.

Discussion of possible motives for going revealed possibility that *some illegal activity may have occurred.* Boy uses Houston (local café) regularly.

Decision: Worker to telephone Headmaster of school to determine the possible motive for departure, and find out other information about his school record.

Contact with Head effected during lunch-break, and large amount of information obtained. This substantiated the 'hunch' that illegal activity had occurred, and apparently *Robert was one of the boys suspected of a breaking and entering job. He had denied that he was involved, but ran away the following morning.*

Decision: that worker should endeavour to effect direct contact, and use brother Freddie as an assistant if possible. In view of the . . . [school] . . . information, it was decided that great care should be exercised in making direct contact, as it was thought that *this boy is not likely to respond if he sees the worker acting as the 'ears' of either the family or of outside authority.*

Planning

JACK. A Bridge Café contact and school playground footballer, this boy has had a lot of group contact in 5-a-side expeditions, and has played a number of times in the second division football group this season. A tall, thin, highly active boy with good verbal ability. Has a marked interest in girls. One of the elder members of a large family, Jack is not popular within the football team. He has determined not to play as goalkeeper, and has thereby lost his place in the team.

Decision: To make no effort to help this boy regain his place in the team. Worker to maintain personal contact in Ada's (local café). To explore possibility of voluntary worker going with Jack and two others on visits to youth clubs, or, second, more general visits to places of interest with Tick and Jenny.

Evaluation

SIMON. Simon is a quiet, socially isolated boy. In a white-collar job. Living on the fringe of the project area. His only contact with workers has been through playing in the second division football team, following earlier contact on school playground. *Little personal contact has been effected, but his footballing ability and desire to*

play means he was a fairly regular attender on Sunday afternoons.
He does not attend gym [football training] on Mondays. On the
field his competence as a footballer is sometimes marred by
outbursts of verbal aggression, and this has also been noted off the
pitch. The home circumstances were thought to be unusual with the
probability that the father had been out of work through illness for
some months.

Decision: To help Simon maintain his membership of the football
team. The worker to make specific contact with the home on a
regular basis (ostensibly with football information) to endeavour to
make a closer personal relationship with this boy away from the
match setting.

All the above extracts were from one meeting of the professional team
held on 15 December 1966. A more extended analysis of team meetings
in the period April 1967 to March 1968 has been carried out to show
the relative numerical weight of each procedure (see *Table 1*). In
addition, each worker would also be giving independent consideration
to work with groups assigned to him, and these would be the subject of
frequent discussion with the project director and colleagues.

Table 1   Frequency of use of social-work procedures April 1967 to
March 1968

Assessment	Planning	Evaluation	No. of meetings
343	288	140	45

The steady and systematic examination of work programmes
throughout the project is further indication that above all else the
workers' view was intended to be a highly professional and responsible
one, presenting their services in such a way that deviant boys would
find it possible to respond to the relationship. This professionalism
informed every part of the social-work process, whether it involved
full-time or voluntary workers. It will now be helpful to look in more
detail at each of these fundamental procedures – assessment, planning,
evaluation – and see how the workers saw the job at each step in the
process.

ASSESSMENT

Most social workers recognize the necessity for a careful assessment of their client's situation in order to establish his true needs and the best manner of helping him.

In seeking the information required to make an assessment, the project workers could not be as direct in questioning young people as, for example, a probation officer. Although workers perceived the young users of the Bridge Café as people who might have problems, any attempt to interview them formally would have been self-defeating. Since the adolescents had not sought the help of the workers in other than a very superficial way, the workers were limited in their understanding of the factors underlying the request. 'Give us a couple of bob, mate' might be a warning sign of a boy in trouble, but any attempt by a social worker to confirm such a suspicion might easily frighten the boy away. The workers' view that the young people were potential clients was not yet complemented by the young person's view of the adult as a helping person (see discussion in Chapter 3). Most workers were content to bide their time, and not to trespass where they were not invited. Some were content to meet the simpler needs of young people by providing, in the café, somewhere to sit down, a warm environment, somewhere to meet friends, and somewhere to play cards. Other workers offered to take a hand in the games, sharing in social activities, and showing the users they were people who were interested in listening but not in prying. At some time or other everybody had to take a large amount of verbal punishment or endure a stony silence.

Workers began to make their assessments of individual and group needs as a result of observation from physical proximity and involvement, rather than by orthodox questioning, and this was to be the characteristic approach to assessment, whether operating in the Bridge Café, on the streets, or in commercial premises. In this way some of the difficulties of piercing the front presented by adolescents in orthodox social-work settings were avoided.

Initially, workers in the Bridge Café tended to concentrate on the physical setting — indeed their role was one of coffee bar helper — rather than on the users. Although this served to take the spotlight of attention away from the adolescent, the real purpose of their presence was never far from the helpers' minds and few, if any, were much interested in the mechanics of the coffee bar as an end in itself. In order to get into a position where help could be provided to those needing it, it was necessary to observe, make relationships, learn facts, and determine needs, and the reports analysed statistically in Chapter 4 (v) p. 172 provided most of the raw material for preliminary assessments and initial plans. In the early stages of the work, prior to the assembly of the full team, most effort was directed to identifying particular people and, through friendly contact, learning about situations, attitudes, and behaviour that would help later assessment.

Building up information in this way is of necessity a slow business, and results in a patchy or sometimes downright inaccurate picture. Some users gave false names; others offered extracts from their fantasy lives involving marriage, divorce, unwanted children, criminal exploits, and false relationships. One example of a boy's fantasies will reinforce the view held by workers that open curiosity yielded little useful information. A worker reported that 'Johnny had married a German girl of 18 but was divorced nine months later because of her promiscuity. He was sad about this.' All of this turned out to be false information. Workers recognized the danger of calling the story-teller's bluff and in any case some highly bizarre stories subsequently proved to contain a good deal of truth. In attempting to relate to these boys it seemed wiser to steer a course nearer apparent gullibility than cynical disbelief.

Early assessments were therefore built up tentatively, and based primarily on observed behaviour. There were frequently questions workers very much wanted to ask in order to facilitate a more accurate assessment. For example, 'Is this very dirty ill-dressed boy living at home?' or 'How can we verify that this particular boy is at work, and doing the job he claims?' Obtaining such basic data, and checking its accuracy, proved to be a very long process, but when information came from young people (as it did increasingly) it came naturally, arising from the level of the relationship and in the order determined by the young person. Much later in the project the team might set out to get some vital piece of information to answer a question such as 'Is Gerald's mother as irrational as she is described?' in order to make a more balanced assessment of the boy's need, but in the early stages they were content for the information to come piecemeal. This is not to say that the workers adopted a careless or *laissez-faire* approach to assessment, but rather that it forced them to use themselves intelligently and exploit lines of conversation with greater skill in order to add to the jigsaw picture of individual personalities.

As relationships strengthened the team was able to move beyond the level of superficial assessment, but in the face of a serious crisis the course of action taken did not always stem from a rounded understanding of the total situation. Workers, helping the client to talk about his current difficulty in some detail, still had to avoid too direct questioning, and accept refusals to follow certain leads of conversation judged by the adolescent to be irrelevant to the matter at hand. Even when workers had begun to show their usefulness, the boys were not always sufficiently self-aware or articulate to anticipate what the workers might need to know in order to help effectively. But in this way the problem never ceased to be the client's problem. The workers never saw themselves as 'taking over'. For, however much the professional team assessed the situation behind the scenes, whether or not a plan of any kind materialized depended upon the client. The worker's assessment could lead to practical action only if it was the expression of the client's need, and felt by the client to be so. This applied as much to the work with groups (the bulk of the programme) as to the crisis intervention requested by certain adolescents. Helping groups and individuals to do what they wanted to do (within the bounds of law) was a view shared by all the professional team primarily concerned with the day-to-day running of the project. Underpinning all assessment lay a shared non-directive, person-centred philosophy. [1]

Assessment could not have a once-and-for-all character where a continuous programme was to operate over three years and more, especially when it covered some of the most formative years of the lives of the participants. At the beginning of 1966 nearly half the boys were still at school; by mid-1968 all were of working age. Their growing interest in courtship and marriage made different demands from those stemming from peer-group relationships. While most of the participants lived in the parental home, this period marked the beginning of the transition from dependence to economic and emotional independence. Much else happened in their lives. Some moved from the neighbourhood when their families were rehoused; some were excluded from the family home, while others left it. One lost a parent through death, others through desertion. Some were forced into unemployment by the effects of the economic squeeze of 1967, and others by the introduction of the Selective Employment Tax. A few were faced with several personal problems simultaneously, and their situation changed daily. No assessment of the needs of participants could therefore hope to be more than a temporary one, and a long-term programme of social work of this nature necessarily implied a continuous process of review.

In a number of situations assessment was unusually difficult because workers were unable to make sense of the observations upon which assessment had to be made. Boys who exhibited highly disturbed behaviour with bizarre or asocial symptoms made assessment impossible because of the team's lack of specialist knowledge in the field of mental health. The fact that the project was working with an unscreened population made it almost inevitable that some of the 'unknown quantities' with whom contact began would need specialist help. But the situation was not one in which specialist and 'sufferer' could be brought together easily, and it was not until late in the project that workers were able to call upon specialists. In any case, the team's judgement of the degree of disturbance, and its origins, was open to criticism. In one case the team was perplexed by the extremely violent behaviour of one 16-year-old boy in the Bridge Café:

> With the arrival of Victor things worsened rapidly. He walked up to the counter and joined Alan (a mate), and immediately grabbed a pack of cards, and began to tear and eat them, chewing a wad of cards and then spitting them out ... Victor didn't appear to hear anything that I said to him ... he grabbed a hammer from a boy doing a repair job and wrenched off the head and broke the stale in two pieces — a task that demanded considerable strength. In the kitchen ... in various bursts of aggressive behaviour he broke a chair, sawed a washing line in bits, broke a bottle and brandished it in the worker's face, snapped a piece of wood into four and chewed one piece for about 10 minutes, laughed silently and aloud, snapped a coathook, broke the sink bowl, snapped a broom handle (ignored another — 'that's a new one'), bent a metal floor brush, and then tried to set fire to it.

This boy had given many previous indications of his violence, but it proved extremely difficult to determine whether the incidents were caused by mental disorder, excessive drinking, frustration in intolerable home situations, or his desire to display his exceptional physical strength. Quite apart from assessment difficulties, this boy presented major problems to workers at every stage in the social-work process, as can easily be imagined from the above extract.

During the re-establishment of contact following the final closure of the Bridge Café, the workers also encountered strange pieces of behaviour in commercial settings which challenged their understanding:

> Rex hogged the conversation the whole evening. He was in a bizarre
> mood. He continuously talked about what he had done to girls, e.g.
> beaten them up, refused to sleep with them. It is difficult to fathom
> out how much of it is true and how much is false. Interspersed with
> this he kept saying various people fancied him and asking them for a
> kiss. He effectively kept other people out of the conversation.

At the outset, assessment was further complicated through an
inability to exercise accurate judgement as to the meaning of certain
attitudes and behaviour in the local cultural background. It took time
to begin to identify the significance of deviant behaviour which was
accepted from that which offended against local standards. It was
important to guard against importing the workers' personal or cultural
standards into the client's environment, and some voluntary workers
tended to consider the young people more disturbed in their behaviour
than local people did. Many participants had what in middle-class terms
would be described as highly disorganized family lives, with one or
other parent absent, or given to violence, drunkenness, or deviance, but
much more irregular family behaviour was acceptable in the project
neighbourhood, and this had to be taken into account in assessing the
needs of clients.

Workers were not entirely dependent upon their personal observations in assessment since information was obtained from other sources.
But what proportion of the workers' time was used in the operation
and to what extent did this vary as the project developed? What form
did the assessment take and how did the team develop methods of
recording assessment in the ongoing process of the work?

The year 1966 opened with a full assessment by the professional
team of each boy designated as a participant. Almost all of the 54 boys
had attended the Bridge Café at some time, and were therefore known
to at least one member of the team. But the team also had the research
data which focused upon two views of the boy's behaviour – his
delinquent record and his behaviour in school. Some of the boys had
already appeared before a court on two occasions, others were included
because of their high score on the Bristol Social Adjustment Guides
completed by the form teacher, and some met both criteria. This
objective assessment of participants into the more-or-less delinquent
and the more-or-less maladjusted at school was, however, rarely used by
the social-work team in assessing current needs, although the fact of

selection as a participant on those more objective measurements confirmed the fieldworkers in their judgements.

In the team discussions workers preferred to avoid knowledge of the extent of an individual's delinquency (nature of crimes, etc.) or maladjustment (reflected in the personal BSAG score) as it was felt that such knowledge might affect the workers' attitudes towards boys assigned to them. But there was another reason why research information could not easily be shared with fieldworkers. Some of it had been obtained under confidential seal. In the case of certain participants the workers' judgements had been validated by research inquiry. With most of the boys the degree and nature of individual disturbance would still have to be discovered by experience, and the programme would have to be adjusted as a result of reassessment in the light of personal interaction between worker and participant.

The full-time workers met each Thursday from October 1965 and usually devoted the whole day (about five hours) to discussing the work. Part of each session was given over to assessment, and every two months a complete review was carried out at which every participant was discussed.

Discussion was based on a written report from the professional worker to whom any particular boy had been assigned. The worker's report and verbal comments would incorporate the assessments of any voluntary workers in close contact with the boy or his group and would draw on written fieldwork reports. The bi-monthly assessment took a different shape. Using a *pro forma*, workers in turn gave their judgement based on the discussion and on their personal knowledge of work with groups of which any particular individual under consideration was a member. This gave a 'snap-shot' of the current contact with each participant and so provided a discussion point from which the team could consider maintaining or changing the programme of work and also make decisions about future action.

The fieldwork was carried out in a relatively small geographical area and every team member, while having responsibility for certain groups and specific individuals (a group load and a case load) would come into contact with many participants in the course of a month's work. Because of this it was possible for several team members to contribute to discussions of a particular boy from first-hand knowledge. Sometimes participants were in more than one group and other workers would service groups other than their own and opinions could be shared to get a more objective picture of the current situation.

A section of the form is reproduced below:

	No contact (concerned)	*Occasional personal contact*	*Frequent personal contact*	*Occasional group contact*	*Frequent group contact*	*No contact (unconcerned)*
Harry A					X	
Peter B			⊢——→ X	⊢——→ X		
Fred C	⊢————————————→ X					
Gordon D						X
Albert E		X ←———⊣				

NOTE The arrows indicate the direction and extent of change in the position since the previous assessment (denoted by the tail of the arrow). It was by no means uncommon for participants to receive two ratings (for example, Peter B above) as a result of individual personal contact with one worker, and involvement in a group assisted by another worker (see text).

The perspective of the worker changed as relationships strengthened and he gained a deeper understanding of the client. At the beginning of work most of the information available at team meetings was the result of fieldwork contact with the adolescent, 'hard information' was scarce, and most information was presented tentatively. It was most important in what was known to be likely to be a long and piecemeal social-work operation, to proceed economically with the little information that did become available. Careful recording of discussions was essential for the ongoing assessment of needs, and a record of team meetings was circulated to all professional staff by the research worker who attended all meetings. An extract from such a record has been used earlier in this chapter to illustrate three social-work procedures. Longer case and group studies were also prepared and circulated from time to time.

Longer case studies came before a slightly different group – the project team meeting. Here, the professional staff were joined by the agency chairman and by other members of university staff as well as the project research worker. Although the emphasis of these meetings was on clarification of policy and forward planning, assessment of the overall situation was always evident. Extracts from the study material will show how the twenty-one project team meetings, held during the period November 1965 to April 1968, were concerned with the discussion and clarification of policy in the light of the fieldworkers' assessments of the current situation.

Periodically, professional staff, voluntary workers, and members of the Trust Committee came together for full project staff sessions. Twenty of these sessions were held, usually in the evenings to enable volunteer workers to be present. In addition, the full project staff came together for two training days and for two residential training weekends. All these sessions included a large element of assessment and drew together various strands of information which aided subsequent planning. In 1967 arrangements were made for voluntary workers to receive photocopies of their fieldwork reports, which not only helped them to look more objectively at what they were doing but gave them a more comprehensive record of their own work.

Most of the early information was obtained through face-to-face contact with young people, but it was not many months before information from other adults in touch with adolescents in the neighbourhood began to come into the fieldworkers' hands. The team had been very much aware of the need to draw upon the knowledge and experience of other social and educational agencies in the assessment of a boy's needs, and though this information began to flow it did not flow as freely as had been anticipated. The reasons for this require close examination. One reason was the fieldworkers' anxiety to avoid bias in their work resulting from the judgements (whether positive or negative) of other adults in touch with the young people in different settings. It was also important that the client should not believe that discussions were taking place in his absence and so until a strong and confidential relationship could be built up with the other adults our fieldworkers remained cautious of discussing their clients. Indeed this caution was enhanced by a situation early in the project where 'behind the scenes' action led to repercussions on the field-workers. A fracas in the Bridge Café had led to a decision to discuss the boys involved with their probation officer, whose subsequent handling of the situation was not sufficiently discreet to prevent the boys deducing what had happened, and reacting with further threats of violence. Over two years later the affair still rankled when a drunken youth accused a worker of having 'shopped our John'. However much the statement was a distortion of the true facts, it served to indicate the danger to the detached youth workers of being 'in the know'. That early incident certainly increased the workers' caution, but there were other factors preventing a very rapid or helpful flow of information from reaching the workers from other sources.

In the case of the teachers in the schools there was not only the difficulty of gaining access, there was the much greater difficulty of seeking information about their educational failures. There was a marked reluctance to discuss with any degree of objectivity those young people who were difficult to control and impossible to teach. The project workers were relatively unknown, and discussions tended to minimize staff-pupil problems. It took many months of informed contact before these could be ventilated freely and then only with certain teachers.

The closest links were with the probation officers in the area but here a further barrier was present, that of professional confidentiality. Project workers were relative newcomers to the area, operating in unorthodox ways, and so it was hardly surprising that statutory officers exercised considerable discretion in what they communicated. If early experiences made the project unsure of how other social workers would use information, the latter must have been equally unsure as to the ways in which the project might utilize material they passed to us. At the early stages neither party was very good at sharing information or in describing the precise limitations on its use. It was only after several years, and then only with certain officers, that some freedom of exchange was possible.

The workers were rarely in a position to obtain an open exchange of information with teachers and social workers until well into the second half of the project. Where reputation, skill, or confidentiality were threatened (and the information most wanted was on boys whose behaviour did just that) progress, understandably, was slowest. The flow of information was easiest in contact with the school welfare service and the police juvenile liaison officer; yet in the first instance information tended to be unsystematic and anecdotal, and in the second related to children rather younger than those in the project. Information although free flowing was therefore not as useful.

So, for a variety of reasons, workers in related services were rarely able to extend full cooperation during the first two years of the project and their assistance in the initial assessment was therefore less than it might have been. As with the young people so with the adults — information and confidences were given when they were ready to give them. This weakness in cooperation, with a direct bearing on the assessment of individual needs, can be traced to three sources, of which the principal one was the newness of the sponsoring agency. The absence of an established reputation in the city's social and educational work made other workers chary of passing on information. The second reason stems from the fact that in 1964 and 1965 the workers were seen as youth workers, not as teachers or caseworkers, and this further inhibited an easy entry into teaching and casework circles. The workers were themselves on trial by their professional colleagues. The third reason was that the work was being carried out by a voluntary agency which had stressed the heterodoxy of its approach.

Besides difficulties inherent in the situation, and in the agency, there were also difficulties created by the project fieldworkers. Their ambivalence to cooperation with other agencies was frequently apparent in an unwillingness to risk damaging trust built up with a boy. They felt an uncertainty as to how statutory officers would use information and a lack of confidence in the professional standing of some workers. These factors, along with the apparent inability of teachers and statutory social workers to understand the vulnerable situation in which the fieldworkers were operating, all served to make the development of close cooperation almost as difficult, slow, and frustrating as that with the youths the project was trying to reach.

PLANNING

Intelligent planning is vital in work with the 'unattached' for workers are likely to find that day-to-day operations are so full of incident and crises that they will make little headway unless they know in which direction they want to move. At the outset the clients can be expected to contribute little to the thinking ahead process, since this is seldom what they have been brought up to do. It was the expressed intention of fieldworkers to involve young people in forward planning for themselves and their groups (if only a few hours ahead) and it was this planning for the young people's involvement in planning that fell heavily upon the adult workers for much of the project. First-hand observations provided plenty of evidence that many of the predicaments the young people experienced were in part the result of a failure to foresee the consequences of their action and also that much of their boredom and frustrations in leisure time stemmed from both lack of confidence and ability to plan effectively.

In work of this kind it is necessary to have both long- and short-term plans, the latter helping to resolve each crisis as it occurs, yet not at the expense of long-term goals. To achieve this it is important that workers always have some room for manoeuvre and, with this in mind, the fieldwork team tried to ensure that total fieldwork time was not fully committed in advance each week. When workers got boxed-in through overcommitment in a crisis, an essential breadth of vision was lost. Sometimes workers reached a point where they were running to keep up with themselves, and drawing on their private leisure time to maintain programmes of work. In the spring of 1967 the workers' field commitments had to be cut back firmly, not only to protect their health but also to preserve their ability to carry out the essential function of planning ahead.

A good deal of straightforward planning was needed to ensure that the slender resources at the Trust's disposal were fully and efficiently deployed. It was important to make sure that these were used to maximum advantage, but also vitally necessary to see that the interests of groups and individuals did not clash accidentally. Certain boys and groups were not ready to co-exist (let alone cooperate) in the small house available for group meetings, and planning was essential to prevent escalation of internal or inter-group rivalries. Accommodation had to be obtained in church halls and school gymnasia; football pitches and changing accommodation had to be hired; youth-club leaders had to be approached to arrange for visits to clubs or to arrange for use of rooms or equipment. Overnight accommodation, camping equipment, and other supplies had to be made available for trips away.

Inevitably, groups began to be possessive about the rented house and the offices used by the Trust for group meetings, and this fact, along with the desirability of having somewhere for workers to drop into when they needed, meant that all of the team had to be kept informed about the week-by-week use of premises. Although as a rule this kind of organization presented few problems, it sometimes necessitated very elaborate planning where clients became possessive about workers as well as premises. It also presented a further problem for the fieldworker resulting from the disintegration of a friendship group, where fragments of the group continued to make demands upon the workers. Familiarity with the worker's weekly programme enabled individuals and sub-groups to force a demand for service, or disrupt carefully laid plans. This problem will be given further examination in Chapter 4, but this incident illustrates the need for detailed planning of a worker's time and physical resources:

There was to be a party for the Senior Football Group at a worker's house on Friday, and arrangements had been made for the group to assemble at the rented house (their normal meeting place) at 7.30 pm. The problem was whether other boys (and one boy in particular) might not be present at the house and cause a disturbance before the group departed. The boy, Dennis, part of a friendship group which had broken up, had also broken contact with the worker at whose home the party was to take place. If he learned that others were to go to a home he had recently cut himself away from (and probably regretted having done so) there could easily be trouble, especially if he was accompanied by certain other lads. It had already been arranged for another fieldworker to meet him at 9 pm in order to prevent him turning up accidentally at the party. It was now thought that this might not be enough, and that workers with the football group (and the group) might be severely embarrassed, and the evening's activities spoiled. A decision was made that the '9 o'clock worker' should be in position near the rented house prior to 7.30 and if Dennis and the others arrived, he would draw them away by vehicle to another part of the neighbourhood immediately.

Planning the most effective use of workers' time became increasingly important when crisis demands by individual young people threatened the workers' plans for working with groups, or where threats of impending trouble meant the work priorities had to be rearranged. Planning time itself was sometimes eroded by telephone calls and urgent requests for immediate action. Attendance at court hearings also tended to cut into planning time as it was so difficult to predict how long it would take. Attempting to minimize such a variety of conflict situations, setting aside time to plan and to carry plans through, and at the same time retaining a flexible approach to the use of fieldwork time, placed workers under considerable stress. Yet, given the objectives of the work, time had to be found for the exchange of ideas and discussion of detailed planning. Here, the existence of broad objectives, already set out in Chapter 1, provided useful guidelines for project workers:

(a) to work with young people in need of help, and assist them in finding a dynamic adjustment to society, and thereby among other things to control delinquency

(b)   to develop methods of working with difficult young people in an unstructured setting.

The interpretation of these objectives and the formation of programmes of fieldwork were essential functions of the staff meetings and the project team meetings described above. The staff sessions not only worked out an overall strategy of approach and method, they spelled out plans for each youth and each group in detail and then revised the plans in the light of feedback from workers directly concerned with implementation.

The precise determination of the list of participants was a further aid to detailed planning, and made it even more important. It would not have been possible to focus the resources upon them merely by offering an open facility such as a youth club or a dance café, or, as the team were increasingly made aware, by a teenagers' coffee bar. The fieldworkers now had to ensure action with a precise number of very different adolescent boys, trying to direct maximum resources to meet their needs, and this meant a special programme for each of the 54 participants. It had to allow for changes of need arising not only from developmental changes mentioned earlier, but also from changes in friendship and conflict in the activity groupings. These boys had already shown their incapacity to follow sustained interests in school and the workers found that many of them soon expressed similar characteristics in their approach to work, to youth club membership, to friendship groups, and to their associates on the streets. The idea of regular meetings, or fixed times of meeting, were unfamiliar to many, and their unreliability at keeping even their own arrangements showed the haphazard and random elements in their own personal lives. Any plans had therefore to take into account cultural and psychological factors which militated against consistency in work, friendship, and social behaviour. The unreliability of 'other people' in the young person's life was used to justify unconcern for the feelings of others and the unimportance of sticking to agreed plans. Out of line with the more usual apathy, there was sometimes over-enthusiastic planning for grandiose schemes well beyond the practical abilities of the group members, and here it was of major importance for the worker to be able to help the group to overcome the threatened breakdown in relationships and work towards more achievable goals.

The following example highlights some of the difficulties facing the workers in their planning for each participant, over a period of years:

Benny is one of the youngest participants. Over a period of three years, eight workers had contact with him for periods of several months, and, of these, three were professional workers, two of whose contact extended over several years.

The first work with Benny was through the Bridge Café during November and December 1965, where relationships were established by workers, A, B, and C. At the closure of the café, C tried to re-establish contact on the streets but was unable to locate the boy. In March 1966 Benny arrived to take part in a session that B had planned with another group, and the small group subsequently took part in several visits, and also arranged a trip to C's home. Benny was offered the use of a room in the rented house in May 1966, and accepted eagerly and brought several friends for weekly sessions of table and party games, and there met worker D. This programme lasted until mid-July, when the group rejected him because of his domineering behaviour. The group continued and plans to facilitate Benny's return were prepared, but they were not realized. Workers A and C continued to see the boy from time to time in commercial cafés, and during a period when he had run away from home, closer contact with his family was obtained. On his return he intimated that he would like to go back to the room, with other friends, and in November this new programme began, and worker E became involved. From the beginning Benny was not a good attender, and as with the previous group, had conflict with others and some difficulty in remembering which night of the week was which. During this time he continued to telephone C and made arrangements to visit — but failed to arrive. A reassessment of the work in May 1967 following the abandonment of the room programme led to the offer of the use of a vehicle, with a male worker (most of the earlier workers were females). Worker E re-established contact and Benny and a group of yet other young people began to meet weekly, and took part in a wide variety of outdoor activities. Girls joined the group, which went on to meet at new premises, where worker G was introduced, and the group spent more time talking and playing table games. Although the groups lost some stability after several months, Benny was a most regular attender and became very attached to one of the girls.

Benny again ran away from home in February 1968, but maintained intensive contact with E and returned home of his own volition, and the group meetings continued. Frequent visits were made to the home of worker C and this further helped in stabilizing his relationship with the girl and with his home. Other members of the group began to go bowling each week with workers G and H, and, although Benny and his girl-friend went several times, they were now more interested in each other than in group membership. Worker E therefore concentrated work on the 'pair' and by June 1968 was withdrawing from 'what seemed to be an extremely stable situation' with the boy settled at home, settled in regular work, and 'going steady' with a girl.

This greatly condensed survey of work over three years indicates the extent of planning and re-planning needed to reach and work with an elusive, difficult adolescent who in his school report was described as 'a moody boy who finds it hard to concentrate on a given task. All his work tends to be slapdash – he is certainly a potential delinquent. He appears to be on the fringe of a lot of trouble. He has the potential to do good, but unless carefully watched he will find himself in trouble. He has been known to play truant quite frequently'.

The record shows plans to contact Benny; plans to offer group activities to him and his friends; plans to circumvent his failures to turn up, his lying, and deception, and his apparent inability to give any shape to his week or to his life; planning to offer and provide help during his absences from home; planning to re-establish contact and introduce new workers; planning to retain contact with past helpers he wished to keep in touch with; planning to encourage and develop his need for mixed company and, finally, for more exclusive company; planning to provide opportunities for him to shape a strong and healthy self-image. Through all the twists and turns of work with this boy, the team persevered in order to be available to help, without in any way making such help obvious or 'official'.

When and how were these plans discussed and decided upon? Planning sessions took place every Monday afternoon from mid-September 1965 to the end of October 1967. By the latter date workers' programmes were more firmly established (due to fewer breakdowns in group programmes) and such changes as proved necessary could be dealt with prior to the Thursday staff meetings, which continued until the end of the project. In the early stages the Monday sessions were often largely concerned with establishing the identity of the participants, and it was also necessary to spend time devising ways of reaching the more remote, silent boys and of sharing some of the considerable hostility shown by others. After the café's closure, the major planning concern was in reestablishing contact with the participants in the open community, and then to plan ways of involving them in regular group meetings of increasing challenge and sophistication.

One function of the staff meetings was to ensure the maximum effectiveness of the team of workers, and avoid overlapping of workers and groups. The extensive use of volunteer workers over the whole period of the work (between twenty and forty at any one time) increased the need for this kind of staff planning. Each worker had to be briefed and to be kept in touch with other work that might impinge upon his own. On any one evening there could be as many as twelve adults working independently in an area little more than a mile square. Each group had to get staff and resources appropriate to its current needs: some groups needed transport; others accommodation; others some piece of equipment. Each worker had different needs – some required the support of the professional workers for longer periods than others, some preferred or needed to work in pairs, some needed transport if they were to be able to begin work at the time and for the duration necessary. Rearrangement of plans following breakdowns of the kind typified in the earlier example with Benny were numerous; such changes of plan involved difficulty, disappointment, and frustration for voluntary workers and emphasized the importance of planning to ensure discussion between professional and voluntary workers, and planning a fresh approach to the task based on a reassessment of the position.

In planning its programme it was also important for the team to keep in sight the Trust's peculiar contribution to the social services of the area. The fact that it was not identified with bureaucracy, government, or orthodox social work put the workers in a unique position to act as mediators between the young people and "them". It is always easy to criticize the shortcomings of overworked statutory services, and tempting to be drawn into providing another set of services to meet clients' needs, yet such action, apart from its presumption, would have been largely ineffective in that the limited resources of the project could not have coped with the demands. The workers also had to guard against taking independent action merely because of difficulties associated with consultation, while at the same time avoiding damage to fieldwork relationships (as an earlier illustration on page 57 indicates). The mediating role is illustrated in the following two examples. The first boy concerned was mentioned in the opening lines of the book.

Tom had very few peer group relationships, and spent much of his leisure time alone or with an older brother. He drinks fairly heavily, and, more important, gambles incessantly. He rarely works, and has no other interests, apart from crime.

Our second period of work with Tom, on his release from detention centre, saw the introduction of a voluntary worker with considerable knowledge of dog-racing and horse-racing. The volunteer became a 'mate' prepared to accompany Tom to real racing (as opposed to the Bookmakers' Saloon, one of Tom's regular haunts). This permitted the professional worker to take a more direct approach to helping with everyday needs in relation to home, and occasional direct help with accommodation and work, and to make discussion more 'problem-centred' and to include discussion about the probation officer's task.

Throughout the period of work close consultation with the responsible probation officer was maintained by the professional worker, and in this way the three men sought to fill different but complementary roles in the work with perhaps the most hard-to-reach boy in the project.

Henry, a participant with whom the team had contact throughout the project, left home to live with a girl-friend, Anna (a married woman). There were several problem areas where fieldworkers were able to assist. One fieldworker concentrated on Henry, helping him to find work, and supporting him in putting matters straight with the Ministry of Social Security. Another fieldworker centred attention on Anna, helping her to arrange with the children's officer for the return of the girl's baby. Following the birth of another child, the worker supported Anna in her efforts to attend a Family Planning Clinic. Over a year later, towards the culmination of the project, the couple were still living together and close consultation with the Family Service Unit led to the introduction of an FSU worker to the family. All the work with Henry and Anna took place within the context of group work with them and their friends, centred on the family home.

The two examples above serve as reminders that workers had at all times to bear in mind their role as 'honest brokers', interpreting the young people to the existing services and the services to the young people, so that clients could learn to use the available services unaided. Independent action was only appropriate where rigid attitudes prevented understanding, but wherever possible workers tried to create bridges between the social services and the potential users. As the project developed, this policy brought an increasing number of voluntary and statutory services into consultation over plans for specific young people.

A small but by no means unimportant aspect of planning was the arrangement of 'covering' procedures during all staff holidays or absences, and fitting in the essential in-service training and supervision periods for the full-time workers. While it was vital to ensure that workers could rest, it was also equally necessary to see that work with individuals and groups did not suffer during such times. This balancing of professional and private lives was an essential aspect of staff meetings. Without such emphasis on planning in all the aspects mentioned in this section, fieldworkers, project and Trust, might well have collapsed in the deluge of demands from individuals and groups in response to services offered at the point of adolescent need.

EVALUATION

Some form of judgement about the achievements of social-work action may be regarded as a professional obligation for all professional workers, though very few approach it in a systematic manner. Success is often measured by the rule of thumb that the client is no longer making demands on the agency. Evaluation in the present project was given high priority, as the appointment of a senior research fellow, whose primary task was to evaluate the work, demonstrates. However, the social workers did not cease to have responsibility for weighing-up the value of the social work they were doing. The research criteria, though precise, as fitted their purpose, were of necessity too narrow to measure all that was happening in the complex relationships of the workers with the young people; also, many adolescents other than participants were receiving service, and these were of no direct interest to the research. The social worker's evaluation was therefore part of the ongoing social-work process, essential if plans stemming from the assessment were to be developed or revised. This need was certainly heightened by the presence of the specific research component, which spurred the workers to evaluate day-to-day work in a more objective manner. The interim reports of the research on certain aspects of the work also served to highlight discrepancies between the social worker's impressions of the work programme and reality, and so introduced a more rigorous objectivity into the whole process.

The simplest level of evaluation was to establish how often the young people met fieldworkers. A target of at least one contact each week was agreed in December 1965, and subsequent counts showed the level of achievement. (These findings have been set out in some detail in Chapter 4.) The purpose of this analysis was assessment and evaluation, as in the case of the form from which the list below is taken. Every two months it proved possible to check records and discuss how frequently the workers had achieved their self-imposed target, and to give special consideration to those with whom workers had failed to make the desired contact or had exceeded the minimum. Although this did not always result in avoiding the tendency for the rich to get richer in terms of frequency of contact, it certainly forced workers to take positive steps to make and maintain contact with those slipping out of treatment situations. But there were several objections to a simple index of this kind, for it allowed no differentiation between contacts of varying length, setting, and duration. Because of the considerable additional work required to analyse these, the information obtained could not be processed until the end of the project (see Chapter 4). Whatever the objection to the simple frequency-of-contact count, it proved a most useful guide to workers in their forward planning, and helped them to share time and resources more effectively.

A further chart devised in mid-1967 helped workers evaluate the progress of work with individuals and groups. The chart itemized a number of levels of contact and enabled workers to plot development towards previously stated objectives over a period of time.

The terms used in this chart require further explanation. Generally the first step in making a relationship was that of *nodding*, followed, quickly in some cases, by use of *first name*, or nickname, and *conversation* of a neutral character, from which, in time, came the *full name* and a willingness to include *personal material* in the verbal exchanges. Some attempt to *exploit* the developing relationship was experienced with most participants before or during movement to a more *personal level* and the receipt of requests for assistance in a *crisis*. Some joined groups on *occasional visits*, and although these groups often continued to involve an element of exploitation, signs of *reciprocity* within the group or towards the fieldworker were some-

No contact
Nodding terms
First name
General conversation
Full name
Personal information
Exploitation
Personal conversation
Crisis support
Irregular (occasional) group involvement
Reciprocal group
Regular group involvement
Democratic group
Enlarging group
Sophisticated group
Concern group
Self-programming group

times evident, more so in those groups which came to meet on a *regular* basis. Initially, such groups centred on a dominant adolescent leader who dictated activities, but time brought a greater element of *democracy* in the groups as they implemented majority rule. The most stable groups were encouraged to invite new members and to accept adult guests, and their ability to *enlarge* the group was adjudged progress in group life. Participation in events requiring travel, organization, cooperation, and social challenge was recorded as an approach to *sophistication* in the use of leisure, as were group actions which demonstrated *concern* for less-privileged individuals and groups of any age. The culmination of work was seen as the full *self-programming group*, a group operating effectively without the intervention of an adult worker in the full process of idea, planning, action, achievement, re-planning, and fresh approach.

It should not be thought that participants moved smoothly through the progression to membership of a self-programming group, or indeed that many of them reached an ideal position. Some remained firmly fixed at one point; some regressed to earlier stages on more than one occasion; others operated, with typical adolescent inconsistency, at two levels simultaneously. However, the chart and the concepts it represented helped workers to measure progress.

Only rarely were workers able to take a long look at what they were doing with particular groups or individuals. There were only two occasions when the team prepared very detailed case or group studies for seminar discussion. In May 1967 a study of a group of boys (two of whom were participants) when it was written up ran to some 15,000 words. The size of the study in relation to the time (2½ hours) available for the seminar did not produce a discussion in any depth, or enable any radical rethinking of action or development of theory. Certainly it was less useful than a similar discussion session the previous year when each professional worker presented a brief paper outlining and evaluating work and progress with one group. These papers, although much less substantial, provoked stimulating discussion and helped workers in their attempts at evaluating other ongoing work.

An evaluation of a different kind was made early in 1967. At that time pressure of work had reached its highest point and the team were often working a 15-session week (as against the 11 sessions required of them), and so a special evaluation was made of the way workers spent their time, in order to effect economies of effort and establish priorities. In terms of its influence on the direction of the work, the discussion on this paper, in early March 1967, was undoubtedly as useful as the earlier discussions on the group studies mentioned in the preceding paragraph. The discussion paper posed the problem . . .

'. . . Relationships with both Participants and Non-participants are developing and leading to added demands on staff — on what basis do we accept new demands — need or expediency? Whatever the claims of expediency it is extraordinarily difficult for workers in group situations to make decisions . . . discouraging personal relationships, yet we recognize the unfairness of a situation in which those who shout loudest ultimately get service. Operating in a free setting, where the role is open to a variety of interpretations (and misinterpretations) increases the difficulty for workers of defining limits to each relationship . . .'

As will already be clear to the reader, the work of the project included many young people who were not participants — indeed, they usually formed the majority of any group including participants. Difficulties arose when these non-participants made demands upon workers away from the group, or when they withdrew from a group and formed new alliances. Fieldworkers faced considerable difficulties in making objective judgements in the hurly-burly of the neighbour-hood, though there was little disagreement with the discussion paper's statement that

> 'for the purposes of the project, the prime concern must be with those individuals in the Participant group, and nothing must be permitted to stand in the way of this work, or we shall later be forced into an explanation as to how we became sidetracked. This may need determined and apparently ruthless decisions, but these are necessary both to safeguard the worker and the project . . .'

The resulting analysis and evaluation of work programmes of all the workers, both full-time and voluntary, led to decisions which were greatly to assist those 'torn between the professional response to expressed need, and the obligations of the terms of employment'. It enabled decisions to be made regarding the use of the most valuable of project resources, the fieldworkers' time.

Evaluation was not only a scientific or intellectual exercise aiming to arrive at a more objective judgement about progress. The full-time workers were encouraged to maintain a continuing evaluation of their own contribution to the work, and this was carried out in three different ways. The first was through the close professional and personal relationships within the team; the second through personal recording of the work; and third through a form of independent professional supervision.

By working together over a period of years the members of the team built up a supportive environment in which team members could express personal uncertainty and self-doubt. All the professionals were acutely conscious of the struggle involved in reaching and working with participants. A sympathetic rather than destructively critical discussion of colleagues' fieldwork actions was therefore more useful in maintain-ing the workers in precarious work situations. The team also realized that when the worker represented the sole channel through which communications with participants could be effected, then it became essential to recognize the strengths and limitations of the human medium in any given situation. Each worker brought different personal experience and training to the work, and the team had to learn from each other that the work could be approached in very different ways, and the objectives attained by very different methods. What worked for one sounded impractical for another. But over the months workers modified their own methods and incorporated pieces from each other, and so enlarged their own ability to function in the no man's land of the streets. These differing fieldwork approaches led to lively staff discussions and re-evaluation of individual contributions, as attempts were made to try to see the situation through a colleague's eyes, and weigh the merits of action on grounds of theory, practicality, expediency, or humanity. In learning about the young people and in fashioning approaches to them, all the team members learned a great deal about themselves. On occasions members disagreed violently (and sometimes found themselves acting in a way contrary to agreed decisions), but generally a shared vulnerability kept individuals from throwing too many stones at a colleague's work, and a complete absence of rancour meant that everyone derived personal support from involvement in the team.

The second source of personal evaluation resulted from making accurate and detailed recordings of action. Although a byword in casework practice, its use in recreational group work in this country is relatively new and rarely put into effect. Staff members were sometimes irked by the need to maintain comprehensive records, yet there is little doubt that all derived benefit from the process, which necessarily required systematic observation and introspection to determine the cause and outcome of group interaction.

The stress of grappling with new situations in detached youth work made the use of supervision particularly important. [2] The Trust was able to put each full-time worker in touch with a personal supervisor who was not part of the agency structure and whom the worker could arrange to meet for regular discussion. Within the supervision relationship, workers were able to look at any aspect of their work. Examples of material discussed in supervision sessions include an examination of agency objectives, agreed work plans, the fieldworker's personal contribution to the work, personal differences with colleagues, feelings about specific aspects of the programme, and a wrestling with the immense difficulties (and personal repercussions) which at different times faced every fieldworker operating in an unstructured setting. One of the team has described the usefulness of this process:

'. . . the main factor that emerged from supervision was that I obtained encouragement and reassurance. I would raise a problem, he would listen and ask for points of information, pick out some factors for more detailed discussion, and ask questions about how I felt with regard to certain issues. Essentially, the main focus was on my perception of the situation and my ability to cope with it, and through the process of supervision we would try to enlarge and amplify both.'

The evaluation of self and the evaluation of work which resulted from supervision benefited the project considerably. All the supervisors shared a basic understanding of human relations theory, and all possessed in some degree the ability to assist workers to look at both themselves and the work with an objective eye, and to do this without damaging their confidence in themselves or in the agency. Once the supervisor-worker link had been set up there was never any question of the supervisor making any kind of evaluative report to the Trust; supervisors were usually provided with basic material on the Trust and on the project, but any detailed information came via the worker who was being supervised, and the very process of explanation and exploration helped to achieve the underlying purpose of the exercise. The complete confidentiality of the relationship between worker and supervisor was felt to be essential if the workers were to feel at liberty to raise matters which involved criticizing colleagues and ventilating personal opinions at variance with policy, and there is some retrospective evidence to suggest that the availability of supervision facilities siphoned off feelings that might otherwise have found expression in the staff group. In supervision these could be expressed freely and discussed in such a way as to lead to greater understanding and ability to handle the major tool of the group worker – his self.

Through the use of these methods of evaluation the workers grew professionally, and their overall perspective of the work, and their own contribution to it, was clarified.

Social workers in general, and youth workers in particular, are often deflected from evaluating work by the weight of the daily task; for some, even assessment and planning lose a recognizable place in the working week. The emphasis on evaluation in the project was a salutary exercise for the fieldworkers and, as this section is intended to show, it led to increased self-awareness and increased professional expertise, and resulted in more consciously informed action in the field.

The process of assessment through planning to implementation and evaluation was the method used to carry out an ordered and systematic approach to working with groups. The broad perspective of the workers was refined and reshaped through experience, analysis, and staff discussion on the lines developed in this chapter, which has concentrated on three of the four parts of the paradigm; implementation will be covered in some detail in Chapter 4. By constantly focusing the workers' attentions on the relationship of all their actions to the ultimate objectives of the project, the workers became more effective in diagnosing the participants' problems, more skilled in reaching them, and more incisive in treating them.

NOTES AND REFERENCES

1 This philosophy was very close to the ideas of Carl Rogers, for example, *On Becoming a Person* (Constable, London, 1967), although his work was not generally known by the fieldworkers.

2 For a useful discussion see Joan Tash, *Supervision in Youth Work* (National Council of Social Service, London, 1967) and Bernard Davies and Alan Gibson, *Social Education of the Adolescent* (University of London Press, London, 1967), especially Chapter 9.

3 · The client's perspective

The young people of Wincroft did not invite the attentions they received and it took them some time to realize what was to be the significance of this strange missionary band of social workers. Their early perceptions of the workers had been largely influenced by the context in which they first saw them, the Bridge Café, and here for some time the visitors to the neighbourhood were seen as commercial operators of some new kind of café. It was not long, however, before the special links with the university began to reveal themselves and the helpers could be identified for the most part as students. Students were not unknown in the neighbourhood, since the University Settlement was only a mile away and many of the customers had also known student helpers in a local youth club.

The people 'at the café' were viewed with some considerable suspicion by the local community, and also by the young people who found it convenient to use the place. Not only was there the suspicion that the police were using the café as a front to keep tabs on boys with criminal records, but there were fears that some of the male workers were homosexual. Later another fertile source of mistrust emerged when the male customers saw the male helpers as competitors for the available girls, or the female customers felt the same way about the female helpers. These attitudes were seldom verbalized and the workers were left with the task of interpreting why certain youngsters took up a particular stance with them. Adult gestures of warmth or affection were frequently misinterpreted, as in the following description of a visit to a fairground.

'John was only too pleased to be asked, and when I won a coconut for him he appeared no longer afraid of me. Yet when returning home he happened to fall behind us, and when I turned and stretched out an arm to bring him level with us he ducked back as if he was expecting me to hit him.'

The adolescent's conception of the trustworthiness of the workers was particularly demonstrated by what he chose to talk about. The use of nonsense material; the avoidance of offering any information about himself; an unwillingness to identify others (turning a 'deaf ear' if

75

workers were so indiscreet as to ask); all these indicated their uncertainty about how adults would use this information and the general expectation that it would be 'used against us' in some way. So, although the young person's perspective changed radically over the years, their relationship with workers was not a total one, and neither party attempted to make it so. But in the early Bridge Café days, workers and young people were not concerned with such an embracing concept. Both young and old were busy trying to remember who was who in the teeming and ever-changing environment of the café. Young people constantly confused names and workers, and they took a long time to work out that helpers had regular nights in the café. Although some clients virtually ignored and avoided the adults for months on end, others began to ask questions. Workers noted:

'Roger asked sensible questions re why coffee bar opened: who ran it; how much it cost, etc.'

'Who owns it; why I wanted to help'

'Did I get paid?'

This type of questioning gave workers opportunities of showing that they would treat clients seriously. It usually led to a more detailed questioning of the worker as a person:

'Are you a student?'

'What's your job?'

'Where do you come from?'

'Are you married?'

'Do you go to clubs in town?'

The workers thus began to take on some shape as individuals to the client and, for some, became someone who was interesting to talk to; but initially the topics were kept either strictly neutral or abstract — views on 'politics and the bomb', 'gambling and the church', or 'What are the mods like in London?'.

Workers reported that gradually the more confident customers (also the less disturbed as a rule) tried to draw the workers more closely into their own local affairs:

'I'll show you where to buy some milk'

'Can you come and watch the football on Sunday?'

Others, again the less disturbed, asked for simple forms of help:

'What does it cost to book a football pitch?'

'How can I do a butchery course?'

'What are the rules of chess?'

The preceding examples are the conversational gambits of the better-adjusted boy and girl; these requests were paralleled by more directly exploitative questions from the more disturbed boys. Once their fear of the strange adults wore off, behaviour moved to the other extreme, and an extended period of testing-out followed. This behaviour included jeering, derision, threats of physical assault, personal gibes, and attacks on the personal property of the adult helpers. Other less unpleasant but embarrassing verbal exchanges included requests for free drinks, loans of money, and excessive demands ('Take us to Blackpool'). Adults were also tested by seeing how they would react to crude jokes and obscenities. Other young people expected the adults to be open to participation in illegal activity (homosexuality and receiving were the two most popular assessments) and within a month workers were being offered stolen goods. For some of the young people this was perhaps just 'big talk', but others applied their normal expectations of adults to the helpers.

The willingness of the workers to take a listening role, and to ask little or nothing by direct questioning, may well have helped the more confident customers to express their feelings, despite the noise and general confusion of the coffee bar setting. Workers noted:

'Pat asked "why is it other boys are afraid of me?" Pat seems lonely, and likes someone to talk to'

'Simon asked me questions about the relationship between his girl-friend and himself . . . he wants to go to bed with her, but she will not'

'Mick is going to court tomorrow — for "breaking in" with Bob. A bit worried because he might be sent away as he has had two conditional discharges already. Didn't want to leave home or new girl-friend'

'Jack in trouble with his girl . . . girl "in trouble".'

It is interesting to note that the above 'problem-centred' discussions were with the older boys (17 years plus) in every case, and with the acknowledged talkers in the large number of very loose adolescent groupings using the café at that time. These were the rare exceptions to the general pattern of avoidance, acting out, overt hostility, and nonsense-talking which the great majority of clients used to express their views of adults in the café. Subsequently, as we propose to show, these early perspectives came to be reshaped in the light of experience, but for some young people the time-span needed was a very long one. During the early months the clients tended to know more about the workers than the workers knew about the clients, but in these measuring-up months the workers did get a number of interesting clues about young people's viewpoints on many things — the workers themselves and other strangers, for example. The outside world was particularly threatening when it brought the boys into contact with minority groups. Very violent feelings were projected onto the gypsies who occasionally camped on vacant ground in the neighbourhood, and certain houses occupied by gypsies were ostracized by adults and. children alike. One or two half-caste children living in the neighbourhood were accepted easily, but bitter criticism was levelled at other races in group journeys beyond the neighbourhood:

'We passed through one area of the city, and noticed many coloured people, and I was disturbed at the boys very antagonistic attitude. They referred to them as "niggers", "monkeys", and "bums" and though I took this up with them I could not evoke any satisfactory explanation'.

'On the way back we had the usual whistling and shouting at passers-by. The two girls said little but joined in the fun, though sometimes they obviously felt sorry for the victim with a heart rending "aaah . . . don't".'

In certain cases, the attitude of boys to minority groups (and especially to negroes) bordered on the paranoid.

'Gerald had an "anti-nigger" moan, which it was very difficult not to lose one's temper at. It was interesting to hear how he'd not catch a bus if it has a "nigger driver" and how he couldn't bear to touch the ticket given to him by a coloured conductor. Apart from this his arguments followed the usual anti-immigration lines of economy and "bleeding us to death".'

Such attitudes were a characteristic reaction to exposure to anything strange when viewed from a place of safety; the behaviour was very different when workers arranged opportunities for them to meet foreigners: 'The boys asked a lot of questions of the residents . . . they also talked to one of the coloured boys, and made no nasty comments'.

This example is not used to suggest that contact led automatically to change, rather it is to illustrate the general principle that seemed to govern their behaviour in the presence of anything strange or threatening. In their own area (or in a moving vehicle outside the area) they felt able to express hostility to the unfamiliar. But everything from outside the narrow environment of the neighbourhood was hostile and potentially highly dangerous.

The customers of the café came there to meet their friends and to pass away an evening that they would have otherwise had to spend on the streets. They did not come expecting that they might want to use the services of a social worker, and yet many of them ended up doing so, often making heavy demands on the workers. The key to this transformation in their relationships was their increasing awareness that the problems that confronted them in growing up in Wincroft could actually be mitigated. The boy who, having been kicked out of home, faced a night on the streets, saw that the worker could help him solve his accommodation difficulty and the news of his success soon got around the neighbourhood. This encouraged him, and other young people, to make other demands. The client's growing consciousness of his own needs along with his expectation that the social workers could help him satisfy them thus formed the basic perspective from which he viewed the relationship. While it may be true that he eventually valued the workers for themselves, for much of the project he valued them for what he could get out of them.

The usefulness of the workers was seen in relation to the young persons' needs, and at this age, between 14 and 18, their needs were changing fast. Not only were they growing physically but changes in their social experience were driving them forward emotionally.

At such an age all young people have to adjust to these changes, but the adolescents the project tried to assist were those already demonstrating by their deviant or delinquent behaviour their inability to come to terms with their present environment.

Adult relatives, already inconsistent in their concern for the increasingly alienated child, were unable to understand the language in which the adolescent expressed his developmental needs. The absence of constant patterns of behaviour towards deviating children was evident from workers' contacts with families in the neighbourhood, and this uncertainty of adult response affected the client's perception of the adult worker considerably. However, in general, the natural pressures towards maturation were allies to the workers, for the very processes of growth brought to the surface of behaviour new needs which the worker could help to meet, new feelings which the worker could help to explain, and new anxieties which the worker could help to allay. Even when the processes of growth of one individual lagged well behind others in the group, the worker could afford to be patient, knowing that growth would certainly come. The key factor was the availability of the worker to interpret and assist the realization of needs as and when they became apparent, so that the client's awareness of his needs could lead to a greater understanding of self and a more conscious effort to attain legitimate goals.

Most of the participants left school at the first opportunity. For most of them school was an irrelevance that they swept out of their minds as they swept out of the schoolyard, but this ran counter to the generally positive attitude of pupils in Wincroft towards education (see Chapter 1). Early records of the café in 1964 and 1965 reveal an almost complete blank on the topic of education or school, but when it was mentioned few spoke of school in other than denigrating terms and the sparing word of praise was usually directed to a particular teacher and never to the institution. Later in the relationship, in more private situations, individual young people sometimes revealed a more positive view of education although they regarded themselves as educational failures: 'David said he would have stayed on [at school] for another year, and his parents were willing, but Mr Jones said he couldn't. "They only want you if you're bright".' [There was in fact no fifth-year form in his school.]

During the early months of the project the only boys who offered information about school were the few who attended a technical high school; these came to identify closely with workers, sharing homework problems and discussing issues raised in the classroom. Such youngsters aspired to professional and white-collar jobs, and saw their ability to profit from formal education as a means to that end. Even then, there was evidence ot considerable ambivalence.

'Freddie is in an awkward position, because he is intellectually nearer the student volunteers than most others, and yet he cannot over-identify with us. This seems to show in his sometimes apparently ambivalent attitude; tonight he was very friendly and patient, at other times, he will appear aggressive as if to show the others that he is not one of us.'

For the majority there was no apparent relationship between formal education and the real world. 'Jack starts work next week. Glad to leave school — "Ten years of being told what to do".' The topic was certainly not a suitable one for conversation in the coffee bar, which may have been because the adults in the bar were seen as somehow 'educated people' to boys who recognized that schooling had only exposed their weaknesses. There were exceptions:

'Duncan and Sean talked about school; both leave this summer. Sean thought the few kids who were staying on must be mad, as he wants to get to work and his father is getting him a job. The worker asked why boys stayed on and he immediately replied "to get a better job". (The boys then broke up the conversation.)'

Parents were not involved in attendance at the school on open days and any achievement at school was likely to pass unnoticed at home. 'Eric asked if the worker wanted to buy a box — he'd made one at school and "me dad don't want it, me mum don't want it, me sister don't want it, I don't want it, no one don't want it".'

The more adventurous took time off from school, more frequently and openly, in the final term of their school career.

'Duncan says he will go to school for the last 8 days of term. He didn't go at all last week . . . "me mum didn't know, I just stayed in bed till dinner, cooked meself something and went out to the café".'

'Percy talked about his "wagging it" [truanting] on Tuesday and the reasons for it. He appears under pressure, and rebels by showing complete disinterest'.

What conversation there was about school tended to revolve around the toughness or the stupidity of teachers, and the various tricks the pupils had devised to humiliate their teachers. Although it was known that local schools were run on firmly authoritarian lines, workers suspected that many of the accounts of punitive action by teachers were exaggeration. It is interesting to note that the identification of workers as 'teachers' was quickly discarded by the spokesman of one group because 'you're not like our sort of teacher'.

The schoolboys were much more eager to talk to the workers about their spare-time jobs than about their schooling and this reflected their desire to be seen as adult by those around them. On leaving school they were less interested in selecting a particular job than in 'starting work'. Fathers and other male relatives were often responsible for finding the first job, and this tended to reflect parental hopes, which a number of the young people were unable subsequently to fulfil. Fathers, in selecting trade-training or apprenticeships, were more ambitious than their sons, but the young people put high wages before long-term reward. Although some boasted that they would 'take six months off', all of them began work immediately on leaving school. However, many found difficulty in holding down the first job and one boy had as many as twenty-five different jobs in his first two years of employment. Several boys well placed in terms of job prospects lost them through their own misdemeanours. 'Dick has been sacked for fighting at school [day release]. He said if it hadn't happened then it wouldn't be long, as he could not get on with the teacher.'

The keenness to talk about part-time work reflected the boys' perception of themselves as grown up, but the continued preoccupation with discussing work is perhaps an indication of their concern about their inability to come to terms with the adult status now thrust upon them. Whereas the part-time job was spoken of with pride and a sense of achievement (even such a relatively lowly job as filling coal sacks) the emphasis when in full-time work was often very different. Many boys were easily drawn into conversation about work, and increased their verbal ability as a result of having to describe work routines and people at work. This frequently helped them to sort out their ideas about the current job, to endure what they could not change, and to make plans to change what they could not endure.

The boys perceived themselves as workers capable of earning large sums of money; they saw themselves as workers with their hands — doing 'real work', but many of them were unable to demonstrate this in practice. Pressure from mates to take days off, late-rising (which conveniently rationalized non-attendance for the day), and impetuous reactions to what they saw as injustices (low pay, tax deductions), the aggressiveness of other employees, all these led to their losing their jobs and to a temporary alliance with the small number of more-or-less permanently unemployed youth in the corner cafés. For most of the boys the failure to adjust satisfactorily to the world of work set up family conflicts, and cross-pressures from their peers, but provided a relatively safe conversational topic in the Bridge Café. It also led to the first direct involvement of workers in helping individuals at times of crisis; in some cases it preceded the group-work programme, and in others ran alongside it. In both cases it was the direct result of a worker being available at the point when the young person first saw his need for assistance:

'Gerald very worried — lost job today, and didn't want to go home because of what mother would say. We arranged to meet tomorrow to go job hunting.'

'Duncan wanted to talk about work and a change [of jobs]; wants "hard" job where you can "batter things".'

Whereas the adolescent's need to grow up and become a worker was strongly encouraged (sometimes forced) by his family and his social situation, the need to establish his personal sexual identity could proceed much more at his own pace. Yet even here the personal drive was slowed somewhat by the fact that the cultural background encouraged and prolonged relationships with other boys. Unfortunately, this did not always mean the continuation of secure single-sex relationships, for the boys' own insecurity and lack of personal awareness often led to a frequent breaking-up of what they referred to as 'friendships'. The constant re-alignment of erstwhile friends was a perennial embarrassment to project workers. Young people saw each other as unreliable, and frequently showed no consideration for persons whom two days previously they had regarded as their 'best mates'. This was not as evident among the girls in the neighbourhood who retained more permanent pairings often with the break not coming until a boy was involved. The boys' growing interest in sex was either furtive or demonstrated by crude jokes, obscene language, and sexual gestures. They had little or no experience of non-sexual social interaction with girls, and much of the aggressive display in the Bridge Café masked a desire to impress the girls present. Those with regular girl-friends tended to ignore the girls while with his own sex, often making the girls wait long periods in comparative isolation: 'I came back to talking about Roger . . . could she get used to the waiting around? "If I'm not used to it now I never shall be".'

In this rather harsh relationship between the sexes, some of the girls gave as good as they got. 'The group was difficult for the most part, for the whole evening. The language even among the girls was worse than usual.'

The girls, although they may have been seeking more from the relationship, took their cue from boys, but were more willing to talk with workers about their developing sexuality and their feelings towards boys in general. The older boys demonstrated the familiar double standard in using 'available' girls while discarding them as possible marriage partners. Although most of the girls spent almost all of their leisure time looking and scheming for 'a nice lad' there were several who allowed themselves to be defined as 'communials' (*sic*) and these became practice grounds for those boys unversed in the physical aspects of sex:

> 'A popular girl seems to be Lorna; she seems to have had sex with most of the boys and they often mocked her about it during the evening. Jack was trying to put his hand up her legs, saying that if he wasn't allowed to do it he was sure she was saving it for Keith later in the evening.'

> 'Later Leslie flirted with the girls, and was eventually persuaded to "go with" Mary, as company for Lorna and Ben. Ben and Russ pulled his leg about it saying "you're not going with Roman Nose are you . . . you'll let the family down" and so on. Ben seemed to begin to realise that Leslie (his brother) is no longer a child — his amusement was mingled with amazement.'

Allowing for the boasting and exaggeration about sexual prowess (in itself an indication of how they wanted others to see them) , most boys appeared to get sexual experience before they were 17, and a few of them before they were 15. From their general ignorance of sexual functioning it is unlikely that the younger boys had experienced full sexual intercourse, but the older boys saw themselves as sexually competent.

The extent to which the boys saw themselves as sexually desirable affected their views of female workers in the Bridge Café. The conception of the women helpers as potential sexual partners was difficult to dislodge, and the presence of unprotected women (in the sense of not having boy-friends physically present) led to considerable misunderstanding.

The younger boys rarely saw women helpers in this way, but occasionally as potential 'in fun' girl-friends. The age difference (usually at least five years) and the skill of the women workers in holding contact at 'older friend' level was usually enough to prevent further problems arising.

'Someone referred to me as Leslie's girl-friend — I explained that my boy-friend wasn't here. I impressed upon them that girls would be an asset at the Christmas Party.'

'I danced with Brian (15) as much as I could because he enjoyed it. When I danced with Leslie (17) I made jokes and comments to the others.'

The younger boys were therefore able to rehearse certain social skills with the older worker and where close friendships formed these tended to cool as soon as the boy began dating girls of his own age.

As workers came to be trusted, the boys talked frequently about relationships with the opposite sex, specific conflicts, and problems of sexual maturation. Their increased confidence in some workers permitted direct questions of a sexual nature, and they saw them as experienced, discreet, and, above all, willing to provide facts and discuss issues which the young people found to be important.

In the first year of the work requests for help with friendships came from girls rather than the boy clients:

'Janice had been told by Roger to expect the worst this evening. He said he was fed up and didn't care about the future. Janice said he is going about more and more with Jake and Alan. They got into trouble last Sunday and she thinks Roger was with them. She says he's so weak he'll be led into anything.'

'Later she voiced her worry about Roger's drinking. "He's only 14 you know" and "if he drinks now, what will he be like later on?" . . . "Oh well, perhaps he'll change". I asked whether he ever got drunk. "He got pissed last night".'

Sometimes the requests were very simple. One boy initiated a discussion on freckles and how to get rid of them, although this kind of request was very rare, as the boys were usually careless about dress and appearance. Indeed, their own view of themselves was not sharply defined. Apart from the impression that each boy saw himself as very much 'alone' in a world where it was a case of every man for himself, their own level of self-awareness was very low initially. The girls followed the pattern of their culture and paid a lot of attention to their appearance, often engaging women helpers in conversation about beauty aids, new clothing, and hair styles. Not all the girls were so conscious of the value of a positive self-image, and several very scruffy girls in their early teens had no interest in presenting themselves as attractive partners.

Young people viewed the opposite sex with some hostility. It was a kind of battle in which the boys saw themselves as aggressive and dominant, and played down affection and feeling, and the girls saw themselves as betrayed by their own romanticism for boys 'who only want one thing'. In fact, because the girls were much more competent socially, tempering their dreams of romance with a very practical awareness of the limitations of their prospective partners, the girls exercised considerable power in determining the ultimate outcome of boy-girl liaisons.

The cultural separation of the sexes, reinforced by the educational system, made it difficult for workers to bring the two together without provoking misinterpretation. Older male workers talking too easily with girl customers led to jealousy among both boys and girls, and while female workers could offer a boy a different view of women, it conflicted directly with adolescent perceptions as to the meaning and purpose of such exchanges. 'Worker: I think the women helpers should never ask about a boy who is absent from the Bridge Café, as this is understood to mean that she is interested in him.'

To some extent these misunderstandings were minimized by working with groups and ensuring that girl workers were accompanied. All the excursions from the Bridge Café (which rarely included girls) contained an element of sexual adventure, and workers tried to create opportunities for boys to meet girls of their own age in outside social situations. These meetings, appropriately exaggerated by the boys, formed the basis of many discussions with workers as the boys compared notes and gained confidence in making relationships with the other sex. But some boys found extreme difficulty in relating to members of the opposite sex, and on being rejected by girls of their own age, frequently displaced their anger onto women workers. Generally this took the form of verbal insults, derision, and suggestive gestures by the younger boys, and more skilled verbal innuendos by the older boys. Some of the older boys needed to justify to themselves and to their mates their lack of success with particular members of staff. On several occasions some physical expression of hostility showed itself.

'Arthur challenged me as to why I hadn't been up on Friday for a drink. Accepted my excuse but looked disappointed. Trouble afterwards with Jake and Bert — tried to pull me down Ackers

Street. I broke free after a tussle, and was then tripped up. Hurt knee. Later they apologised.'

However badly the workers might be treated, the young people still wanted them to come. On one evening when events in the Bridge Café led to an early shut-down, the concern of the chief protagonist was that 'you won't come tomorrow night'. After the early difficulties of identification, certain workers were 'missed' if they did not attend. Viewed in retrospect, the young person's perspective of the total situation certainly placed the workers in a more important social position than that occupied by other adults known to them. People who were absent, or came late, or had to leave for holidays, were frequently subjected to the strong feelings of the group members:

'I wasn't sure to what extent it was personal or if I was simply an object to usefully vent aggressive feeling on but I have certainly never encountered such overt demonstration of hostility. Mostly it took the form of swearing and jeering. Most of the evening I was ignored or excluded and various boys continued to jeer "Get out you fucking Russian [she wore a fur hat] , we don't want you here." Several boys made slightly bitter remarks about my being a stranger — said I hadn't been for *months*, not weeks.

'I told them I was going on holiday for a month and Leslie and Stanley were angry and told me not to go. If I didn't come next Monday they would "fill me in" next time they saw me. Very cool towards me from then on. Very off hand saying goodbye.'

The workers had to accept considerable hostility, not only because they happened to be men and women who were strangers by education or locality, but also because they responded to anti-authority behaviour in unexpected ways. The workers represented people who were 'educational successes' against the adolescents' own self-evaluation of failure. The client's perspective of the workers as 'snobs' was accompanied by all the familiar tales of the wickedness and arrogance of the rich. There was much prejudice to be broken down, and a good deal of roughness entered into the process, as young people tried to get the responses they wanted. In this the workers received no different treatment from others. Roughness entered into all their personal relationships. Mating behaviour lacked finesse, consisting in a running exchange of verbal threats, but through the somewhat hard exterior view of the sex relationship a more sensitive consideration occasionally showed itself, and violence had no part during the period of 'going steady', even if it seemed inevitable in marriage.

'Benny and Rhona had had a row. In a dispute over which cinema they went to, Benny had hit her and made her cry. Percy was full of it . . . "it was just like they were married".'

'Argument was inevitable. Jane would like to get married but it's just the beginning of a long argument. "You always argue when you're married, it's natural". She shook her head knowingly . . . you may not argue with your boy friend now, but I bet you will after you're married".'

In private they sometimes spoke with greater gentleness than either the group or the neighbourhood sanctioned, but the rarity of this emphasized the expectation that they would hide such feelings. Once, in a tape-recorded interview, a boy and a girl demonstrated a different level of approach, despite the more traditional interjections by others who were listening:

'The main part of the evening was . . . a tape-recorder, which everyone gathered around and became one group. Dick interviewed Alison well, and she talked seriously about her ambition to get married and have children, and to live in another area "in a new house, it's lovely there". Once Leslie interjected something to which she objected violently ("I don't think that's a funny remark") and it had something to do with her reputed sexual generosity. Later she mentioned Gerald and Leslie interjected "have you been to bed with him yet?" which got a roar of laughter from the boys. But her hopes for the future were sincere, and she took the interview very sensibly, as though these were things she really wanted to say. Alison then interviewed Dick, who also spoke thoughtfully, and without interruption.

A. Do you want to get married
D. I've no time for women, but I'll get married when the right one comes along.
A. What would you consider the ideal girl?
D. She should be small, dark-haired, and have a pleasant personality.
A. Does she have to be beautiful?
D. It wouldn't matter if she wasn't, as long as she had a pleasant personality.'

Some years later a worker met Dick and joined him for a drink on his wedding eve, and he reminded the worker of his first contact with the girl who was to be his wife — 'you know, the one who interviewed me that night in the café'.

Interest in girls became a growing preoccupation in the use of free time, but even so the use of leisure was a major problem for some of the boys. With so little to do in the immediate neighbourhood, they were hanging around 'on the corner' ('our corner' was frequently pointed out to new workers). Describing their own use of leisure they saw themselves as 'messing about' during the week and 'drinking' at the weekends. They made occasional visits to the local swimming baths, and to the local cinema, spending periods when they were banned from one, the other, or both, in even longer sessions on their street corner or, in winter, in one of the corner cafés, and during the summer playing football in the schoolyard.

'The worker passed the cinema and by chance met Freddie, Spick, Derek, Frosty, and Frank trying to get in without payment. Freddie paid to go in, and then opened the exit doors for the rest to go in.

The worker left the group [at the cinema] and by now it was pouring with rain, but the worker noted "several groups, maybe eight or nine, sheltering in shop doorways, obviously at a loose end and out on this wretched evening".'

Many of them had attended youth clubs in or near the neighbourhood, particularly the one-evening-a-week clubs run by the churches, though very few had sustained their membership for more than a few weeks. None attended the clubs run by professional youth workers, which were open every evening, but they criticized these strongly without being able to substantiate their criticism. 'We talked about youth clubs in the area . . Duncan lives next door to one of the biggest . . . says he "hates the place".'

For most of the young people the clubs were outside the neighbourhood, and attending them involved the risks of walking into alien territory. In general terms, it was as though they saw orthodox youth provision as in some way 'not for them', though later in the project, some of the clients revised their views not only of youth clubs, but of their own use of leisure. In occasional moments of insight they saw themselves as bored young people, constantly wishing that something interesting would happen, but with neither the imagination nor the drive to create ways of using leisure more enjoyably. In this situation workers had to take care to avoid being seen as enthusiasts rather than as adults prepared to share the monumental boredom of the youths themselves. The former role would have saved the boys from thinking at all whereas the aim was to change the young people's perspective from an initial hostility to a situation where workers were seen as a source of support and encouragement, so making possible the expression of latent ideas and their translation into action.

A few were so involved in crime that leisure presented no problems. As one of the older boys who owned a vehicle put it, 'the difference between me and you [the worker] is that I make my car *work* for me'. (He used it to get to and from the scene of the crime.) Another refused to plan leisure two weeks ahead because, as he said, 'I'll be inside by then'. But those were exceptions; most of the boys had some acquaintance with crime, but it was rarely a central activity in their lives. Often it seemed to happen when they were bored or when they had been drinking. Even then it was frequently regarded as a 'bit of fun' with little or no awareness on their part of possible consequences. The general consensus seemed to be that most people do it, and provided you don't 'overdo it' then it is excusable, and in this they reflected the views of their parents and the neighbourhood. For most of them the idea of making a living from crime was beyond consideration – it simply wasn't worth it:

'Benny knew there was crime in white-collar society ... "I don't know anyone who works in an office or anything like that, but I suppose they're not satisfied with what they've got". Others might choose crime, but he had decided against it on the "not worth it" basis.

"I'll work to get money – it's safer" but at the same time he savoured the remembrance of breaking into a tobacconist's and getting "70,000 cigs – they were all over the place" ... "It must be great to strike it rich".'

If a life of crime was viewed critically, so were certain types of crime:

'The group also talked about Russ and the others' crime, which includes the possibility of murder, and their horror of this, as opposed to robbery.'

'At the cemetery, we talked briefly of death and burials. Percy thinks that to steal from flower vases (pennies are added to keep flowers fresh) is "the meanest thing on earth. I can't imagine even the lowest crook doing it".'

Between these two extremes of criminal behaviour, most were prepared to experiment in their leisure time with various forms of illegal behaviour, including shoplifting, pilfering from work, stealing by finding, housebreaking, and selling stolen property. Those who got caught and 'sent away' were regarded as fools — not only for being caught, but also for being too ambitious. Parents would sometimes cover for them.

> 'Spick claims he was almost in trouble stealing from yard, but he got away and his father provided an alibi to the police (said he'd been indoors the whole evening). The other boy was caught, and is to be charged.'

Most boys appeared to respect those with criminal records, and were quick to wish to be seen as on their side, showing a fawning approval when in the presence of 'the big men', but criticizing them in their absence.

The use of leisure was very much influenced by the need to get out of the home and away from their fathers.

> 'Frank: There's a lot of fighting and drunkenness at home and I just can't stand this way of going on, so I'm going to leave and get a flat as soon as I can.'

> 'Leslie: I wouldn't accept owt [anything] from him [his father]. He kicked me all round the house.'

> 'Freddie and Tom were comparing who had the worst father. Main complaints — drink and gambling and violence.'

Certainly, a few of the families were highly disorganized, but parents saw their boy's misbehaviour as usually linked to common situations of changing jobs, failure to work regularly, staying out late, and associating with known delinquents. But the adolescent's failure to conform to parental wishes widened the rift in family relationships and caused an atmosphere for which the boy was often held solely responsible. A few of the boys actively hated a parent, and whereas most tolerated their parents, there was little evidence that any were very close to them (although they were always quick to defend their parents in the face of outside attack). The sheer pressures of competition for space in the home and the growing demands of this new wage-earner both played a part in creating tension between the young person and his parents. This tension had to find release elsewhere.

Of the 54 participants, 18 lived away from their parents at some time for reasons that often included inability to maintain peaceful coexistence under the family roof. Sometimes leaving home was seen as the boy's solution; sometimes as the parents'. In some cases the boys were physically excluded from the home, while in others the family made arrangements for a fractious son to live with relatives. Leaving home was seen by everyone as a step of great significance, a step both desired and feared. Most of the boys verbalized their wish to leave as they found it increasingly difficult to sustain relationships within the home, and in cases where relationships with workers were good, changes in boys' attitudes and ability to endure or modify difficult home situations became apparent. This will be looked at more closely in Chapter 4. In fact, the hard and critical judgement of home masked an underlying attachment, which indicated their own inadequacy to survive without it. Those who made the break were seen by their friends to survive, but hardly to prosper. A number of them were glad to return, some creeping back with forced apologies, others to a negotiated settlement. Other boys noted the outcome of these events and continued to complain, but did not act. They criticized those who did and sympathy was given only to those who, because of parental breakdown, were thrust into physical independence. Even here, however, much as they wished to help their age-mates, they could not interfere in the lives of another family. Although they sometimes envied the apparent independence of those ejected from the family, they were also quick to perceive the disadvantages and perhaps especially the way in which their mates would be largely powerless to help them.

'Morris was thrown out of the house. Mr Willitt said he'd let Morris (who'd been brought home by his own son Terry) stay just one night more. (The boy had stayed one night unknown to the father.) Mr Willitt says he doesn't want trouble with Morris's family — "they're a rough lot, he'd soon tell me it was none of my business".'

For this reason young people who found it necessary to fend for themselves tended to turn to project workers for help in this situation and, impelled by the pressure of crisis, one or two young people did much to encourage others to recognize these adults from outside the neighbourhood as having something to offer. Workers came to be seen as people who could help in serious situations.

The demonstrated need for greater independence was shown not only by violent clashes with parental authority, but in the client's desire (but not always ability) to explore new areas of experience. The stresses caused by the physiological and psychological drive towards hetero-sexual experience have already been indicated and, where the striving for independence and new experience over-reached the abilities of the clients concerned, they became increasingly willing to accept support. This was especially evident as courtship and marriage drew together the various strands of movement towards full independence.

These changes in role came later in the project, after the workers had established a strong relationship with the young people concerned. So despite the shift away from 'mates' which occurred when boys began to 'go steady' and prepare for marriage, the workers were able to retain contact, and were seen as suitable people to share some of the intimate problems of young people on the eve of their independence. The freedom with which the latter discussed future hopes, differences of opinion, family planning, separation of duties, and other problems of the about-to-be-wed or newly-wed, demonstrated not only the limita-tions of some clients' knowledge, but the changed views held by the young people, which enabled uncertainties to be verbalized, often in the presence of the marriage-partner.

Other boys, starting to 'go with' a girl, and breaking away from peers in order to devote all leisure time to 'the bird', occasionally invited workers to share visits to smarter clubs and more respectable public houses. As with the young couple (Dick and Alison) mentioned earlier, preparation for marriage often involved them seeing themselves as living away from the neighbourhood, although this did not necessarily mean they were aspiring to a higher status.

The early part of this chapter has given the young people's view of the outside world, but how did they view their own environment? And how did this affect their approach to the workers? On the point of marriage this often became very clear, but there was also plenty of evidence at an earlier stage in their development. An attitude of hostility to outsiders who threatened the uneasy *status quo* was coupled with a stoical acceptance of life within the neighbourhood. There were times when they rebelled against the standards of the area in which they lived, and it was during these crises that young people demonstrated very fiercely that they were unable or unwilling to internalize the rough and ready but respectable standards of the neighbourhood. At the point where their own physical and emotional drives became violently opposed to the settled ways of local life, the workers were able to assist clients to look at themselves more objectively, to examine their neighbourhood more critically, and to consider ways of changing both.

The discontent of adolescence was frequently brought to the surface by the poor living conditions and the imminent renewal of the area. The prospect of changes in his environment presented challenges to the adolescent that had to be faced, no matter how ill-equipped he was to handle change, and such instability was not always a beneficent factor. Rehousing proved a difficult burden for adolescents already confused in their personal relationships. Yet such issues provided workers with something to go on and they were able to assist in a more mature adjustment by clients to changing conditions.

'The worker talked a lot with Benny, who said it was impossible for the worker to understand what it was like to live in a slum. We defined what we meant by a slum — differentiating the people from the actual physical environment. Benny felt he was trapped ... "I've no choice have I? I don't like my job — in fact I hate it — but what can I do about it?" The worker noted afterwards that the conversation gave a strong impression of a boy who'd like to break out, but was helpless — trapped in his case by family circumstances in addition to social environment and physical surroundings.'

If many verbalized a desire to leave the neighbourhood few turned words into reality:

'Derek told me about his application again to join the Merchant Navy. On the previous occasion he passed the medical, but his father dissuaded him. This time his mind is made up — especially he is fed up with his dull existence, the job, etc., and in particular sitting on the corner bench each evening, and wants to see the world. He rather liked the idea of seeing the world and the thought of young women queueing up at the ports ... "it will be better than sitting on that bleeding bench".'

Knowledge of the world outside the neighbourhood was remarkably limited among clients, and their attitudes to the unusual and the new were predictably uncompromising. At the seaside they behaved like small children. Their reaction to what was strange was a blend of fear and disgust. The outside world was a disquieting place where the worker's presence was a valuable protection. Taking work outside the area required massive encouragement from the worker, and a careful examination by the client of the routes to and from work. Many of them soon lost their bearings upon leaving the neighbourhood and had little or no sense of direction (contrary to their own view). Yet at the outset they confidently proclaimed an ability to find anyone, any-where. This oddly unrealistic approach to the outside world, by which they tried to make it controllable, persisted for much of the project.

'It was decided that I would drive the group to a house outside the area where Percy was to acquire a fishing rod in exchange for his guitar. The four of us then went on a wild goose chase. Percy did not know the address, nor the surname of the person he was looking for. After knocking on two or three houses they decided to give it up as a bad job.'

Whatever their views of the outside world, they were usually glad to get back to base — although they rarely had a good word to say for that either! A number of the boys referred to the neighbourhood as 'this dump' and earlier examples indicate the intentions of some of them to get away from it, though their solutions were not always realistic ones. For others the desire to get away had a plaintive ring: 'During a group excursion, we saw some ducks. "It's alright for them" Clive said "they just have to get up and go".'

Some admitted to liking life in their own neighbourhood, and indeed most of them were singularly unable to cope once outside it. The reality was far more painful even than the imagination, and the dream world of new housing turned out a disappointment: 'John says there's nothing to do on the estate. He is bored.' Some subsequently travelled back to spend their leisure time in Wincroft, and at least two moved back to stay with relatives still in the area.

Differences in wealth were accepted as one of the facts of life and not worth discussing. Some local families were living on very low incomes and while this affected the programme of work with youngsters from these families it is problematical as to whether the youngsters' perception of themselves as 'poor' was a very clear one, except that they expected the adults in the Bridge Café to be in some mysterious way 'rich'. The lack of realistic comparisons (as opposed to symbolic ones) played some part in preventing them from perceiving their own total situation with any clarity. Therefore the critical situations in their lives (court appearances, ejection from home) presented opportunities for some radical assessment of self in relation to environment, and some action to produce a more satisfactory future state. [1] Crisis intervention by the workers therefore developed naturally out of casual contact and small group contact sessions, when a young person's mistaken or hazy conceptions of workers could be discarded and a clearer picture established. Some never discarded the misconceptions. Severe disturbance within their lives did not lead to closer involvement with workers; in some cases this seemed to be because of fixed views about the unhelpfulness of adults generally, and in others because contact was not sufficiently continuous or frequent to break down preconceived anti-authority attitudes.

In general the adult world seemed a hostile place to most of the boys involved in the project and no adults seemed so hostile as those in specific authority roles. They found it difficult to separate the probation officer from the policeman. Both were firmly established in the category 'them' along with the magistrates, the school welfare, the Youth Employment, and the 'Nab' (the National Assistance Board as it then was), as some continued to call the Social Security offices. Many held a childish view of the law, in so far as uniformed men represented it, acknowledging its power when present, but ignoring it when absent. Workers had many opportunities to observe adolescents jeering at the police from a safe distance, but subsiding to cowed and apparently respectful silence at times of physical proximity. The most commonly expressed attitudes were those of sullenness and deference in the presence of all authority figures, and derision and criticism away from the immediate presence of external power. Baiting various authority figures was one of the recognized ways of filling leisure time:

'Duncan was very friendly, talking about new friends and having fun with them ... "oh, knocking on doors, scattering bus tickets, shouting at coppers, and breaking windows in old houses".'

'Ben said "come on, let's go by bus, then we can fuck about".'

The 'push' of adolescence was thrusting them forward, urging them to experiment, to express dissatisfaction with immediate surroundings, and to determine their own future. It was within this conflict-laden situation that workers had to try to assess the young people's view of the world. In helping them deal with conflict, the workers came to understand that there could be no one perspective shared by all the young people, but for each individual a shifting view of the world outside as he came to handle new experiences. This chapter has therefore given an overview and an over-simplification of the perspective of any one child, although the many facets that it has touched on would at some stage have formed part of the view of every child with whom the project worked. This general picture is presented largely from workers' comments and reports at the time, but the illustrations used are believed to be truly representative of how most of the young people viewed their relationships with the workers, the neighbourhood, and the outside world. There is no shortage of examples to back up the general points made here and, although the pieces included convey the attitudes and mannerisms of particular boys, the sentiments expressed would be shared by all of the participants at some time during the project.

The hostility that met many adult workers in the early months may now be explained by what came to be seen as a characteristic reaction to anything strange. Some young people worked through this easily, but where hostility continued other evidence was forthcoming which indicated that the perception of the young person was more severely maladjusted as a result of family and peer influences. For these young people, the view of self, of others, and of society and its institutions was so blurred as to provoke a generalized reaction of hostility to anything that could not be easily assimilated. Yet changes did occur (this is examined in detail in Chapter 4), and one indicator of this changed perspective was the way in which young people fitted the workers into their lives. The initial view of workers as snobs, crooks, homosexuals, exploiters, rich, do-gooders, and so on had to be discarded in the light of experience over a long period of time. Workers refused to fit into the young person's expectation of their behaviour, and the adolescents found their own behaviour changing to accommodate the new situation. Once the rapport was achieved, the workers' presence came to be validated by the adolescents in new ways, 'he's alright', 'he's a chap I know', and later 'a mate I know', or even 'my mate'. At the end of the project there was an example of an introduction of a worker as 'a good friend of the family'.

It is suggested that over time this gradual change in the adolescent's perspective extended far beyond his relationship with the workers. Other sections of this book illustrate how groups were no longer threatened by strange places or by unfamiliar people and demonstrate changes in attitude to other minority groups, to authority figures, and to the opinions of others in general—to the world around them. It is not intended to imply that these changes took place solely as a result of contact with the fieldworkers, they were also the result of the whole process of maturation and of exposure to new situations. Workers, by being watchful for changes in the client's attitudes were able to boost any increase in the degree of self-awareness and to shape programmes of work in such a way as to reinforce changes within the young person that made his relationships more personally satisfying and more socially acceptable.

The problem is not as simple as it sounded expressed by the father of one of the boys who, in remonstrating with his son, turned on the worker and said 'here, you're a youth leader aren't you? Well, he's a youth — get the bugger led'. Voicing the need is one thing — but it is a considerably more difficult and complex operation to outline the processes of leading recalcitrant youngsters towards competent social functioning.

NOTES AND REFERENCES

1 See Gerald Caplan, *An Approach to Community Mental Health* (Tavistock Publications, London; Grune & Stratton, New York, 1961) for a discussion of the opportunities for therapy in crisis situations, especially pp. 40–41.

4 · Changing relationships

Chapters 2 and 3 have described the expectations that the workers and the young people brought to their mutual relationship; this chapter examines the actual relationship that emerged from their encounter. Not all of their expectations were fulfilled; happily, the suspicion and distrust felt by the young people were dispelled when the workers turned out to be different from other middle-class adults they had met, and different from the stereotypes they had formed about them; however, some of the boys did not respond to the optimistic forecasts of the workers, and these boys have now moved into what appears to be a chronic condition of warfare with respectable society. For something like 14 of the 54 participants very little in the way of any kind of relationship emerged, and workers' contact with them was so fleeting and infrequent that it is difficult to know what they thought of the workers. For the remaining 40 it can be said with some confidence that over a period of two and a half years they reached some common understanding with the 156 adults who at some time during that time had tried to help them.

The main theme running through this chapter will be the changes in relationships that occurred over the 31-month evaluation period; in particular, the shift from a situation in which the client was interested only in exploiting the worker in order to satisfy his own needs to a situation where the client could accept the worker as a person with needs of his own. The young person started by trying to dominate the worker but eventually became dependent upon him. This dependence was itself transitory, since the young person was encouraged by the workers to function on his own and, subsequently, to enjoy the mutual dependence of friendship and marriage. In this chapter the development of the relationships between the workers and the young people will be examined phase by phase. The first section will open with a case study that illustrates each of the phases: making contact with the young person; handling his testing behaviour; helping him to resolve his crises; meeting him on a regular basis for leisure activities; and, finally, ending the association when it had served its purpose. The section will then analyse the preliminaries of the relationships in some detail. The second section of the chapter examines the relationships as they functioned and developed in times of crisis for the young person, and the third examines what these relationships meant in the routine associations of normal day-to-day living. The intention will be to show how each aspect of the relationship, in both crisis and routine, enriched and informed the other. The fourth section describes the efforts of the workers to anticipate the end of the project and to withdraw from the relationships, and the fifth and last section of the chapter gives a statistical summary of the type of work done and the level at which it was carried out. Throughout the chapter extensive use is made of case studies in an effort to show the progress of clients observed by workers, and later in the book it will be possible to compare workers' observations on the impact of the project with the results of the research evaluation.

Henry was one of the most disturbed and delinquent boys involved in the project, and so, apart from contact in the Bridge Café and occasional involvement of voluntary workers in excursions, work with him was done solely by professional workers. The work continued over the whole length of the project. Following contact with the boy in the Bridge Café, a series of informal meetings took place at the family home; later, many sessions took place in the home where Henry and his common-law wife lived together. In both these more fixed periods of contact (Henry frequently lived elsewhere for short periods between residence at the maternal home and his final 'own home') it was necessary to involve other regular or casual callers at the house to aid his social adjustment. Such groups frequently involved his mother, his wife, his married brother and sister-in-law, and two brothers of another family living nearby. It is not proposed to attempt to survey the vast amount of family group work and individual casework given to this family over a period of years by the professional workers, but rather to demonstrate the development of the work by reference to contemporary records kept by workers.

Contact during the Bridge Café period was minimal; Henry, then only 15, attended spasmodically, usually when drunk (so much so that one record notes that he was not drunk), and behaved in an aggressive manner, damaging property and also attempting to steal goods:

'Henry attempted to take some goods from behind the bar counter, and when I challenged him he became aggressive. I put my hand on his arm as the only possible method of restraining his movement, and he threatened me with a bottle'.

In the café it was learned that Henry's behaviour was not modified at home:

'Apparently Henry is up on a wounding charge, and will be "put away". Percy said during the ensuing conversation "You want to hear what he says to his mum . . . I know I'm a twat with my mum sometimes, but I'm not as bad as that".'

A worker later was able to make an opportunity to visit the home where events verified this report:

'Back to Henry's house after ice-skating trip. Mother a pleasant 50-year-old with a married son living away and only Henry at home. Says he is quite a handful, and she took several opportunities of saying things which she probably couldn't have done in private without receiving a mouthful of abuse. Said he has been "talked out of starting work", but "he won't live here if he doesn't work".'

'Henry still treats dog, mother and young cousin in very much the same way . . . masterful, enjoying the power and knowing he can get his way by force. Regards toleration as weakness and cowardice. Mother still worried about him and very pleased to see me (? as a possible ally) and says "he's a bugger nowadays". She is getting trampled on — but lent him 10 shillings to go out with.'

His school report was useful in an assessment of Henry's needs:

'Big for age, and tried to make out he was a "hard case" but underneath he was a physical coward. A considerable amount of bullying of younger children was instigated by him. Not very popular, very much a lone wolf. A vast number of stories of torture, killing and general cruelty to animals, which is rather disturbing.'

In view of this, and worker's experiences with Henry in the Bridge Café, on trips out, and in contact with his home, it was decided to give the boy a more individual approach, and seek to take up the family contact again. This took time, and when it was finally accomplished many factors combined to prevent a positive and helping relationship at that time. Several conversations with his mother took place, but developments outside the family home led workers into encouraging his friendship group, and it was to be some time before the relationships with the family could be developed.

During the next few months, group work with his friendship group predominated. The group was torn by inner strife and conflict, and most members displayed in many ways the fact that they were disorganized young people. They tested out the workers for a long time, making impossible demands on their time, aggressively demanding attention, exploiting situations involving workers in expense, damaging premises and property. Eventually the group split and one worker was able to devote time to Henry and one other boy; this took the group back into the home, and enabled a discussion of Henry's relationship with his mother and elder brother to be taken up again. In periodic conflicts the worker was able to help Henry and his mother to overcome the crisis.

'Henry asked his brother about motor-bikes and this led to a long discussion. Then they started pulling each other's leg about their weights, and their mother got out old photographs of the two lads.

Henry persuaded his brother to come to the pub, and when we got there he told us about the fight on Saturday — his brother pointed out what it might do to his mother if she found out, and I assured Henry if anything happened we would help his mother.'

'Went to Henry's brother's home. Henry is very uncomfortable at his brother's as he feels his sister-in-law doesn't like him. He gets his own back by ill-treating their dog when he thinks no one is watching.'

On a family group outing

'. . . Henry was very warm towards his mother . . . and gave her a good deal of attention. When we returned to the house he began to terrorize the cat and dog (despite his mother's request) and the situation was unpleasant.'

This was a profitable few months of work, but Henry constantly regressed and there are many recorded instances of his deceit and brutality, and of his carelessness about working and his relationships with others.

'Henry in a sulky mood is pretty frightening even to those who know him well.'

'Mrs S. says that she would be quite prepared to throw Henry out of home when he is 17 if he is not prepared to work regularly.'

But within the smaller group (which usually included mother and son) the worker was more frequently giving support to positive feelings and actions, and more frequently involved in problem solving situations. Trouble was never far away, even when the evening seemed set fair:

'Went with Henry and George to the baths and swam until 8.30. Then to his home for a cup of tea. He and his mother had an argument and she threw three darts at him. We went to the pub . . . this evening we were able to discuss Henry's father (deceased) as a worker and as a father. We also discussed male/female differences, and physical and verbal aggression. Not a bad evening at all.'

In very small groups (sometimes just Henry and his mother) the worker felt there was sometimes a real development:

'Henry and his mother and I interacted in a much more positive way than usual. We stayed in and watched TV (Joan Crawford in a play about schizophrenia). There was some disagreement between Henry and his mother, but on this occasion we were able to discuss it; for the most part we all discussed things fairly easily, such as how emotions can affect mental functioning, how it must feel to lose someone you love, etc.'

In the latter part of the winter of 1966-67, however, the situation deteriorated, and despite visits to the theatre, to friends and other relatives, and to local pubs, Henry's work habits declined, and quite a lot of time was spent with him finding new jobs and talking about what was wrong with the last one. He had also stolen a car, and was involved with adult criminals in the neighbourhood. His hostility to his mother grew as she became more distressed (and eventually ill), and at one point Henry left home. The worker tried to bridge the gulf between Henry and his mother, and facilitated his return home. This incident highlighted the conflict situation of the worker – how was he to maintain the confidence of Henry and of his mother in such extreme crisis situations?

Shortly after this another crisis occurred, and Henry left to live in a café with the wife of a man in prison, and several months followed in which the two workers maintained a link with all branches of the family, and helped them to come to terms with the new situation.

Relationships between Henry and his mother and brother were eventually re-established and after a long time his mother was able to accept the girl involved whereas previously her attitude had been one of complete rejection. Henry and Anna moved into a flat and the workers spent much time with them and so the 'family group work' moved its location from the maternal home to Henry's home — sometimes in both homes on the same evening as the worker went with the younger family to the widow's home. So continued a second bout of family group work.

The family group in this case ranged from three to a total of eight persons at any one time, and allied to this work was individual casework with Henry alone. These family group situations enabled the worker to interpret behaviour from all sides in an attempt to increase self-awareness in what was always a potentially explosive setting. Workers had constantly to guard against being used as pawns by members of the group who tried to get each worker to 'take sides' on every issue, and so draw the worker into the web of conflict and mistrust that enveloped the group relationships. Where the workers could retain objectivity within a context of concern for all the group members, there is evidence that a good deal of new understanding took place. Operating the method had many drawbacks, not least the unanticipated presence of people who 'dropped in' to the households during the course of an evening session, but the alert worker could always use these group changes to stimulate conversation, whatever the topic, and so raise the general level and frequency of interaction.

As the project drew to a close it became evident that Henry would need support in the months and years ahead. Although workers saw a growth in ability to cope with stress, both Henry and Anna were living on a knife-edge, just surviving in a world that to them was confusing and threatening. In shaping the rundown programme, it was clear that some continuing support would need to be provided, and careful plans were made to introduce the ongoing support in a way likely to prove acceptable to the young couple concerned.

They had moved with her two young children and a large dog to a small terraced house that despite Henry's efforts (and help by the worker) was in poor condition. They had for some time been a family, if a highly disorganized one, and as the partnership seemed likely to continue, the introduction of a family caseworker into the setting appeared most appropriate. In this way Anna could be helped to care for the children without neglecting Henry and could have the opportunity of discussing her difficulties. The worker would also be able to interpret Anna's difficulties to Henry and help him to see how best to support her and maintain his precarious family.

Discussion with a professional casework agency led to the introduction of a female worker. No mention was made of the agency initially. The new worker simply accompanied the fieldworker, who cleared the way by asking if she could bring 'someone like me who will be around when I've gone'. The preparation for withdrawal had for some time included verbal statements about the date of departure of the workers, and some anxiety had been noted. The new arrangement was welcomed by Anna, who was increasingly aware of her needs as she became stronger in trying to hold together her oddly assorted family; Henry was less interested as the new worker had less to offer him, but he could see that there were some advantages in the new relationship. The new worker did not go to the house alone until just prior to the end of the project, and by this time the contact was quite firmly established and the more specific role of the new worker had been explained in greater detail. The transfer was accomplished smoothly, and contact continued for many months after the conclusion of the project.

In the discussion that follows the development of relationships will be traced in terms of a development from one-sided to reciprocal obligations. In the early stages, the days of the Bridge Café, the obligation was upon the workers to provide the café and the services that went with it. The customer's obligation went no further than paying for his tea. Later still, the customers began to exploit the situation when they no longer felt the restraints that would be imposed upon them in the usual café and where there was no obligation to respect the workers. But when this stage had been worked through there were signs of reciprocity in the development of occasional group excursions or, for some, in the joint solution of crises. Eventually, and in terms of time this accounted for most of the project, most young people were able to enter into the give-and-take of regular group relationships with their peers and with the workers.

Contact had first to be established before the workers could use any social-work techniques, and for this purpose the Bridge Café was opened in the area in February 1964. It had been a shop used previously for storage and had now to be converted for use as a café that could stand a good deal of wear and tear. The café was open five nights a week and staffed entirely by voluntary help until the project director arrived in September 1964. Thereafter he was always on duty when it was open until the supporting team arrived a year later. From then onwards one professional member of staff was always on duty, but the number of evenings the café was open dropped to three a week, and then to two. It was closed in January 1966. Attendances at the peak point of the evening were substantially higher in the first months of opening — from February to July 1964 — than they were in subsequent phases; in March 1964 about 50, but after the Easter break in that year they fell to half that figure and never again approached it. For the first year of the project director's service the peak hovered at around 20, but in the last phase of the café's existence from October 1965 to January 1966 the number dwindled to around 10. The overall nightly attendance was, of course, higher than this peak figure, from anything between one-third and two-thirds higher, but the general trends in attendance were remarkably similar.

In evaluating the capacity of the café approach to effect contacts it is worth noting how frequently the customers came, and how far, after work had shifted outside the café, the workers were able to use their café acquaintance to re-establish contacts. It is clear from the records that a substantial number visited the café once or twice and were never seen again. This casual trade accounted for about one-third of attendance between September 1964 and September 1965, and thereafter for about two-thirds. At the other end of the spectrum from casual trade there were a number of intensive users (with over a 50 per cent attendance rate) but never more than 20 in any period and accounting for only 5 per cent of attendance in the last phase (October 1965 to January 1966).

The café provided opportunities for physical proximity and also a setting in which the users could make contact at their own speed, but this presented workers with two problems — how to make satisfactory contact with these young people who virtually threw themselves at the workers and challenged the establishment of a meaningful relationship, and how to reach those who used various methods to prevent the establishment of any kind of contact. Those in the former category were the hardest to handle, in that they posed problems of social control for the workers, and so challenged the very basis upon which the approach depended. The adoption of authoritarian methods of control at the outset would certainly have prevented continuing contact with a number of young people most in need, simply by putting them beyond physical reach. These youngsters challenged the workers 'not to like us' and by their aggressive manner tried to set up barriers to effective communication. Yet acceptance of unprovoked hostility proved difficult for most workers, and the toleration of destructive behaviour even harder. By absolving workers of personal responsibility for the premises, and by encouraging them to look beyond the immediate situation to the needs of the child and the reasons for his behaviour, it did prove possible to get from workers a fairly high level of consistent acceptance of these young people. Workers tried to accept young people as they were on any particular evening, accepting 'the bad evenings' in order to be able to make contact when the adolescent was more open to profit from it.

Other adolescents minimized all contact with the adults. For some of them the behaviour of other Bridge customers proved too threatening, as staff members were rarely in a position to protect them. With these young people the workers used a number of neutral techniques to indicate a willingness to be helpful: offers of a small service (for example, a light for a cigarette) or the offer to play a game (for example, joining in on a game of cards).

The workers tried to accept all the café-users, but no attempt was made to initiate head-on contact with isolated young people. Both the aggressive and the withdrawn showed a degree of ambivalence to the workers, wanting contact yet resisting it, and workers at times found this difficult to handle. Yet the maintenance of a tolerant and accepting environment did in the long run lead to the development of relationships. The symbolism of the café's title, the Bridge, was never made obvious to the users, the café did indeed provide a means of access whereby adults from one cultural background could meet adolescents from another. This neutral meeting-ground, uneasily kept open, eventually led to the formation of ongoing relationships extending far beyond the café where initial contact had been made.

Most of the participants found it necessary to work through a period of exploitation, in which the worker was tested in a variety of ways, before further progress could be made. For some young people it was a prolonged period that stretched the endurance of adult workers to considerable lengths; for others the stage passed quickly or they were satisfied by observing the testing behaviour of others. This testing included constant attention-seeking behaviour, abusive language, complaints about service or the quality of goods sold in the coffee bar, and refusal to leave the premises at closing-time.

Different clients demonstrated different ways of challenging adults.

Bert carried a sharp instrument and carved on anything in sight; Leslie was adept at spitting through his teeth; Percy would work discreetly at loosening a café fixture; Simon complained about his coffee; Frank pretended to have 'just paid' for his drink. In a wide variety of ways, of which the above are only a selection, the clients tried to force a situation of rejection by workers and a resort to coercive authority both of which would confirm their negative view of adults. These attempts to give workers the 'run-around' and to 'play up' seemed to represent an important part in the establishment of the relationship, and the workers appreciated, at least theoretically, that the more disturbed the young person the longer and more violent the testing time would be. Such behaviour certainly shattered any illusions well-meaning adults might have harboured that the clients would immediately respond to kindness. For most workers it was an unusual experience not to be liked and respected by children and in a few cases attitudes hardened, since some doubted the value of a tolerant or bland attitude in the face of 'excessive cheek' or personal abuse. But in the two cases where workers resorted to physical control the results were that in one the worker was injured and in the other the boy severed all future contact with the worker. Banning, or a report to parents, or referral to the police were quite out of the question if contact was to be maintained. The policy of acceptance of testing-out was not only theoretically desirable, it was, in practice, the only possible course of action, given the intention to reach those outside the grasp of other socializing agencies in the community. Most workers hung on grimly — others were more ironical: 'I suggest we give Percy 2/6 every evening, so that he can go to the pictures.'

The testing-out stage of relationships between client and worker were largely accomplished during the Bridge Café period of the project (1964 and 1965). The re-establishment of contact carried out in 1966 after the closure of the café and the introduction of new workers brought repetitions of this behaviour, but rarely expressed in the earlier, fiercer forms. The change in workers' attitudes provoked by such behaviour swept away all illusions based on middle-class benevolence and made many workers acutely aware of their own limitations. Coping with difficult young people certainly helped workers to be less starry-eyed, but in what way did it change the young people? For most it seemed to fulfil a need to be convinced that these adults cared enough about them to withstand such attacks. Once this point was established the young people seemed to need to reassure themselves from time to time, when under personal stress, for example, and also to project the animosity they felt for others on to the workers, who by this time had become 'safe' targets for anger.

All these aspects of testing behaviour were evident in the use one boy, Andy, made of the café and its workers:

One of the earliest customers in the Bridge, he was an extreme example of a boy who needed to test every new adult at some length and possessed an extraordinary ability to vary his testing behaviour to achieve the maximum irritation of the adult under attack. Café staff became the focus of much of his hostile feelings for his father and for authority figures at school, which he was too afraid to voice to them. It is suggested that the testing period led directly to Andy's realization that there was one place where his very considerable personality could express itself without self-damage. On some evenings he seemed to have stored up his emotions for release on the café staff, and he would return home empty and exhausted. One worker, complaining more in anguish than in anger, asked Andy why he kept up such a constant barrage, and received the reply 'Because you're the only one who'll put up with me'. A collective 'you' perhaps as every staff member came in for Andy's attentions and all demonstrated a considerable ability to put up with him. During the testing period, and the months following it, there were never opportunities to discuss his behaviour with him (he did not permit them) and his level of self-awareness was very low. But the willingness of the staff members to absorb sustained and devastating hostility played a large part in changing Andy's behaviour and his attitude to adults. In moments of quietness it became possible to discuss neutral matters, and much later in the relationship, his behaviour; after certain excesses of aggressiveness he felt it necessary to offer some kind of halting apology; there were occasional indications that he was beginning to think about his behaviour and make efforts to adjust it. Yet his conflicts elsewhere, and the contact with more repressive and sternly authoritarian adults at home and at school meant that for many months he needed an 'escape valve' for his feelings.

But in the developing relationship with certain trusted workers he felt able to verbalize his hatred for his father and his own feelings of powerlessness in his presence. He was also able to talk about the [to him] injustices of school life. At first these were only glancing comments, but as confidence built up it was possible to discuss matters at greater length, and he was able to talk seriously about coping with the feelings he had about his father, and dealing with then in a much more mature way. The amount of insight was never very great, but the fact that this resulted in an adjustment of external behaviour is important evidence that learning had taken place. Later in the programme he was able to discuss his father objectively, revealing some understanding of his father's position in the total situation.

Testing-out behaviour did not in every case lead to observable change in the young person's understanding of his own emotions, but it was always a prerequisite for the implementation of informal group work which could and did lead to emotional and cognitive learning. The reliability of the worker was established, and young people had opportunities to escape for a while their own sense of powerlessness in society by 'taking it out of' adults who went on caring (though sometimes through gritted teeth).

But change was soon evident. Workers came to understand some of the young people through the brief conversations that interspersed the hostility. And for the young people some reassessment also had to take place, as adult workers not only accepted them despite the insults and exploitation, but also appeared to bear them no grudge. Even the most provocative of their comrades seemed to be accepted and supported. This support often involved sharing goods or time (in playing cards, for example) or in facilitating trips out of the café, and involvement in small groups on an *ad hoc* basis (a game of indoor football or a visit to another café). The provision of this kind of accepting relationship enabled the young people to move, at their own pace, to a position where they could request and carry out numerous visits and activities of a 'one-off' nature. Gradually workers were seen to be of use to the clients, though the early excursions were often further opportunities for testing the workers, for example, with such comments as (boy to shop owner) 'Oh, this is a friend of ours (deadpan expression), he's a queer.'

During trips away from the area, group members could gain confidence in new situations from the assured behaviour of the worker. Youngsters could even show a generosity they found difficult to show in the neighbourhood café, and could be more dependent upon the worker's protection and skill than they could in the local streets. On these trips, boys and girls saw things sometimes for the first time – the airport, the sea, the country at night. They became people who had 'done things' and 'been to places' and this changed their conception of themselves. Travels through prosperous or immigrant areas of cities and visits to different kinds of homes provoked discussion and a change in attitude. Satisfaction with these occasional excursions played a large part in encouraging the confidence necessary to move to more systematic meetings in groups, and also enabled young people to ask for specific assistance in times of crisis.

However, apart from the extra embarrassment that could be caused to workers, these group outings strengthened relationships and there were numerous examples of a young person listening to the worker in addition to trying to dominate him. In this, and in the occasional offer of cigarettes by the young person, small reciprocal exchanges took place. Generally the worker was viewed as a 'mug' and although this tested some helpers (who had sometimes gone a considerable distance in order to accommodate the group), the workers welcomed these opportunities to get to know their clients. Individual boys and girls came more clearly into focus and, if there was little reciprocity, at least the young people began to demonstrate by their requests that they were beginning to fit the workers into the neighbourhood situation, and find a place for them.

Within nine months of opening the Bridge Café, a variety of *ad hoc* trips were carried out, and these continued to increase. Over twenty groups were involved by March 1965 and their excursions included such activities as playing indoor football, ice-skating, watching football matches, camping, and table-tennis, as well as visiting such places as workers' homes, street fairs, seaside resorts, and the airport. The suggestions usually came from the boys, but even at this early stage the worker tried to facilitate those visits likely to promote most satisfaction among the members.

On group expeditions young people sometimes asked to include a stranger (to the worker) or someone who was a highly disruptive element but whom the group wished to placate. Workers rarely had any chance to structure groups, and it was only later in the relationship that a worker's ideas would be listened to and considered by the group. If at this stage the young people saw the worker as in some way useful, then the worker was glad to take the opportunity of involvement with any group, however impractical (in group work terms) the object of the group outing appeared. However difficult the group, these expeditions gave many opportunities for discussion with individuals, with sub-groups, and with the whole group, of matters unconnected with the expedition. Although the worker was prepared to be a good listener to his younger partner, the latter's low level of verbal ability and lack of experience in talking to adults meant that frequently conversations were halting and limited in scope, and initially lasted for not more than a minute or two at a time. But the presence of an interested adult who could skilfully draw out opinions and expand the client's ability to express himself brought results. Later in the project it was not uncommon to talk with individuals or groups for upwards of an hour, and 'having a good talk' was seen as sufficient justification for spending time together. Even in the café, some clients would seek out particular workers who they had come to know would listen to them, although these clients came to be seen as the more regular users of the café. The less stable, and generally less articulate, saw and used the worker as an active facilitator (e.g. for getting them to somewhere desirable) rather than a passive listener. These small-group activities were excellent opportunities to blend personal and general conversation, and the achievement of the limited goals of the expedition made further excursions possible. These activities also provided a number of situations in which young people interacted with each other, which helped the worker to understand the individuals better and to strengthen the cohesiveness of the group. As a result of seeing individuals in a variety of group situations, workers were able to appreciate more easily the degree of disturbance and could adjust their own actions accordingly. Inclusion in group activities was never seen as a reward for good behaviour, and the worker's willingness to reverse the expected pattern of adult approval may well have played a large part in convincing difficult boys of the continued concern and care of the worker.

Just occasionally these group excursions were as satisfying to the worker as they were to the group members — when there was some progress in developing relationships, and in understanding individual attitudes, or some expression of satisfaction from the group or evidence of cohesion. These were the shreds of reward that compensated for the majority of evenings where little if anything seemed to be achieved and for frustrating sessions where groups argued and fought, where the worker was misunderstood and misused, and where the hopes of both the worker and of the group were dashed.

Some boys continued the pattern of casual expeditions over the whole project, though at times their group activities became more stable. Leslie was one of these.

Winter 1965
(i) Leslie and his friends formed a five-a-side football team, and the worker helped to get fixtures at clubs in and around the area. They stayed close to the worker, played enthusiastically, if erratically, usually lost, but found someone or something to blame for the defeats.
(ii) A school gymnasium, obtained at the request of an older adolescent group, became available to Leslie and his group for the earlier part of the evening. Activities revolved around indoor football and other ball games; Leslie occasionally stayed on a short while to play with the early arrivals of the older group.
(iii) After using the gymnasium, the group was able to make use of a room in a nearby house for refreshment, talk, and table-games.

Spring/summer 1966
Through conversation with the worker, gear was borrowed and transport made available for weekend camping trips. Sometimes a worker accompanied the group; at other times Leslie and two or three friends were transported, and visited by workers.

Winter 1966
(i) Leslie and his friends, helped by the worker, formed a football team, entered a league, and played for a period of some six months. The meetings for training at the gym continued, as did meetings at the house afterwards.
(ii) Leslie wanted to meet with a couple of friends on another night of the week, and a room was made available at an office about one mile from the project area. The group talked, played table-games, used building bricks, and experimented with the telephone.

Spring 1967
The group planned a weekend visit to London; 3 of them, including Leslie, travelled with the worker, stayed with a family previously unknown to them, and travelled to various parts of the city (for one session entirely unaccompanied).

Winter 1967
(i) In addition to indoor football, Leslie also requested an opportunity to take part in weight-training. The group survived only a few weeks,

and it was thought that he may have used this request to hold on to workers whom he felt were spending more time with other boys.

(ii) Receiving information through the café network, Leslie and a friend joined another group making excursions to a bowling alley. Regular visits followed, and then came the opportunity to take part in a mixed group in a more sophisticated setting.

Spring 1968

One of the bowling group suggested visiting a youth club and the group agreed. A large mixed club was chosen, and the worker was asked to arrange a visit. After several visits, Leslie (and others) joined the club, and spent more and more time away from the worker who accompanied them. Leslie seemed to grow quickly at ease in the club, and made no demur when the worker attended for shorter periods, and, finally, withdrew completely.

In addition to these group activities, Leslie was frequently involved in contact with workers in casual groupings in cafés and on street corners, and often took part in kickabout football games on a school playground. He also took part in swimming, table-tennis, soccer matches (as a spectator), and visits to city coffee bars. Work with him was almost exclusively in group terms, a sporting activity (football, at which he was skilled) was used to lead into a range of social situations in which he could be helped towards adolescence and maturity. At the commencement of work Leslie was a very small 14-year-old, a bright-eyed, sharp child, admired by his peers for his daring and for the delinquent and criminal reputations of his older brothers. He rarely felt able to discuss his feelings about his brothers, or his 'tough' father, but workers felt that his ability and intelligence, given scope and encouragement by those who did not regard it as automatic that he would follow in his brothers' footsteps, would be enough to permit him to shape his own life in a different way. He was able to talk enthusiastically about his work, and about his ambitions to learn a craft which combined both 'hard work' and 'skilled knowledge'; his attitudes to formal authority were always wary, but he made friendly (though not warm) relationships with adult workers. He always saw himself as exercising power over other young people ('I'm a natural leader'), but towards the end of the project it was clear that he recognized the positive uses of this leadership. Having slipped the chains of his reputation, Leslie now had too much to lose by getting into trouble, and the workers felt that he had every chance of making a very good adjustment to adult life.

(ii) CRISES

Out of workers' initial encounters with clients came requests for a more regular series of meetings, and, more important to the workers at the time, requests by individuals for help in some kind of personal crisis situation. (The term 'crisis' is used here to mean an immediate and major difficulty to which no solution is evident. The many minor difficulties discussed in group situations or with workers at various other times are not included, but only those provoking in the client an urgent cry for help.) Requests for help in a crisis permitted a more rapid readjustment of both worker and client perspectives, and presented an opportunity for a more radical, if at times painful, change in behaviour.

How did the young people come to see our workers as people who could help in a crisis? Workers did not always realize that their behaviour in the café and in the group excursions was watched carefully by the young people. At any point the young person could break contact — by not coming to the café, by rejecting or avoiding the worker, or by refusal to participate in group actions. The decision to 'use' the worker in a situation of stress was therefore a decision that could only be made by the client. The worker could assist only through his demonstrated concern for young people and by his physical accessibility. Most of the requests for help were made to the workers most frequently present, and generally stemmed from an established relationship. Some extended opportunity to 'weigh up' the worker would seem to be vital if young people already wary of adults and of commitment are to be able to ask for and use help in times of crisis.

The workers' ambiguous role in the detached work situation, one might almost describe it as being that of a 'professional stranger', made it easier for some young people to select workers to advise, share, and assist in dealing with a major personal crisis. This not only meant a breakthrough in the relationship, but was also an eloquent testimony to the effective working of the relationship to date. Of the 32 boys and 2 girls involved in the group excursions in the winter of 1964-65, 10 boys and 1 girl requested assistance during a time of acute personal stress. Help in a crisis, if correctly handled, usually carried the relationship onto a new level of intimacy. The range of problems that provoked requests for help was highly predictable, and included relationships with parents and with girl- or boy-friends, loss of work, accommodation, feared illness and pregnancies, criminal behaviour, and financial debts. The point that should be underlined here is that demands for this kind of help stemmed from the previous acceptance of testing behaviour, a willingness to cope with exploitation, and the provision of opportunities for informal group action.

Help in a crisis went beyond the individual. It furthered relationships with others in the group, and with those in the café network of the neighbourhood. It helped to convince clients of the usefulness, the interest, and the discretion of the adult workers, and so represented a vital stage in the development of a relationship of trust. It drew workers into touch with the client's parents and other relatives, and permitted an extension of knowledge about the total situation in which the client found himself. This in turn helped the worker to treat the relationship with much greater understanding, and superficial views of individuals had to be discarded in the face of the complexities revealed through awareness of the facts leading to the crisis.

It is not suggested that every relationship developed in the same way, progressing from occasional group contact to a demand for help. In some cases the crisis help was requested much later in the relationship; in rare cases it preceded group contact of any kind. The pattern outlined in this chapter is the most typical. This kind of work has always been seen by professional social workers as requiring the use of casework techniques, but it was through the provision of extended programmes of group work that the project workers saw the major contribution of the project in assisting young people to greater social competence. Yet the inclusion of young people in group situations where they could get close to the adult worker, test him, and learn to trust him, led to numerous requests for assistance on matters that, for cultural and personal reasons, could not be treated in the group. Whether casework or group work methods were employed, the worker's availability at the point and time when he was needed was vital to further progress, as is evident in the case of Roger and Janice.

Roger and Janice were a boy and girl friendship which, despite numerous rows, achieved a remarkable consistency. Both had been particularly difficult to get to know in the Bridge Café, Roger especially keeping his distance and holding conversation to neutral themes. The separation of male and female roles in the neighbourhood meant that Janice and Roger rarely came together until the end of the evening, and there was little chance to involve them in joint discussion. From Janice we learned that Roger's family was in danger of breaking up, and that Janice's parents disapproved of the family and Roger in particular. One of their periodic rows separated them, and both talked about it independently to workers. Janice's behaviour and appearance deteriorated. Roger began to associate with older, known criminals, and, despite the workers' efforts, got involved in a couple of street brawls. He assumed an even greater carelessness of consequences.

The crisis help began when Janice was found by a worker in a café, tearful and in some distress, saying she had been thrown out of her home. The cause appeared to be her continued attachment to Roger and her resumption of this relationship. The worker's knowledge of the girl led the worker to conclude that an immediate return home was out of the question, and he got in touch with the caseworker, who provided overnight accommodation and helped the girl rent a room the following day. Discussion with the worker led to Janice letting her parents know her approximate whereabouts, and permitted the caseworker to open contact with the parental home provided her address was not revealed. Another worker was able to find Roger, and because of the crisis, force a discussion of his feelings, intentions, and hopes, and led ultimately to the workers supporting Janice and Roger in working towards a permanent relationship. This involved close contact with Janice's parents (where the major objections lay) in order to prepare the foundations for Janice's eventual return home to an atmosphere where her relationship with Roger could be based on personal choice rather than reflecting opposition to parental wishes.

The caseworker became the liaison between the mother and Janice, interpreting each to each. Another fieldworker shared time with both the young people, providing opportunities for them to discuss their feelings more openly and decide ways in which they could help each other. Occasional visits home ended in Janice returning to live there after an absence of six weeks.

The contact with the young people and their families did not, of course, stop there, but the availability of workers to carry out intensive work during that crisis helped to bring all the parties concerned to a greater understanding of each other's attitudes and behaviour. The workers were able to 'take the heat out' of the conflict, and so enable and encourage a more mature assessment and a more helpful action by both the young and the older people concerned.

Eventually Roger and Janice became engaged and were married with the approval and support of both sets of parents. The issue here is the way in which involvement in the crisis led to a change in these young people. Roger was never given to expressions of warmth, but there was no disguising the sincerity with which he now invited the company of workers. Janice regarded the workers with greater affection anyway, and following the crisis recognized that they had helped her to resolve conflicts. Both were trying to make sense of their experience, and perhaps all that the workers did was to help them to determine what they really wanted and then assist in removing some of the barriers. Yet at one point in time the relationships were near to irretrievable damage, and the break that enabled help to be offered depended upon a worker being in a backstreet café late one night.

Relationships between people are always likely to change as a result of their sharing a crisis, but if left to chance or in the hands of an unskilled third party, the relationships might well worsen, attitudes harden, and the situation become intolerable. The worker's contact with Janice and Roger was just strong enough to permit his involvement in their crisis. The worker's function was to help the couple identify objectives and decide about action, and to encourage their participation in working out the solution to their problem. As a result of his involvement with them, and the contribution he was able to make, the worker formed a steadier and deeper relationship with them, which in turn helped them to achieve personal, parental, and socially approved goals, and to learn a great deal about themselves in the process.

Although many of the crisis situations involved conflict with parents, there were many others that arose from breaking the law or being in trouble at work. Indeed, as will be shown later in this chapter, about one in eight of the sessions contained reference to representation in court on behalf of the client, and one in seven referred to help with work problems. Often this representation and help was given in crisis situations. It needs to be stressed perhaps that in the main the following observations about social services used by the boys rely on *their* statements. Although these are extremely relevant, they can only be a limited view of the way in which the services actually did function.

The 'mediating' role of the workers was at no time seen more clearly than when boys had been arrested. Of the thirty-eight court appearances made by participants in the evaluation period, twenty-one were with a report from a probation officer, and in sixteen of these instances (covering twelve boys), the workers were in touch with the officers concerned. Sometimes it was purely a matter of exchange of, and request for, simple information — such as when a boy would return from approved school — and sometimes it was a more detailed discussion of planning and implementation. The latter tended to occur with only a small number of officers and in some cases the discussions remained at a general and rather superficial level. In the case of three officers there was a refusal to cooperate or discuss clients.

Almost invariably the project workers initiated contact with the probation officers in the crisis situation, and undoubtedly such situations helped to develop cooperation between them and assisted in clarifying the project workers' role to officers. Where the team had decided to support a boy in court, either by attending with him, speaking for him, or writing to the court or magistrates on his behalf, communication and cooperation was further developed. Support in the actual court situation was very important in the development of a relationship with the client, for it was an overt demonstration of the helping role. In terms of total work it consumed a great deal of time, not only in the actual court appearance, which frequently meant being available for a whole day, but also in the necessary prior planning sessions, discussions, and explanations with the client or clients concerned. Also, in some instances, remands could mean that a participant might make two or three appearances for each offence or set of offences, and it would be necessary for the worker to be present at each of the stages. The following figures do not include remands but list them together as one appearance. In ten of the thirty-eight court appearances made by participants in the evaluation period, a worker either spoke or wrote a letter to a magistrate on the client's behalf. In a further eleven instances a worker was present at the court hearing, but only offering more general support.

In the fieldwork situation, when suitable opportunity arose, workers attempted exploration, interpretation, and alteration of a participant's attitudes to probation, to after-care, and to the particular officers involved. In the data sheets completed by workers at the end of the project for each participant (usually only one worker was responsible for completing the information on each client) the attitudes of 14 of the participants to those agencies was reported. Although there must be an element of subjectivity in their rating, they were helped by information from participants' casefiles which included information from other workers. Out of 14 participants 8 were reported to be indifferent to the supervising agency and officer. Some participants tried to ignore the whole business, but for most it was simply another thing to be endured. In contrast to this passive attitude 6 showed varying degrees of cooperation with and trust in the officers, but even in some of these cases the workers felt that the relationship was a superficial one. The 4 participants who expressed the most positive attitudes did so because they felt they could easily 'put one over' on the officer. In part, the participants' attitudes to probation and after-care followed the local cultural response to outside agencies, that is accepting them but not believing in them. However, a number of other factors associated with the administration of the system probably intensified clients' reactions. The Probation Service offices were located outside Wincroft in places not familiar to their clients; staffing changes within the department led to rapid changes among personnel; and movement out of the area by participants put them under the care of strangers. Indeed, these changes also presented their own problems for the project workers who often had to start almost from the beginning to develop a relationship with the new officer.

Discussion of Probation and After-care Services between the project worker and the participant might only take the form of allowing the client to 'sound off' about the situation, but even this could have a useful cathartic effect. On the other hand, in some instances help would be of a more practical nature – discussing with the adolescent the possible consequences of non-attendance for his reporting session or else actually facilitating the boy's attendance at the office after he had been warned by the officer of a possible return to court for non-attendance.

Workers' contact with these agencies was usually known to the participant concerned, as was similar contact with other agencies or figures within the boys' milieu, although the precise content of that contact may not have been known. In the relationship between the probation officer and the mutual client the worker saw his own role as one of mediator, although this description was not always clear to the other parties. In the case of 6 of the 13 participants who started probation or after-care in the evaluation period the mediator role became more explicit, but in the other cases it remained blurred, except when crisis points such as court appearances brought the three parties together.

Contact between the workers and probation officers on other than a superficial basis was limited to a small proportion of the total number of officers in the neighbourhood. The level of contact and cooperation in these cases was undoubtedly far above that experienced with the schools, but in some instances this liaison could have been developed further, to the benefit of the clients. One reason for the failure to achieve fuller cooperation was the large caseloads carried by the officers.

At certain times during the project and throughout the whole period for a small number of boys the problem of unemployment loomed large. As the report of the YWCA Project by Goetschius and Tash has shown [1] the field of employment is an area that holds special difficulties for socially deprived youth. They lack training and qualifications in work skills; often, personal instability means that they are unable to accept industrial discipline; and they are likely to be in marginal jobs that are the first to be affected by the trade-cycle or by government intervention in the economy. In addition, in Wincroft there were unsympathetic employers who would fire a boy with very little notice and, seemingly, for very little reason. This problem was aggravated for the clients, and in turn for the workers, because some parents refused to sleep and feed their sons if they could not pay their way. The sequence – no job, no wages, no bed, leading to crime – was identified on a number of occasions. Also, whether or not a boy had left home following the loss of his job, unemployment provided the motive and opportunity, and for some the need, to turn to crime. Again, if a boy had followed the above cycle and was, as a consequence, appearing in court, the lack of a job could well influence adversely the sentence imposed by the magistrates. Of the fifty-four participants twelve presented workers with employment problems on either an intensive short-term or an intensive long-term basis. In addition to this there were ten who were helped on a less intensive basis. Work with these twenty-two usually involved finding jobs somehow; this ranged from actually taking a boy to a job that had been found by a worker to suggesting possible jobs picked up from advertisements in the newspaper. The level of the worker's involvement varied according to the ability of the participant concerned to cope with the situation. Participants were encouraged to take at least some of the initiative themselves, rather than rely on the worker to make the necessary arrangements, and workers would not force the issue if clients were not prepared to make any movements themselves. In addition to the 22, 7 other participants were helped with problems arising out of their job situation. The work here was on a more general support basis, and meant discussion with clients on such topics as attitudes to the boss, prospects within the job, and stealing ('fiddling') from work.

At least 24 of the 54 participants were unemployed for one week or more during the evaluation period. The workers therefore found it necessary to accumulate a list of sympathetic employers whom they could contact if no other vacancies could be found through normal channels. This list proved invaluable on a number of occasions where clients were desperate for jobs but were unable to obtain them. Participants were encouraged to use the Youth Employment Service or Department of Employment and Productivity, but this proved difficult since the participants' almost unanimous opinion of these services, of the former especially, was that they were 'no fucking use'. This statement was often supported by real or imaginary tales of being sent for jobs that were no longer vacant or of officers giving out only the lowest paid jobs. No doubt the basis of some of these attitudes was to be found in prejudice rather than reasoned experience, but the fieldwork discussions with participants after visits to these agencies, and visits by the client with a worker, show that the youth employment officer and Department of Employment and Productivity official sometimes lacked tact and understanding in dealing with this kind of boy. Thus, although it was often insisted that a client report punctually at 8.30 the following morning for a vacancy and/or to sign on, he was often kept waiting by the officers for no apparent reason, and, perhaps most damaging of all to the boy, the staff often made their feelings of disapproval and disdain clear. At least 18 of the participants used one or both of the state employment services, some on more than one occasion, but at least 11 of these were in connection with claiming unemployment benefits. Only two boys were known to have obtained a job in this manner. Nine of the participants were accompanied by a worker to the Youth Employment Service or Department of Employment and Productivity, some on several occasions. In one case there was contact with the officer concerned before the visit. Contact between workers and employment officers was minimal, apart from in the early phase of the project, in 1964-65, when the director had made visits to all the agencies in the area. In three cases only was there consultation with the Youth Employment Service on participants and their jobs, but this contact did not persist over time.

A number of private, as distinct from state, employment agencies existed in Manchester and the workers were able to develop contact with three of these. All proved useful in providing, on occasions, jobs that were urgently required and the director of one proved particularly helpful in providing jobs for several of the participants who had poor work records. Certainly some of the clients were more amenable to using these private agencies and generally the workers found the latter more helpful with their specific problems.

The state employment services were not active in placing participants in jobs, although it is true that this was often because of a reluctance on the boys' part to use them. But some boys used them for another purpose. Where participants wished to claim unemployment pay or supplementary benefits they had to 'sign on' at the appropriate agency, depending on their age, in order to receive their benefits. In such instances visits were regarded as a regrettable necessity. Eleven of the participants claimed one or other of the forms of benefit ment.oned above during the evaluation period. Usually it was supplementary benefit, since many clients were ineligible for one reason or ancther for unemployment pay. In fact, 24 of the participants were out of work for a period of longer than one week during the project, but only 11 were known to have claimed benefits. The reason for this is partly to be found in the traditional Wincroft attitudes to such state payments, which are described in terms of offending 'my pride' and 'accepting charity'. People who did claim such benefits regularly lost standing in the neighbourhood, being regarded as 'parasites'. In some cases this may well have been a rationalization in order to hide an inability to deal with the process of claiming benefit. No doubt some of the participants were exploiting the system, and indeed there were two who were known to have made illegal claims, but the picture for the majority was of either reluctance or failure to claim entitlement. Project workers encouraged and assisted participants to obtain benefits when unemployed, but this was often difficult because of their widespread prejudices and because of the treatment they received when applying. Social security officials were often very rigid and unsympathetic in administering the rules. On a number of occasions participants were threatened with suspension of benefits and, as in the case of the employment services, disapproving attitudes were made abundantly clear. Long periods of waiting, being sent to other offices, often a considerable distance away, and having to complete complicated forms, all had the effect of deterring clients from seeking benefits. On one occasion a worker spent a whole day with a boy just going through this process. Another, applying by himself but after encouragement from a worker, was told to return the next day and when he mentioned that he had no money for food was informed that this was his misfortune. In all 8 participants received help in applying for benefits and this ranged from verbal encouragement and explanation of procedures to actually accompanying the boys to the relevant offices. Contact between the workers and Ministry of Social Security officials was confined to that arising out of visits with a client and at no stage was there discussion with them about clients.

The examples given in the preceding section of relationships with other agencies in periods of crisis may seem to have unduly stressed the shortcomings of the services. It is once again acknowledged that the examples rely largely (though not wholly) on accounts given by the participants.

(iii) PROCESS

The development of worker-client relationships noted in the crisis situations was also to be seen in the more frequent group meetings that began to take place on a regular basis. Here too relationships swung from being largely non-reciprocal to being an exchange in which more and more the worker came to be recognized as a caring adult with whom young people chose to share their time. Progress was never smooth, and even when the worker was enjoying an easy, shared relationship in the group its members were likely to regress when faced with frustration. As the reciprocal relationships within a group grew, so its members enjoyed more trust (for example, in the use of facilities in the absence of the worker), but they also had new opportunities for exploiting the workers. Yet, despite all these exceptions, it still seems possible to trace a thread of development in the relationship itself that makes transition from the non-reciprocal to reciprocal action worth this detailed examination.

In discussing the earlier levels of relationship the emphasis has been on the worker/client and worker/group, and the overall impression is of young people with little concern for adults and their feelings. But the non-reciprocal nature of relationships extended to other young people also, and even to members of the peer-group. It was by no means uncommon for 'friends' to be excluded from sharing pleasures, and they were frequently deprived of companionship by 'mates' who decided arbitrarily to go elsewhere. No concern was demonstrated for absentee group members, or individuals less privileged than themselves. Workers came to see that they had not been singled out for harsh and unfeeling behaviour since for young people in the neighbourhood such behaviour was commonplace in their dealings with each other. This apparent unconcern and superficiality in relationships extended through the peer-group network of the streets and, for many of the boys, into their family network also. Reciprocity was an enforced obligation in the family and not a freely undertaken response.

In retrospect, workers came to understand that progress from superficial, exploitative contact with the worker to a request for regular meetings was in itself an indication of a change and a growth in social functioning. Some of the requests were very direct — to play indoor football, to do some weight-training, and so on. But generally the request was more oblique, extending contact week by week, and culminating in an agreed regular meeting. These meetings provided the worker with an opportunity to use more of his group work skills to assist the group and its members, and so the worker came to be seen as someone willing to offer consistent help to the group. The meetings also changed the worker's view of things, for he could now begin to plan ahead in the light of the more relaxed and intimate atmosphere of regular group meetings. He could feel confident in pressing the group to act over absentees, and so further stabilize the group. He could do this because the responsibility for inviting boys had been placed squarely on the members of the group.

The stabilization of groups now became of considerable concern to the worker and many months elapsed before the same young people turned up regularly each week. The early period saw constant changes, and promising groups were disrupted from within by the inadequacies of the members. Some of the regular group meetings were seen by the young people as straightforward activity groups. *Ad hoc* opportunities to play table-tennis led to a number of regular players beginning to regard themselves as 'the group'; boys who wished to play football pulled in others to make up a team, and so on. Other groups were primarily friendship groups, which moved from *ad hoc* social contact with the worker to a regular weekly session. The young people determined the group membership on the basis of friendship rather than skill at an activity; the programme of action each week was decided in discussion with the group. A few groups were a combination of friendship and activity skill. The 5-a-side football group was formed by school-mates with some ability at the game. In another group, later in the project, a number of friends decided to form a guitar-playing group.

By the time that regular meetings had developed, the worker was very much an accepted part of the group. Frequently a relaxed and easy atmosphere prevailed in the groups, and the worker found himself receiving confidences, jokes, conversation, cigarettes, and sometimes money for petrol or contributions towards the group's expenses. With notable exceptions groups no longer exploited the workers, but were able to demonstrate concern and even affection for the worker.

It is necessary to examine briefly the methods employed by the workers, and some of the difficulties in using them in a neighbourhood setting. The main method, *social group work*, is still a relatively unused method in British social-work practice, and though many social workers and educators encounter groups in their work it is seldom that a conscious effort is made to put the resources of the group to systematic use. But young people are especially sensitive to the opinions of other group members, and so the method of social group work is particularly relevant to working with them. It is important to stress that this method deliberately and consciously encourages the group to help its own members, 'the mobilization of their strength' to use Gisela Konopka's explanatory phrase. [2] During the early meetings the worker played a large part in sustaining and stabilizing the group, but his primary task was always to support and service it, turning its attention to its problems and helping it to reach an acceptable solution. The worker's attempts to understand the group process — 'the totality of the group's interaction' (Konopka) — were directed towards releasing and canalizing the contributions of each member and of the group towards the attainment of socially desirable goals.

The programmes of group work in the Wincroft Project were accomplished entirely through the use of recreational group activities and carried out by informal friendship and activity groupings. Group work did not include therapeutic group discussions. Occasionally there was some assessment by the group of relationships within it, and the workers often discussed the group experience with individuals or pairs when apart from the main group. Generally, however, the workers' task lay less in interpretation and much more in supporting groups and the individuals who made up the groups, and in assisting their functioning in society.

It was not the worker's intention to structure groups, and he played little or no part in the formation of the groups or their composition. The onus for this was placed firmly on the individual boy or boys around whom the group was to grow. At all times the worker was available to play an instrumental role in locating a boy the group wanted to include, and to implement a decision by the group. Later in the project it was possible for the worker to ask the group to consider inviting someone whom the worker felt would benefit from the group, or to tolerate a visitor to the group for one or more meetings. It was also possible to bring groups together for short periods in order to test, and to increase, their competence in different social situations. In the early months the method was chiefly to make opportunities for groups to be formed, and to be available to nurture them. 'Starting a group' never achieved the formality evident in American practice, though sometimes friendship groups asked for activities or for the exclusive use of a worker or of premises. Once the group was formed it was the worker's short-term objective to help it enjoy satisfying group experiences, and over a period of years carry through to a more sophisticated level, and so achieve the long-term objective.

Most of the work was with groups of friends of the same age, though some difficulties were encountered in the constant interplay between the participants and older boys in the cafés and public houses. In general the workers tried to reduce such interaction and with it the possibilities of criminal influence. In fact much of the group work took place outside of the immediate neighbourhood, and this increased the possibility of objective discussion and comparison with different sets of standards.

One of the major assumptions in applying social group work methods is a concern for the individual, but this concern was not enough to deal with the needs of some boys. A different social-work method was required in certain situations, and this method was *social casework*. The relevance of this method in crises has already been explored, but what about its relevance to routine situations? The need for casework procedures derived from two manifestations of the same root difficulty – the lack of trust and interpersonal concern showed by young people for each other, shown in one way (by far the simplest way from a treatment viewpoint) by the unwillingness of individuals to reveal or discuss certain types of personal problems in group situations. Admittedly, the groups were largely recreational and social, but there seemed to be more than the group's character preventing discussion at other than a superficial level. Greater trust in the group worker than in each other enabled a number of boys and girls to talk when away from the group, and here a programme akin to casework became necessary. Young people whose group involvement was practically nil posed a particular difficulty. Their inability to sustain any friendships or any kind of group membership made it extremely difficult to use group work methods at all. Other literature has demonstrated the inability of emotionally deprived children to cope with anything more than very simple group life, and this was confirmed in this project. [3] Only on a one-to-one basis could change be effected where an adolescent's group experiences had been consistently unsatisfactory.

The unusual work situation rarely permitted the taking of a detailed social history. There were no opportunities to conduct formal interviews in an office setting, and only later in the programme was it possible to obtain an invitation to the family home. Discussion sometimes took place in the relative seclusion of the worker's home, but more often in the noisy setting of a public house or café, or perhaps in the course of a journey. Where the young person could present a problem (but one he could not easily ventilate in a group), there was a clearer awareness of a 'casework relationship' in which the adult was consulted by the client. But in situations where work was undertaken with the severely isolated person, or with one excluded from the group, there was rarely much if any awareness, on the client's part, of personal difficulties in a way that could be discussed in casework terms. With these boys the one-to-one relationship became more of a friendship relationship, with the worker seeking to maximize the trust necessary before touching on areas where there appeared to be problems of which the young person was only partially aware. It has already been suggested that getting to a position where systematic use of group work skills could be employed demonstrated a change in the young person's understanding of his relationship with the worker. In the same way, getting to a point where individuals felt able to share and face problems with a caseworker also demonstrated a positive development.

In the project casework grew out of group work, and both grew from the pre-casework and pre-group-work stage of efforts in the Bridge Café, where workers had taken neutral positions ready to step into group work or casework roles as and when the young person permitted them to do so.

Use of both group work and casework led to changed relationships between clients and workers, but both methods had acute disadvantages, which should be kept in mind when considering the detailed studies later in the chapter. The first major problem confronting workers when undertaking group work was the existence of the network of informal relations in the neighbourhood. [4] The constantly shifting alliances within this network caused practical problems for the workers when trying to stabilize the groups. Informal friendship groups mushroomed and collapsed with startling rapidity, and it was against this background of relationship failure that the workers operated.

The second major problem was the existence within the network of older and more delinquent adolescents, some in their late teens or early twenties. In facilitating the formation of groups by participants the workers had to try to avoid the selection of older experienced delinquents, but at the same time avoid being the centre of rivalry between the older and the younger groups. Here the pre-group work period of the Bridge Café was useful in assisting the workers to identify and seek to negate the influence of young adults who sought to involve the adolescents in more actively delinquent groupings. In encouraging boys to form groups from immediate peers, and in providing opportunities for independent group action, workers offered an alternative to 'going around with' older men. This, of course, produced difficulties for the worker, and skill had to be used to avoid getting into a role of 'opposition'. This necessitated maintaining nominally friendly relations with the older groups and individuals, without a regular commitment of time or concern.

An associated problem was the need to maintain relations with the proprietors or managers of the coffee bars and other places where the young people gathered, for in some cases these were known to be profiting from the illegal activities of the young people. In providing opportunities for the young to get away from the neighbourhood and to be more objective about their lives, the workers were introducing concepts and values which did not go down well with those individuals who needed teenage trade. It is particularly important to emphasize here the strong pressures placed upon young people in the neighbourhood to conform to the expectations of the powerful figures in the network. In order for the project to continue in the area the opposing values of workers and older delinquents had to be left largely unstated, and this presented problems of method and of conscience to the worker. He sought to maintain an uneasy neutrality while, in other settings, offering the participant group more positive ways of spending their leisure and looking critically at the world around them.

Even in working with the participants, workers had to exercise considerable caution in where they went, what they did, and what they said. The small size of the area, the café network, and the fragmentation of groups made it difficult to work with one boy or one group without it becoming known to others, and there were a number of instances of 'sibling rivalry' among participants.

We propose now to look at work with two typical friendship groups and two typical activity groups.

This first friendship group was created around Donald, one of the participants with whom contact had been made in the Bridge Café. Their weekly group meetings were entirely social in character, and the period of meetings extended over eight months. At its largest the group totalled six (five boys and one girl) plus Donald. Including a few home visits, thirty-five arranged contacts were made, plus some accidental street encounters.

Donald was a slim, hyperactive 17-year-old when the meetings started. He came from a very disturbed home background, which included a delinquent older brother. In social situations Donald showed a lot of inappropriate and sometimes bizarre behaviour. A number of his age-mates did not show such disturbed behaviour, but they enforced Donald's role in the informal group as someone who would shock by his outspoken homosexual and heterosexual imagery, and who was therefore 'good for a laugh'. Personal contact with the boy showed workers that although he was limited in verbal expression when dealing with ordinary conversational topics, much of the 'idiot' behaviour could be shed. Donald came to be able to say that he felt he was trapped by his reputation. [The parallel with Benny's comment on page 94 is striking.]

'We discussed difficulties experienced by comedians off-stage, who were often expected to be funny in their private lives too, and Donald was able to understand and apply the comparison. "But what can I do . . . they say 'here comes Donald, now we'll have a laugh'. They all think I'm a fucking idiot so I behave like a fucking idiot. That's my problem – how do I change my fucking image? " '

The worker and Donald then set about to draw together a group of boys who could be helped to see Donald in a new light. It was decided that meetings should take place away from the neighbourhood area in the 1930s estate to which Donald had moved some months previously. The boy also felt that other adult workers in the neighbourhood knew of his reputation, and that he would find it difficult to change his behaviour in their presence; so a new adult was introduced to him who, so far as Donald knew, had no knowledge of his previous wildness.

Two visits to Blackpool were arranged and the worker went with Donald to invite two carefully selected mates. The trips were relaxed and enjoyable. The natural skylarking of adolescent boys on a night out never began to look like getting out of control, and the worker reported very favourably. The conversation on the journeys was sensible, and there was a high degree of interaction. Twenty-one sessions followed the Blackpool nights; almost all took place in public houses. Talk and card- and dart-playing occupied the bulk of the time.

	Age	*No. of sessions:* 21
Donald	(17)	21
Lionel	(17)	19
Ian	(20)	16
Rose	(17)	10
Oscar	(17)	7
Lloyd	(17)	3
Chris	(17)	5

Lionel, Ian, and Oscar had taken part in the Blackpool trips; Rose came to the group meetings with Ian; Lloyd and Chris came fortuitously on occasions, not because they were invited, but because it proved difficult to exclude them. Work with groups in neighbourhood settings permitted boys to invite themselves to take part in events, and the nucleus group (and the worker) were not in a sufficiently strong position to reject them.

The three boys invited by Donald were all passive, slightly withdrawn young people. In fact, he made a wise selection in terms of his objective of putting across a different and more serious aspect of his personality. Rose was a very quiet girl, already coping with very great problems in her own personal life, after leaving home. At no time during the group meetings did Donald demonstrate bizarre behaviour, and, with the help of the worker, the group talked about experiences and opinions, and about current national and local events, which would not normally have been possible unaided in their social group. Group members expressed personal surprise at Donald's more acceptable behaviour, but put this down to the new social situation rather than intention on Donald's part. Certainly on his return to the old neighbourhood (the project area) some deterioration in behaviour occurred, and under stress his behaviour wavered regardless of the situation.

Although the group existed primarily to help Donald, each of the other members appeared to derive benefit from it. Lionel found himself and his opinions listened to more than in the neighbourhood, and often brought facts and 'things I've heard' to the group. Ian, more cynical and worldly-wise than the others, was forced to think and to give reasons, once even producing a newspaper article to support his argument. Rose emerged from her abstracted silence to become an occasional contributor, and her presence was acknowledged by delaying the card game which would exclude her. Oscar, taciturn and suspicious, contributed least to the discussions. Donald, extrovert contributor, introduced many of the topics for talk, spoke sensibly to the group, and learned to relax and listen to the views of others. The worker helped them to express their views, listened, tried to introduce helpful facts and get opinions, and in this way maintained an increasingly mature, if at times somewhat inconsequential, discussion. The group members were inexperienced in marshalling their thoughts and verbalizing their feelings in connected sentences. But if the conversation was sometimes superficial and tangential, they were surprised at their own intellectual and verbal ability, and as a result of the exchanges each of them came to view himself as a slightly different person. The evenings also helped them to be more confident in a strange environment, and in new social situations.

The group rarely touched directly on personal problems, but discussions in areas relevant to such problems were frequent: behaviour with girls (and how to get them); parents; work prospects; house purchase; pre-marital sex; hire-purchase; marriage. They were also encouraged to talk about their past and to share their experiences with the group, to help them see where they were going. Above all the group generated a warmth that made the evenings buoyant and friendly. Conversation often bubbled, and the card games which formed the central section of most of the sessions were always free from acrimony.

The group gave Donald a chance to present his new image. It also gave Lionel status, and gave Ian a chance to be 'with the lads' while also fulfilling obligations to Rose, who enjoyed the more sophisticated settings in which the group met. For all of them it was a group situation very different from anything they had experienced in the project area.

During these months they had got to know and like adults from very different social backgrounds, becoming increasingly willing and able to share things with them. Despite involvement in illegal and criminal behaviour in their own past, they were still able to show genuine concern for the worker when his car was stolen during one evening's visit to town and also during his brief illness. But the flow was not entirely one way — the worker's perspective changed also. The adults came to see the world of officialdom a little more through the eyes of these young people, and became more aware of how incomprehensible many of the rules and regulations of society must appear to them. The workers came to appreciate the personal qualities of the boys although those had been muted by the social situation in which they found themselves.

In the second of the two friendship groups described the boys were neither as intelligent as Donald nor as socially sophisticated. Indeed, Roy and Laurie were both educationally sub-normal and targets for juvenile aggression in the neighbourhood. Although a continuous and intensive programme of work was carried out for three years the workers were never able to link this pair up to the wider society.

The two boys concerned (both participants) attended a special school; both were 14 at the commencement of work; neither appeared to have other contacts with adolescents, yet they had little in common with each other. Roy and Laurie formed an inseparable partnership as a kind of defence against the outside world; the workers gained admission and helped them through a varied programme of activity and adventure (doing, rather than talking) to gain greater social competence. This is illustrated by extracts from the diaries and reports of voluntary workers.

November 1965 Tonight I was to meet two new boys, and when I arrived with the professional worker only one boy, Roy, was there. When asked if he had a friend he would like to share his evening with, he found it hard to think of anyone he could really call his friend. Eventually he decided on Laurie, and when we found him we drove into town in the van.

December 1965 As arranged I met Roy at the cinema and we collected Laurie. [Later] I showed them the new place [the rented house]. Before they began to play draughts they noticed that some of the paint-work had just been done. They asked who had done it. I told them ... and then asked if they liked painting and that perhaps they would like to do some to improve the place. They both liked the idea.

January 1966 The two boys were waiting. The boys enquired about the paint, whether it was there [at the house]. With some encouragement ... they made quite a good job of the door and window.

January 1966 They told me they had painted the staircase in two hours – they were bursting to tell me. When they had had enough of painting, the boys went exploring down the cellar.

January 1966 I suggested they might bring some friends along to help with the painting. They seemed enthusiastic . . . and wanted to know how many more they could bring.

February 1966 I told the boys that there might be some other people at the house tonight. The boys glanced in the back room and nearly left. I put myself between the two boys and the door . . . and managed to persuade them to get their brushes from the kitchen.

February 1966 They expected two more boys . . . but nobody appeared. The worker with the other group, seeing that we were packing up, suggested that if they wanted a game of hide and seek now was the time . . . and the two boys readily joined in the game.

This period, with work centering mainly on the rented house and in decorating work, laid the foundations of the work with these two boys. Gradually they became able to share the premises, to verbalize more freely, and to repose trust in the adult worker. This worker was able to introduce new workers on his departure, and the following record some months later indicates an extending range of ability and confidence, but no expansion of the group.

June 1966 Went on trip to country – climbed up Mam Tor – tried to stroke sheep. Both exuberant – talkative and excited.

Went to Derbyshire – definitely wanted to walk up 'biggest hill'; inquiring and much more constructive conversation than usual. Went swimming at local baths; boys appeared to have no contacts.

September 1966 Boys wanted to go to town – went to coffee bar. With their agreement, left them in town so they 'could find their own way home'.

November 1966 Visits to workers' home. Boys commented on baby clothes; stunned at our suggestion of a baby due – had not previously occurred to them!

Went shopping with workers, and home to lunch. Lots of rough and tumble in the evening. Met workers' young relatives.

February 1967 Going to try to come out by bus themselves on Sunday [a distance of some 15 miles. They didn't make it on this occasion but did so later in the year]. Surprisingly sympathetic; offered to and more or less efficiently did wash up. Brought a friend; watched TV film.

Went to town for coffee; talked about one of the boys' girl-friend, and girls generally. [On way home] . . . whistled at anything suitable.
April 1967 Spent day with workers; one boy brought records to play. One boy concerned to meet friend to go to cinema after tea.

Visit to art gallery while shopping to follow up one boy's interest in painting. Other boy learns basic moves of chess from worker.

A full-time worker was in touch with the adult helpers and with the boys throughout the whole period, and the above records should be seen in this light. The extent of contact varied, and was dependent on the flow of information from the adult voluntary worker, and an assessment by the team when certain crises were discovered.

Much happened that is not recorded above, and perhaps this is most effectively indicated by the following account of a meeting arranged with their first worker, who agreed to return to see them in October 1967, just two years after their first contact.

'Called at their homes. Laurie much smarter than two years ago; Roy still seemed to have the same indifference to appearance. Laurie asked if a friend could join us, and we went down to the city for coffee. I was looked upon as an "old friend"; this was more noticeable from Laurie than Roy who seemed to find difficulty in expressing his feelings — possibly this is due to his low intellect.

Laurie is making other friends; Roy stays at home unless out with Laurie. Friendly atmosphere, but I felt Laurie rather conscious of Roy's behaviour (for example, his loud comments to girls in mini-skirts).

Roy still displays a lack of maturity and seems to be at an impasse. Could easily be influenced by stronger, more forceful characters.'

The work continued through into 1968, with the rift between the two boys widening as one became more socially competent than the other. For one the relationship with the workers became a pleasant addition to many other relationships that he began to make for himself; for the other there seemed to be little movement towards the local community and thus the probability of no more than fringe membership of it, with the possibility of illegal behaviour stemming from his very limited ability to appreciate cause and effect.

Group-size, except on rare occasions, had not increased. However, in terms of providing adult models, opportunities to explore, opportunities to relate to friendly people and to verbalize their situations and their feelings, the workers achieved a great deal through the painstaking week-by-week involvement of these boys in group situations where they could relax and express themselves in ways that would give them strength as they moved into adolescence.

The varying adjustment of Laurie and Roy has been stressed. Laurie, because of his slightly greater intelligence and a warmer, more accepting home, seemed able to benefit from the relationships and work programmes, and achieved a very fair adjustment. Roy, because of his level of intelligence (having been adjudged at school to have an IQ of 61) coupled with a chaotic home-life centred around a drunken, inadequate father, changed only very slowly, and slipped back all too quickly during the brief breaks in the relationship with the workers. There was some progress but probably not enough to be permanent, and the possibility of his living other than inadequately on the fringe of working-class society is unlikely.

In all of the work with groups and individuals there was modification in the worker's perspective as well as in that of the young people, and in no group was this more apparent than in the first activity group examined below. This is one of the several football groups that work was done with, and is the largest group and the one with the longest life. Several participants were involved, two for the full duration of the group's existence, which covered three footballing seasons. The following abbreviated survey will inevitably omit much work carried out by a number of workers over the full period. The material selected covers the broad history of the group while devoting more attention to changes in relationships, especially those affecting one of the participants.

Progress was determined by the speed of the group's awareness of its needs and difficulties. The role of workers was to support the group and to encourage all forms of socially adaptive behaviour likely to lead to satisfying and mature group experiences. Problems of non-attendance, team selection, heavy defeats, discipline and poor sportsmanship, internal conflicts, financial costs, and so on had to be tackled by the group or members of the group, assisted by the workers. This was alien to the adolescents and, initially, baffling and painful. They would have preferred to let the adults take charge and then challenge or resist the decisions. This was particularly true for Jack, a skilful footballer and a sharply intelligent, verbally aggressive young man, who disguised his insecurity with an arrogant, self-opinionated manner which gained for him a reputation as a 'big-head'. When faced with making decisions rather than expressing opposition, he was less sure of himself. His initial leadership was due to his skill as a player and to the fact that the idea of the team originated from him. The three seasons of work helped him to progress from an edgy, emotional, verbally dominant group member to a player who could respond to the group's needs, lose himself in its action, and command a higher status within it.

How the group began. Workers made contact with 4 boys in the Bridge Café; this led to informal football on a school playground and enabled the group to ask for help in forming a team. A meeting in a church vestry, and the presentation by Jack of a list of potential players, led to entry in an amateur league. Team selection, shirts and equipment, and fees were discussed and decided upon. The initial phase was one of constant activity among the boys, discussing, recruiting, practising. The adults were supportive, but brought reality into the conversations, and were also active in ensuring that the facilities would be available for the group to function effectively.

Jack's imagination and energy were endorsed by the workers, and his arrogance and his hyper-critical views of other players were softened but not directly criticized at this stage. His determination to create a vehicle for himself to display alleged footballing talents helped him to temper his views of others enough to avoid their withdrawal from the team; workers were content to bolster those hurt by criticism while overlooking the major source of it.

The first season. A series of early defeats (with compensating goals for Jack) shattered the early illusions of greatness. Workers helped players talk about the origins of the team's difficulties, and plan to overcome them. When morale was at its lowest (because of heavy defeats in bad weather on a poor pitch) workers had to redouble efforts to avoid the break-up of the team. Team changes, scapegoating, withdrawals, failure to turn up to matches, displays of petulance, excuse-making, and much verbal aggression were evident in the first half of the season. After discussion a gymnasium was obtained for training one evening each week. The second half of the season brought a couple of victories, but more important the defeats were less decisive, and the team members felt they were improving. Even so, the team finished firmly at the bottom of the table.

Jack's skill allowed him to displace the blame for failure on to other team members, but his intelligence also enabled him to recognize the reasons for failure. These included lack of fitness, small physical size, unwillingness to tackle, lack of team play, etc., and, in association with the workers, he was able to help the team members to take action. He was not, of course, very good at seeing how his own individualistic approach to the game and obvious lack of confidence in others affected the team's performance.

It is appropriate here to illustrate how much at odds the project's methods were with more orthodox approaches. During one practice session a potential adult volunteer, a trained teacher, came to consider helping, and in discussion with the group worker said that the first thing he would do would be to 'get rid of that lad — he's no good to you'. The 'lad' concerned was, of course, the very boy for whom the group was formed. Many in the group did not like him, but he was too good a player to drop, and his assumption of the captaincy from the outset was not at the time challenged by boys who did not seek such responsibility. Workers, unlike the potential helper mentioned above, tolerated Jack, tried to understand him, admired his restless energy and through a growing relationship with him helped him to modify his view of other players and to begin to make positive and helpful, rather than supercilious and negative, comments.

The second season. The core group of the first season (8 players) was joined by new recruits, and they trained harder than ever. A short course with a professional footballer made a great difference to their fitness, their skill, and above all their self-confidence. A new set of shirts acted as a morale booster, and an early victory gave the team members the success they wanted. They asked for a place to meet to discuss tactics and team selection, and at these meetings such practical matters were soon overshadowed by social interaction and discussion about a wide variety of non-footballing affairs. Subscriptions were raised, and money-getting schemes started to repay the cost of the kit and a new football. Girls began to watch the matches, and to come to the meetings, where women adult workers involved them in decorating the meeting-room and catering for the players as they came from training for the weekly session of tea, discussion, records, and cards. The team finished in the top half of the table; fewer players had been involved in the matches and those who were showed all the signs of enjoying the training and the social sessions; players were increasingly recognized as friends rather than people who made up the team. As one boy confessed 'I don't come for the football — I come for the friendship'.

Jack's pride took a considerable blow, when, attempting to hold the team to ransom by withdrawing his services, they continued to play competently without him. Only the skill of the workers drew him back into the team without obvious loss of face. His involvement in team selection was shared with others, and late in the season his 'team position' was no longer fixed as (reluctantly at first) he used his skill in other positions. Although sometimes regressing to childish behaviour and criticism of others, he more frequently took a thoughtful, positive line in relation to the adult workers and fellow players. By the end of the season he was less in evidence on the pitch, demonstrating more effective team behaviour, and giving more support to others. The results spoke for themselves.

As with Donald's group in a previous case study, Jack and other individuals in the football group also had access to workers on a one-to-one basis. At a low level of service (e.g., uninterrupted personal conversation) every member of this very large group would have received something in addition to the group experience.

The final season. Steady and skilful play brought regular victories. Few new players joined the team. The old players continued more for what the team meant in terms of friendships with each other and with workers, than for the weekly game of football. Girl-friends were an important part of matches (as spectators) and of social sessions; in some cases girl-friends became fiancées, and in one case a fiancée became a wife. Removal from the area involved some difficulty in attending regularly, but confidence in the team and its arrangements was high and players often travelled long distances unaccompanied to play fixtures. Financially the team was self-supporting, and had paid off earlier debts; those able to attend practice sessions organized the group themselves, with workers merely observing. There was a more realistic approach to individual performances, and with greater social maturity a diminishing in the importance of the game itself as a means of self-expression. By the middle of the season it was evident to most of them that to continue the team for a further season was neither necessary nor practical, and here the workers' willingness to 'let go' was an important factor.

The year saw the absorption of Jack into the team as a playing member, involved in selection but not acting as captain. Contacts in the social sessions brought a regular girl-friend, and a greater security and self-confidence when in serious discussion. In the relationship with the adults whom he came to accept as friends he had learned a lot — but he had learned more from the help he received in understanding the group and the other players in the team which his initiative had created for quite a different reason.

The football group provided for Jack and others a period of group membership that led them into experiences far in excess of their expectations: relationships with each other in greater depth; relationships with adult workers and with a variety of other football teams; travel over a wide area of the city; and an increasing involvement in social gatherings with objectives remote from football. Their group experiences in the team enabled the lessons of football to be extended to other aspects of life. It provided a chance to do something for themselves, to solve problems, and to overcome frustration and difficulty. Initially, the unwillingness of adults to take charge of the group frightened them, but the preceding example indicates the extent to which they overcame fears and coped with self-government.

This view is perhaps too flattering; it omits a number of factors — the frustrations of the first year (and how narrowly the team escaped disintegration) and the internal arguments and irritations, which were never long absent; the many missed opportunities of creating greater member-involvement and therefore wider learning experience; the element of good fortune needed for any group enterprise to survive the interpersonal conflicts that spring up in any group of socially unskilled and egoistic adolescent boys.

The last case study to be presented is also an example of a group focused around a specific activity — playing guitars. However, when the project workers first met the four boys concerned three could not read or play a note of music.

The boy in whom the project was most interested, one of the 54 participants, was first encountered in the Bridge Café in late 1964. He reappeared as one of a quartet of boys who began visiting the worker's office in the neighbourhood. At this time Brian was in his first year at work, but was not yet 16, and living with his mother, step-father, and their children. He quickly voiced his dislike for his 'uncle', spent little time at home, and was usually in local cafés or messing around on the streets. A quiet, pale boy, rather stiff and doll-like in movement, he rarely laughed or smiled. Initially he minimized contact with the worker, but later he revealed a critical, cynical view of the world and of adults. It was soon known by the worker that Brian was stealing from his work place very regularly. During the early months the group not only helped clear out the cellar beneath the office and carried out some decorations there, but also went on to do garden and house-decorating jobs with the worker at the homes of elderly people, and took part in numerous social and drinking sessions. Most work sessions ended with a visit to the local public house, and slowly Brian began to open up and reveal a greater willingness to engage in conversation with the worker. It became possible to discuss his illegal behaviour and his difficult home situation.

Later in 1966 two girls joined the group. There were parties at the home of a voluntary worker and a visit to London for the weekend. At one of these parties, a volunteer worker who could play a guitar was present, and this resulted in two of the group (including Brian) voicing a desire to play. Informal practice sessions began, using borrowed guitars. Despite the boys' lack of knowledge, both responded to the encouragement of their 'teacher' and after twelve months became quite competent. One of the non-players became the vocalist and later he also learned to play, helped by the group. The girls continued to attend and support the group, and Brian got his brother-in-law (himself a teenager) to come into the group. As he was already a competent player this enriched the group experience. Brian was the next most competent performer, and spent much time practising, selecting music, writing out words and scores, and planning programmes. Brian was enthusiastic about his skill as a player, but still very critical of others and demanding a good deal of tolerance and understanding from the workers during group practice sessions and discussions. The London weekend was repeated, even more successfully, and, late in 1967, they did a number of concerts for the elderly, and appeared twice at a club for mentally handicapped adults. More important, they played informally in public houses and took part in the pub concerts that were part of the life of the area. By now Brian's stealing from work had almost ceased, and he was finding the home situation less of a strain. There were still signs of tension in his face, and difficulties associated with courtship were brought to the worker for private discussion, but now he often laughed and a marked increase in confidence was noted. Whereas at one time he had been unwilling to play in isolation, even at rehearsals, Brian could now take a solo spot in public.

A new worker who possessed little musical knowledge was introduced to the group, and this encouraged them to take more initiative in planning the group's musical affairs, calling upon their old 'instructor' to join them at public events. The group devoted one New Year's Eve to entertaining an old people's club, and then the whole group (enlarged now by regular girl-friends) went to the local pub and played informally until midnight, to the applause and encouragement of the patrons. Brian was clearly enjoying himself considerably. Although the group continued to play and meet socially in 1968, when the professional worker (whom they had known throughout the four years) and the current voluntary worker both planned to leave the area there was only the disappointment of losing friends rather than losing vital support. Brian was by now engaged to be married; he was one of the few boys who appeared to like work; the pilfering had stopped. The cynicism and hard-faced approach to people was less in evidence, and he presented a much more open and relaxed manner in the company of other people, and even showed considerable concern for the less privileged and the elderly. In the friendship group he became more tolerant, and willing to help those less competent than himself. But perhaps the major gain was his ability to play the guitar, for this gave him confidence and a feeling of achievement he had not experienced before. He had earlier expressed a doubt as to his ability and indeed his whole approach was one of criticism of others coupled with personal inaction. But given the support and encouragement of the workers (and progress was painfully slow) he surprised himself. He also surprised his parents, and it may well be that his interest in this one thing gave his parents more room to treat him in less critical ways, and ultimately to be proud of his achievement. Brian revealed himself as a good conversationalist with a lively mind, and he is now well on the way to making an excellent 'dynamic adjustment' to adult life. This adjustment will not be merely a narrow conformity to traditional patterns of behaviour in the locality, but will lead to involvement in the changing community, of which he has now the resources to be a helping member.

The groups described are only four examples. They do, however, illustrate some of the main features of group work in the Wincroft Project: the need to offer boys like Donald the chance to break out of groups that defined them as deviant people; the need to offer boys like

Jack the fairly normal experience of taking part in a team activity; the need of timid boys like Roy and Laurie to be offered wider horizons; and the need of boys like Brian to cultivate a natural ability that will gain him status and prestige in his family and neighbourhood.

(iv) TERMINATION

One fact dominated the workers' thinking during the planning and implementation of what came to be called 'run-down procedures', and this was the ending of the project grant in August 1968 and thus the end of the project. Section (iv) attempts to trace the way they acquitted themselves professionally in the last nine months of the work. The aim was to draw the work to a close with minimum interference to the social development of participants, and the further 120 adolescents associated with the participants at this point in time.

The team began its discussions in October 1967, and based its plans on a paper which outlined possible action, and was intended to 'assist in making the overall problem clearer, and spotlight the areas of particular difficulty.' It did this by categorizing the participants according to the way in which their needs were being met currently, as an indication of the degree of difficulty that might be experienced in withdrawal. The emphasis of this approach was on a reassessment of the situation and, although it was recognized that individual run-down plans would have to be made for each young person (rather than each category of persons), it seemed helpful to make certain general statements about possible action regarding all clients in a certain category. That action was to be directed towards facilitating movement away from Category 1, and towards Category 5.

Category 1   5 boys in this category. The most difficult clients, receiving long-term support from the professional workers.

Category 2   17 boys in this category. Receiving short-term support from a professional worker, assisted by a voluntary worker or leading to the introduction of a volunteer.

Category 3   11 boys in this category. Receiving long-term support from a voluntary worker, with assistance from professionals where necessary.

Category 4   8 boys receiving long-term support from voluntary workers exclusively.

Category 5   1 boy where support was no longer adjudged necessary.

Category 6   5 boys where contact by professionals was only occasionally possible, and 7 boys where workers had lost contact completely.

In order to help the forward planning, work over the last nine months was presented schematically as shown in table opposite.

It was thought to be 'vital that each worker prepare a personal run-down programme defining the change in his/her relationship with each young person on the workers' list'. In attempting to spell out the exact method of withdrawal in each case, it helped to relate it to the 'ideal' process set out in the form, but it was important to remember that, in the volatile situation in which the workers were involved, 'movement' could be in either direction.

It is useful to look in more detail at the problems associated with each category of client. Category 1 contained the most intractable problem clients and little immediate movement seemed likely. The team agreed that 'even the linking, on a long-term basis, with voluntary workers is unrealistic ... The nature of the maladjustment, the frequency of crises, the cost in money, materials, and emotional energy, make it unwise to burden voluntary workers in this way'.

For clients in this category an intensification of work was agreed, with the professional team spending yet more time with them. It was further decided that 'if they do not make rapid progress ... [they] ... must be provided with another professional crutch in the spring of next year'. It was recognized that some of the boys might require ongoing support beyond the duration of the project, and the nature and extent of this support will be discussed later in the chapter.

Some of the boys in category 2 might also prove intractable it was thought, and several were already in a no-man's-land between category 1 and 2. The too rapid withdrawal of services, non-availability at a time of minor crises, and the unexpected crisis which only the presence of the worker could help the youngster to cope with, all might lead to deterioration in relationships. In the work with adolescents in this category workers were constantly in danger of precipitate action, for the youngsters might reject the planned transfer to exclusive contact with volunteers, and, in any case, it was decided that 'each volunteer so engaged ... [must have] ... easy and effective access to a professional youth worker or social worker to advise ... as necessary'.

The boys in category 3 did not create the same concern, as it was

Project withdrawal scheme

Category	No.	67 Nov	Dec	68 Jan	Feb	March	April	May	June	July	Aug	Sept
1	5	Full working contact			Joint YDT/other agency				Other agency only			Other agency only
2	17	Usual contact, and hand over to voluntary worker					Sole responsibility transferred to volunteer and/or other agency					Volunteer backed by agency
3	11	Full-time support of volunteer		Sole responsibility transferred to volunteer								Volunteer
4	8	Sole responsibilities on voluntary worker										Volunteer
5	1	Watching brief only				No further action						
6	12	Exploit opportunities only		Refer to other agencies								

reckoned that 'there seems every chance that some will become independent of any worker during the remaining months of the project'. Here the difficulty of termination lay not so much with the client and his needs, but in relation to the voluntary worker and his skill in making a personal withdrawal. The team tried to help volunteers to do this. 'One practical step of value may be the preparation of withdrawal procedure notes, so that voluntary workers can feel free to put these procedures into effect at will.'

This material was prepared subsequently and it helped workers to see how they could introduce withdrawal into discussions with the groups. They tried to explain what was to happen and using a variety of methods (reducing frequency of visits and duration of visits, limiting involvement, and so on) eased the transition from a role of regular commitment to the group to one of only occasional contact and advice. Policy for termination was further discussed at the residential training weekend in December 1967, and in role-play situations workers were. encouraged to practise verbal explanations to 'their group', and then to discuss their feelings about consciously setting out to terminate contact.

As with some category 3 boys, the contact with boys from category 4 would also be subject to a natural break as a result of 'marriage, courtship and the continued demolition of the Project Area'. It was adjudged that, with care, work with category 4 clients would have reached a point 'where complete withdrawal of all worker support will be unlikely to have a negative effect on the young person's social development'. These boys, already receiving long-term support from volunteers, would either lose their workers by natural turnover of staff who would not be replaced, or else workers would use the withdrawal procedure described above.

Category 6 consisted of 12 boys. Workers were no longer in contact with 7 of these boys. One was living abroad, one was in an approved school, and of the remaining five, one was thought to be no longer in need of help, as he had left the area and broken all contact with the group with whom he had been on the fringes of trouble with the law. One other was known to have left the area, and the remaining three were no longer involved in the café and street networks and had completely 'gone to ground'.

Professional workers had a little contact with the other 5 boys in category 6 but an increase in contact and reawakening of relationships at this late stage of the project would present the same difficulties as

Changing Relationships · 147

contact with those who had been 'lost' would have done, and so it was decided that during the final phase of the work the team would 'maintain superficial contact only' as workers would face 'considerable difficulties if one of these boys . . . presents major relationship and other problems' at such a late stage in the proceedings.

The ideal framework required a programme where worker-client contact had ceased entirely by the end of July 1968, and where the period March to May 1968 involved a 50 per cent reduction in contact, by full-time and voluntary workers. In this way, it was hoped, plans could be devised to taper off most demands and effect referrals where this was found to be essential to the needs of the individual adolescent.

In retrospect the whole operation appeared less difficult than workers had expected. Whether this was related to the achievement of satisfactory adjustment by the clients or was affected by the workers' skill in communicating the process to the volunteers is open to question. Certainly there were fewer problems connected with interpreting run-down to the volunteers than had been anticipated.

By early 1968 most relationships between voluntary workers and clients were relatively trouble free, and, indeed, in some cases workers were already questioning the need to continue contact. In other situations workers held relationships at a fairly superficial level – partly through lack of skill and partly through lack of motivation to go deeper. With these clients there was little chance of relationships escalating. Where clients were still exhibiting consistently anti-social behaviour volunteers saw their own inability to continue unaided and were keen to discuss alternative arrangements.

How well were these plans received by the young people? Here there were problems, but mostly among category 1 and 2 clients. These more difficult clients reacted more forcefully to hints of withdrawal, and their reactions will require closer examination in a later section. Workers noted:

'Paul said he "hoped I would get the job" – yet also said "deep down I hope you don't". Said he was quite depressed; seemed worried at my leaving. I told him of a possible resource person and mentioned all the positive achievements that Paul has made in the last 18 months or so. This seemed to cheer him up. I reassured Paul that all was not lost when I left.'

'. . . told them about going away. Robert seemed annoyed briefly and then he and Freddie devised plans to come too.'

'Peter wanted confirmation that the worker was going; would I [another worker] still be around etc. Said quietly, "So he won't be coming to see me Monday evenings any more" — in a reflective, sad way.'

Clients in other categories, more socially competent and active, no longer found the workers important to their social and emotional growth. For a number, the worker had served his purpose and he recognized this: 'I will attempt to effect a gradual withdrawal ending at the beginning of June. I do not think this is a serious problem, as I do not feel they are greatly at risk and they are quite sophisticated'.

For most clients the problems of termination were slight and there were two major reasons for this. When the project began in 1964 it was known that replanning of the area was scheduled to take place within five to seven years. The beginnings of compulsory purchase and rehousing began during the final months of the project, and this served to remove a number of clients to new housing estates. Although it was policy to continue contact with participants after rehousing, it was seen to be impossible for workers to remain in as close contact as in the brief transition period during which they helped participants to settle down.

But a more important factor in participants' loss of interest in the workers was their increasing interest in the other sex. Several participants acquired regular girl-friends, two got married. This change of social situation, although it did not by any means end contact with the workers, made the presence of adults less desirable and less necessary, and so the frequency of contact was reduced. These young people welcomed the workers, but rarely sought them out, and (with certain exceptions) this was true of all the participants who moved into marriage or stable courtship relationships. The workers were happy to withdraw into the background. Other young people, not yet dating girls regularly, were increasingly involved in the young adult world in their neighbourhood, and were finding an acceptable place in the local community — sometimes this was no more than becoming a known regular customer of a public house, but workers were content to move into the background when the young people were seen to be involved in a society of adults of their own choice, for example: 'Francis seems to be settled into the labour club and is now also moving into the working-men's club, thus increasing his contacts.'

In addition, the role of the worker had become much clearer to some of the participants over the years, and in identifying a helping role some were able to verbalize their move to a position where such help was no longer necessary. 'I don't think I need you any more' commented one boy, hastening to add that it would be good to continue contact on a friendship basis. The reaction of Leslie to the withdrawal of workers, set out on p. 114, is another indication of the participants relating worker-contact to needs.

From Christmas 1967 the workers were beginning to introduce a note of departure into their conversation with groups and with individuals, and throughout 1968 these comments became more explicit as the young people became involved in facing the reality of change. The withdrawal from the premises rented by the Trust in the late summer of 1967 had already caused certain groups to find other meeting places and also prepared them for the loss of the worker.

The nature of adolescence and the other factors mentioned above made for changes in groupings and changes of interest, but even where groups remained stable in membership or in activity the group members did not appear to be unduly worried at the impending departure of someone who had helped the group to achieve its recreational goals. It must again be emphasized that the place of the worker in these later stages was never so important that the survival of the group depended upon his continued presence. By this time, workers were no longer in the position of sustaining the life of groups, but merely of supporting and encouraging them.

All workers reduced both frequency and duration of visits to 'their' clients, and this is shown in the analysis of contact later in this chapter (pp. 151–61). Generally the once weekly contact was maintained until the spring of 1968, but visits were of shorter duration. This was usually accomplished by arrangement with the group, the worker absenting himself for a part of the evening by arriving late or leaving early. Groups were encouraged to continue functioning normally, as the group worker became an onlooker. Later in the termination procedure, workers made excuses to miss a weekly meeting, and where arrangements for regular meetings were broken the participant was encouraged to use the telephone to make *ad hoc* arrangements. In some instances the interest of the worker became more pastoral, visiting to observe groups in informal setting, or calling for brief social exchanges at the homes of the participants. This gave opportunities to help adults to understand the change of circumstances that would take the worker away from the neighbourhood later in the year. In some cases, the withdrawal of a volunteer for personal reasons linked with removal of the project from the region brought a situation where the individuals concerned did not expect a replacement. The young people had by now begun to come to terms with the fact that many of the workers followed a way of life that took them to different parts of the country. The professional workers also talked about changes in their own work, and of the probability of leaving the region also, and this was used as a reason for slackening the contact between the workers and the bulk of the participants, for example: 'I managed to talk about my new job and the difficulties lying ahead to future meetings. Seemed to accept this, but insisted that I visit the new house (when they move) . . .'

When considering requests from participants the workers, by the judicious use of various limitations such as lack of time ('I can only manage a Friday, later on in the evening'), difficulty of access to equipment ('I can't get the minibus so often now'), and the need to travel outside the area ('I've got to go away for a couple of days next week') aimed to help the young people to face the reality of the situation and to make plans for themselves which did not require additional servicing by the workers. Another more positive approach was the strong endorsement of group decisions to use commercial or club facilities.

'These two evenings at the club have been quite successful considering what an ordeal it must be for any child to go into new surroundings like this. They all appear quite relaxed with the exception of Stephen who I worry about. They like Mr Marshall and he understands the position and will encourage them to go when we are not there.'

In encouraging them to use existing recreational and educational facilities the workers were reassuring them of their ability to cope with new social situations.

Many of these actions would have been taken by the workers regardless of the need to terminate work. Had the project not been of limited duration, work with some would have been ended in favour of taking up new clients, and especially those of a younger age-group, some of whom were brothers of the participants and some whose behaviour indicated their need of some service. The social-work team was satisfied with the progress made by a number of clients, but the need to terminate the project forced workers to open up gaps between them and the young people in order to see how well the groups and individuals would survive. Most survived extremely well without the workers, and, although this provoked a certain ambivalence of attitude in the workers, the overall reaction of the team was one of pleasure.

By the end of February 1968 the numbers of boys in the different categories read as follows:

	February 1968	*October 1967*
Category 1	5	5
Category 2	9	17
Category 3	6	11
Category 4	11	8
Category 5	12	1
Category 6	11	12

Compared with the position in October 1967 (p. 143) all of the same boys remained stubbornly in category 1. Later, one did make a good adjustment and another was committed to borstal training. The three remaining were joined by one boy who previously had been placed in category 2.

These few clients presented the team with a major dilemma. As social educators the team recognized, with some justification, that these young people would not survive the withdrawal of workers. It was also felt that it would be ethically incorrect to terminate by complete withdrawal, in some cases after more than two years' consistent work with the client. And yet the reality of the grant situation forced workers to balance professional obligations to the client against professional obligations to the employer. Workers had also to consider the implications for long-term research if special supportive measures were provided for the boys who were high delinquency risks. Somehow the team had to devise a means of effecting a withdrawal that would satisfy the agency without damaging the client.

The hard core of clients in category 1, which presented this dilemma, was not large but it occupied a large amount of staff time in the last months as the team wrestled with the problem of disentangling workers from relationships, while giving the clients opportunities to obtain support elsewhere. Thus in two distinct but related ways the use of a fixed-period project with built-in research challenges social-work practice. It not only requires work to be maintained for longer than is perhaps necessary (in terms of delinquency prevention) with some clients, it also inevitably requires the cessation of treatment with clients with some whom it is still a professional obligation, whether in terms of mere prevention of delinquency or the broader concept of aiding dynamic social adjustment. The former is a comparatively minor difficulty, but resolution of the latter issue required much thought and effort.

In certain of the hard-core cases a social worker was already involved and was likely to be so until the end of the project. Here it seemed appropriate to extend discussions to the social workers (child care and probation officers) concerned, and so ensure that they were fully aware of the withdrawal of Trust workers. Then the workers attempted to increase the client's understanding of the usefulness of the appointed social worker. In view of these officers' statutory obligations it seemed unwise to try to recruit a new social worker to become interested in the clients, instead efforts were made to strengthen the existing relationship. It was hoped that the clients would use the officers in much the same way as the Trust workers, and, at the very least, would call on the officer for assistance in crisis situations rather than act impetuously or retreat into apathy.

Such misgivings as the workers had about this procedure stemmed from the rigid views of the clients as to the functions and trustworthiness of social workers, and probation officers in particular. It was also known that the boys were not good probation risks. None of the boys in question showed much evidence of a positive relationship with their officers, and the workers were therefore not particularly optimistic about the effectiveness of this interesting possibility.

However, encouragement towards closer contact with probation officers was accompanied by an intensification of casework over the final few months of the project, in an attempt to get the young people in a position of some stability and personal social control. These efforts were directed not only towards helping them to understand the special difficulties of statutory social workers rather more objectively, but also towards helping them to measure their own progress and be pleased with it, and thereafter to use all the social resources available to build upon it, or reinforce it when progress was threatened. The figures in section (v) of this Chapter show how, in the termination period, casework exceeded group work. This was partly due to the fact that group work services were withdrawn more rapidly than casework service, but also because casework with certain clients was intensified. This intensification also took place in two cases where no other social worker was involved, and where it was thought necessary to try to introduce, from another voluntary agency, a worker who could offer specific kinds of help in future personal crises or in situations that required ongoing family casework. In the two cases where this approach was tried satisfactory transfers were made to Family Service Unit workers. Work with these two families continued long after Trust workers withdrew. In one of these cases it was also possible for a volunteer worker to continue to relate to the family, and provide additional support to certain members, apart from the more specialized family service unit provisions.

The team also discussed the possibility of introducing these hard-core clients to a 'resource person' should any client feel the need for advice or assistance at some future point. In fact, workers made contact with half-a-dozen professional social workers and asked if they would be prepared to act in this capacity. Three accepted. In one case this was made known to a participant who met one of the adults concerned and then arrangements were made for him to reach this person should he feel in need of support of any kind. The introduction and involvement of two other adult workers was, of course, a complex business requiring a great deal of careful discussion, and the preparation of both client and 'resource' adult. It was also necessary to arrange a meeting between them which was not so formal as to stultify the exchange, nor so casual as to imply a continuation of service at the point of need and in the client's chosen setting. In all cases it was necessary for the client to telephone for an informal appointment, and to travel to meet the workers. To get clients to accept this kind of compromise, involving an initial contact with an unknown individual on alien territory, in itself suggests an improvement in social functioning, even though supported by a worker.

Although not more than half-a-dozen young people were involved in these procedures, it took a considerable amount of time to facilitate a workable contact. It was difficult to find agencies in the field who could help, and in fact only the Family Service Unit was able to cooperate; it was difficult to find people willing to act as 'resource persons' for youngsters in difficulty. In all, three adults were introduced to these clients for this purpose. In spite of the difficulties in formulating termination procedure for the few hard-core clients, the social workers felt easier in their minds after considerable effort had been expended in helping these young people to be aware of what they could do in a crisis. Whether these particular young people should have been selected for the programme at the outset is a matter that will be examined in Chapter 6, as work with this hard core has implications for future work in this field.

The small number of such problem cases was due to both planned and fortuitous factors. The early selection of the clients gave workers a clear run of two and a half years, during which time many clients worked through their personal relationship problems and achieved an identity that was acceptable to both the individual and society. Thus the need to terminate contact in these cases, i.e. the majority, was a professional rather than a financial necessity and there were few difficulties associated with the run-down. Although many worries were expressed in staff sessions, in practice termination was a relatively smooth business.

Even the difficulties associated with termination of contact among the hard-core clients were eased in different ways by unforeseen circumstances which affected planning. One of the most difficult boys appeared in court and was sent for borstal training a few months before the end of the project; another got married and, in the changed social situation, led workers to a revised judgement about the difficulty of termination in this particular instance. In some cases then the process became easier, but the relapse of one or two boys who had appeared to be making good progress in the termination period increased the workers' difficulties. The overall impression then is of a total pro-gramme of work smoothly terminated, however, more attention has been paid here to the problems of termination, since they present the more interesting social-work difficulties, and have far-reaching implications.

Before leaving this description of the social-work process, it is worth considering whether the termination phase itself indicates the useful-ness of the programme. As we have seen, for the majority of the participants and the groups of which they were members the with-drawal of workers excited relatively little reaction. Ease of withdrawal may, of course, be thought to indicate that workers had made so little impact that their absence was hardly noticed. The number of client-contacts achieved by workers (see section (v) below) may suggest that this was true for some participants, and the method of operation, which precluded workers from taking a dominant or intrusive role, may also have prevented a very dynamic engagement with certain other clients. While a criticism of superficiality is perhaps valid in certain instances, independent reports from the boys indicate that in general the position was quite otherwise.

It could also be argued that the young people were so apathetic that they were acquiescent to the withdrawal. Workers were certainly worried about two boys whose response to the termination was so accepting and uncritical that they were concerned that behind this front the relationship might in fact be of much greater importance to them. But in almost every case it proved possible to discuss the forthcoming withdrawal. Wherever possible the workers extricated themselves from group situations slowly and deliberately, and even invited the hostility of certain boys. 'I left Andy to 'phone me (his suggestion) on Wednesday week to see if I'm around. No regression on learning of my increasing uncertainty of continuing on Wednesdays.' In these cases it was thought that boys who were emotionally dependent upon the worker must have opportunities to express their feelings, so that they could be discussed in the light of the real situation for both boy and worker. With the majority the worker's departure was discussed by clients sensibly and in a mature way. It was not given undue importance, but accepted as an inevitable accompaniment to life. This may be a sign of their greater social maturity.

The relative ease of termination of most relationships may also open up the question of the need for the project. Perhaps the boys had not needed help? The whole book is, the authors believe, an answer to that criticism. The case material and discussion in earlier chapters, drawing as it does on work with many of the participants and their friends, may serve as evidence enabling the reader to make his own judgement of the needs of these adolescents in 1964, 1965, and 1966. It may be reasonable to conclude that the natural slackening of contact in 1968 represented a real development in social competence and self-assurance on the part of the 54 boys. The ease with which the majority were able to readjust to a situation of change was a small indication of the dynamic adjustment which was the main objective of the project.

Since the end of the project there has been little or no contact between clients and workers; the only evidence of the existence of the project is in the changed attitudes and behaviour of those who took part. The extent to which such changes are permanent is open to argument; some evidence on this point will be provided in Chapter 6, and the long-term effects of the programme will be open to further inquiry at a later date.

(v)   A STATISTICAL SUMMARY OF THE WORK

From September 1964 to July 1968 some 6,000 fieldwork reports were submitted by workers. Great emphasis was placed on report writing throughout the project and it is estimated that less than 3 per cent of sessions failed to be reported, most of these in the period February to August 1964. Thus it is possible to answer very accurately, in statistical terms, such questions as who did the work, who received it, what type of work it was, and how it changed over time.

The topic of fieldwork recording will be dealt with later, but before embarking on an analysis of the data abstracted from the reports for research purposes it will, perhaps, be useful to describe briefly how they were processed, firstly, as they were received and, secondly, for this analysis. Between thirty and fifty reports were received each week from all the workers. In some instances there might be two or more reports from different workers for the same piece of fieldwork, hence there were considerably more reports than fieldwork sessions, about 20 per cent more. Each meeting between a worker and a participant was coded and dated along with the length of the meeting, the initials of the worker or workers, and the number of participants and non-participants present. Factual information on clients, relevant to the social-work process or the research, was abstracted and placed in the client's casefile.

Report forms were divided into certain sections and basic items of information about the session were requested on it. The standard of reporting was not uniform and varied not only between workers, but also from time to time from the same worker. Some reports, not only those from voluntary workers, contained little more than the names of clients present. This is understandable under the pressure of work that often existed, but it did make analysis of the reports difficult. If information central to the analysis, such as the length of the session, was omitted from the report, the research worker would request it from the worker concerned. In some early cases, because ongoing processing of the time element of the fieldwork was not instituted until 1967, estimates of the length of some sessions had to be made. In certain instances this was made easier by the fact that a second worker may have reported on the session or that similar sessions with the particular client had taken place in the past and showed a degree of uniformity of length. Where this was not the case and no other method of determining the length of session was available, a figure of three hours for a group work session was allotted. In only a very small number of cases was it necessary to make an unaided estimate, since information contained within the body of the report often gave clues. Where time spent was omitted from casework and street (casual) work reports a figure of ninety minutes in the former, and fifteen in the latter, was allocated. Obviously this will have led to some discrepancies, but there will be some cancelling out of errors. However, as the number of reports where there was no knowledge on which to base the estimate was less than 100, overall errors are not likely to be large.

Throughout the project the research was faced with methodological problems, and one of the most difficult of these was the quantitative measurement of the fieldwork. Building from the experience of youth clubs, the 'session' might be thought to be the appropriate unit of analysis. But what is a 'session'? This term is far too vague for use as a measuring device [5] and will only be used here in its colloquial sense of a piece of work, of indeterminate length, which has a definite beginning and end. Thus an evening's fieldwork by any particular worker might include a number of separate sessions as he transfers from group to group or individual to individual. Conversely, the evening, or day, might be taken up with one session, the worker remaining with the same group or individual for the whole of the time.

The fieldwork, from the client's perspective, is composed of two quantitative elements: the frequency of contact with a worker; and the amount, in terms of hours, of contact over a given period of time. An example of the first would be that client X was contacted by a worker on 150 occasions during 1966, and as an example of the second measure, was contacted for a total of 300 hours. For the first measure the term 'contacts' will be used and for the second, 'client hours'. It will be necessary to define these further when we come to look at each separately.

There are, of course, two categories of clients termed participants and non-participants, and the amount of work done with each, whether by a professional or by a voluntary worker, will be examined.

(a) Quantity and frequency of contact with the 54 participants

Over the whole four and a half years of the project, workers had some contact with over 600 young people, but it is only possible to analyse the quantity and quality of contact for the 54 participants since this was the only systematic data collected.

The term 'contact' is defined, minimally, as 'an acknowledgement (to the worker) from the boy concerned'. The rationale for this is that the worker was, and was seen to be, available to provide a service to the client. A session might involve a number of 'contacts' depending upon the number of clients present. The analysis that follows is fairly unsophisticated, since it assumes that all contacts are equal in length. This assumption will be corrected in the next section dealing with amount of work in terms of time.

Contact with adolescents in Wincroft started in February 1964, but it was not until September of that year that an efficient recording system was introduced.

Table 2 gives the number of contacts with the 54 participants over the whole period, broken down into three-month intervals.

The large fluctuation in contact in 1965 is to be accounted for by the irregular opening of the Bridge Café (April to June 1965) and the absence of students (July to September), but even so, the level of contact in the January to March 1965 period was not exceeded until the October to December 1966 period. However, the contacts in the Bridge Café (i.e. most of these prior to December 1965) were of a very different nature from those that followed. Most of these early contacts were of a superficial nature, with little precise planning or implementation of a treatment programme. In this early phase of the work, especially up until the middle of 1965, participants were to be numbered with the customers of the Bridge Café rather than identified as a selected treatment group.

During the evaluation period, 1 January 1966 to 31 July 1968, there was a total of 4,837 contacts, an average of 90 per participant, or about once every ten days. A closer look at the fluctuations over the period reveals a peak in January to March 1968 that is to be explained, at least partly, by the policy adopted in the termination phase, of having shorter contacts, thus allowing workers to increase the actual number of participants serviced and distributing their work more evenly over the whole group. The troughs are to be explained by workers' holidays in the April to September periods and also the absence of students and voluntary workers.

In formulating the objectives of the project, and more especially in determining the size of the participant group, the definition given of 'intensive work' was an average of one contact per week with each participant. It was expected, however, that this figure would be modified at any given point in time by such factors as the perceived need of the client and the general level of work with other clients, but that this average frequency would be achieved over the whole period of

Table 2 Number of contacts with participants February 1964 to June
1968

		Actual no. of contacts	Adjusted minimum no. of contacts required to see each participant once per week (see text)	Actual no. of contacts expressed as a percentage of target figure
	1964			
	Sept	28		
	Oct–Dec	381		
	1965			
	Jan–March	424	(In this period the participants	
	April–June	62	had not yet been selected.)	
	July–Sept	172		
	Oct–Dec	332		
	1966			
	Jan–March	247	650	38
	April–June	340	654	52
	July–Sept	340	663	51
	Oct–Dec	584	663	88
	1967			
	Jan–March	655	646	101
	April–June	503	650	77
	July–Sept	523	685	76
	Oct–Dec	525	689	76
	1968			
	Jan–March	680	685	99
	April–June	360	676	53
	July+Aug	101	452	22
	Total	6257	Average	70

Evaluation Period (bracket spanning 1966 Jan–March through 1968 July+Aug)

the project. In theoretical terms there would, therefore, need to be a
minimum of 702 contacts (i.e. 13 x 54 participants) in any three-month
period if this target was to be attained. However, as one participant

emigrated at the end of 1966, and throughout the period there was usually one or more delinquent participants receiving residential training, the average quarterly minimum number of contacts to be achieved was 667 rather than 702. The number of boys not available for contact over the period varied between one and five per month, the average was 2.7 per quarter. The adjusted minimum number of required contacts is given in *Table 2* and it can be seen that the target was exceeded in the January to March period 1967 and came within 1 per cent of it (5 contacts) during the same period the following year. Between October 1966 and March 1968 the actual number of contacts never fell below 75 per cent of the target figure and the average for the total evaluation period was 70 per cent.

Averages are in many ways misleading since contacts were by no means distributed evenly and some participants received many more than others. The number of recorded contacts per individual participant varied from 0 to 298 during the evaluation period, thus the participant most frequently contacted was seen, on average, once every three days. Since it was only in this period that a conscious and planned effort was made to work specifically with participants, these are the figures given in *Table 3*.

Eleven of the participants were contacted on average during the period once per week or more, 33 at least once per fortnight, and 40 once per month or more. Of the 14 contacted less than once per month, 1 spent almost two-thirds of the period in approved school and one emigrated. Contact was lost with another boy when a worker resigned and then at about the same time the boy moved away from the area. Despite persistent efforts one adolescent refused all attempts at contact. Two boys were judged by workers not to be in great need, and, because of the pressure of other work, only a loose, watching brief was kept. Of the remaining 8 participants, 2 were known to have moved away from the area. A further 3 of the 8 were seen on average 22 times during the evaluation period. The contact with practically all of these 8 boys was of a casual nature, especially during the evaluation period, and none were drawn into any extensive group programme.

Considerable time and effort was put into trying to find all the participants and periodic discussions took place on how this could be effected. However, this task had to be set against the demands of work with those participants with whom the team were already in regular contact. It is believed that a common factor behind the failure to

Table 3 Frequency of contact with individual participants January
1966 to July 1968

		No. of participants
134 or more	(i.e. more than once per week)	11
67—133	(i.e. more than once per fortnight, but less than once per week)	22
32—66	(i.e. more than once per month to once per fortnight)	7
15—31	(i.e. once per 2 months to once per month	3
14 or less	(i.e. less than once per 2 months)	11
		54

sustain contact with many of these 14 boys is that they moved away
from their former network.

It can be seen from *Table 4* that the maximum number of participants
contacted weekly in any one 3-month period was 23 (October to
December 1966) or a little over 40 per cent of the total. If the
frequency of contact is altered to once per fortnight or more frequently
then the maximum figure is 29 (October-December 1966 and January-
March 1968) or a little over 50 per cent. The 11 participants who
received a weekly or more frequent contact over the whole period had
an average of 203 contacts and four of these an average of 240
contacts. In many cases this frequency of contact was geared to the
need and demand by the client, but since resources of time and workers
were not infinitely elastic this meant that those who received more than
134 contacts (i.e. once per week or more) benefited at the expense of
those who received less.

It is difficult to find comparative figures, since other projects have
not published such information, but figures from a study of the
Probation Service give the following average number of face-to-face
contacts with the probationer over a one-, two-, and three-year order.

Table 4 Levels of contact October 1964 to August 1968

	No contact	1–3 (1 per month or less)	4–7 (1 per month to 1 per fortnight)	8–12 (1 per fortnight to 1 per week)	13 or more (1 per week or more)	Total
PRE-EVALUATION						
1964 Oct–Dec	34	5	1	2	12	54
1965 Jan–March	29	7	3	1	14	54
April–June	30	18	6	0	0	54
July–Sept	22	18	6	5	3	54
Oct–Dec	15	14	6	6	13	54
EVALUATION						
1966 Jan–Mar	20	11	11	6	6	54
April–June	11	13	12	11	7	54
July–Sept	11	12	13	10	8	54
Oct–Dec	14	8	3	6	23	54
1967 Jan–March	11	7	7	8	20	53*
April–June	12	9	7	8	17	53
July–Sept	11	7	9	10	16	53
Oct–Dec	14	7	10	2	20	53
1968 Jan–March	10	9	5	8	21	53
April–June	15	14	8	4	12	53
†July–Aug	29	14	3	5	2	53

* One participant emigrated
† Adjusted for two months

These figures in *Table 5* have been obtained by Dr Steven Folkard and his colleagues in the Home Office Research Unit for their National Study of Probation. [6]

Table 5   Frequency of interviews by probation officers

	Interviews	
1 year order	18.3	(i.e. about once every 3 weeks)
2 year orders	25.3	(i.e. about once every 4 weeks)
3 year orders	31.7	(i.e. about once every 5 weeks)

(*Source:* National Study of Probation)

The average number of contacts per participant for the 31-month evaluation period was once every 10 days.

The figures for frequency of contact tell us something about the workers' contact with participants, but because a contact could vary between a greeting on the street and a ten-hours excursion, it is necessary to correct these differences by looking at the amount of fieldwork with each participant. This can be obtained by simply summing the length of time of each contact for each participant. The results of this are given in *Table 6* (see p. 164).

(b) Support work

Figures so far refer to direct face-to-face contact with participants, but work in their interests was by no means limited to this. A great deal of work was necessary on their behalf especially with employers, probation officers, and other social-work agencies, and also with their families. All this is treated under the general classification of support work done in the absence, but with the knowledge, of the participants.

In section (ii) (p. 115) of this chapter the use made of other social-work agencies has been examined. During the course of the project as a whole, i.e. from February 1964 to August 1968, social workers from over twenty-five different agencies were contacted.

Support work was also necessary in other areas of individual personal relationships. Some was in the nature of family casework with the worker interpreting the needs of the participant to the parents or siblings. Sometimes, as in the case of peers, it was necessary to continue to support the group in the absence of the participant, who had perhaps

Table 6   Distribution of participants according to number of hours of
fieldwork received January 1966 to July 1968*

	1966	1967	1968	Total
1 hour per month or less†	20	13	23	15
More than 1 hour and up to 2 hours per month	6	4	7	2
More than 2 hours per month up to 1 hour per week	10	9	5	8
More than 1 hour per week up to 2 hours per week	11	9	9	18
More than 2 hours per week up to 3 hours per week	2	7	4	3
More than 3 hours per week	5	12	6	8
Total	54	54	54	54

* No allowance is made for those participants who had a period of
residential training between these dates and who were thus unavailable
for regular contact during this period.
† The actual figures used in the class intervals are as follows
(adjustment was made for 1968):

1966 and 1967: no. of hours   For the whole period: no. of hours

0– 12	0– 30
13– 24	31– 62
25– 52	63–134
53–104	135–268
105–156	269–412
157 plus	413 plus

left through conflict, in order to try to reintroduce him at a later stage.
In certain cases the focus of the work moved from support for the
participant to actual work with the other individuals concerned.

For a number of reasons it is difficult to put a precise figure on the
amount of worker-time involved in support work. Discussions with
other agencies, schools, and employers tended not to be reported in
detail; usually only a brief note of what had taken place was written.
Again, during a contact in the home, a worker might take the
opportunity of the temporary absence of the participant to discuss the

boy with the parents. Support work increased over time as the workers formed a deeper relationship with clients. Thus in 1966 only 13 instances of this type of work were recorded, 76 in 1967, and 54 for the seven months of 1968. All of these were occasions where the purpose of the contact was direct support for the participant and most of them refer to contact with the family. Overall this type of work represented about 5 per cent of the total, but these figures, based on the 143 instances above, are probably an underestimation.

(c) Work with non-participants

An ever-present danger in this report is to give the impression that the team worked only with 54 individuals. It is true that with three important exceptions most of the intensive work was done with these 54; over the whole of the project period contact was made with some 600 young people. In fact, participants formed a minority of members in most of the groups.

In assessing the relative amounts of work with participants and those who were not participants a measure termed the 'client-hour' will be used. An example should help to make this concept clear. If a period of group work lasted for two hours and there were 2 participants and 3 other clients present then this would count as $2 \times 2 = 4$ participant client-hours and $3 \times 2 = 6$ non-participant client-hours.

Over the whole of the evaluation period, using this measure, participants received just over 30 per cent of the workers' efforts in face-to-face situations. There was not a great deal of variation in the proportions in any of the three-month periods. It might have been expected that work would come to be more concentrated on the 54 participants, especially as casework grew in importance, but to be set against this was the tendency for groups to grow in size and for new members to be non-participants.

Using the different measure of sessions it was found that one-quarter of all sessions did not contain a participant. Some of these (see section iii) will have been of indirect benefit to participants, but much of this effort represents work in isolation from the main objectives of the project.

(d) Professional and voluntary work

It will be remembered that throughout the period there were four professional workers, one of whom was part-time, and a team of 151

voluntary workers. [7] To assess the relative importance of voluntary
and professional effort the numbers of hours worked by each of the
two groups of workers is shown in *Table 7*. If a voluntary and a
professional worker were present at the same time, the time spent by
each worker is separately calculated rather than apportioned. No
distinction is made between the various type of voluntary worker (see
Chapter 2), since any such division is likely to be misleading rather than
helpful here.

Table 7 Fieldwork January 1966 to July 1968: the relative proportions of work undertaken by voluntary and professional
workers, by hours worked

| | Voluntary workers | | Professional workers | |
	Actual	Percentage	Actual	Percentage
1966	1267	36	2228	64
1967	2955	51	2820	49
1968	1106	45	1504	55
Total	5328	45	6552	55

Over the whole period of the project just under one-half (45 per
cent) of the work was carried out by voluntary workers. Although
during 1966 the contribution of voluntary workers was increasing
(second half of 1966: 771 hours cf. first half: 496 hours), the work
done by professional workers was increasing more rapidly.

From October 1966 the proportion of work contributed by
voluntary workers grew, and in the whole of 1967 actually
accounted by a narrow margin for more hours of work than
the professionals. As the termination programme got under way the
contribution of volunteers became less important. In this programme
(see Chapter 4(iv)) it was the more disturbed participants, with whom
work had been done exclusively by professionals, who received support
right up to the end of the project. For those who were better adjusted,
those worked with by volunteers generally, terminations came earlier.

If the number of sessions undertaken by voluntary workers rather
than the actual time in hours are examined the following results are
obtained. The first column of *Table 8* gives the actual number of
sessions worked by voluntary workers, the second gives these figures
expressed as a percentage of all sessions. The third column gives the
number of sessions staffed solely by voluntary workers and the fourth
expresses this as a percentage of the number of sessions they worked.

Table 8 Number and percentages of sessions worked by voluntary
workers January 1966 to July 1968

	No. of sessions at which volunteer(s) was (were) present	*Percentage proportion of all sessions worked*	*No. of sessions staffed solely by volunteer(s)*	*Percentage proportion of volunteer sess- ions staffed solely by volunteer(s)*
1966	368	38	127	35
1967	734	45	407	55
1968	318	33	180	57
Total	1420	40	714	50

On the proportion of sessions worked by voluntary workers the pattern is the same as in *Table 7*, a rise in the proportion in 1967 as against 1966, and a decline in 1968. In 40 per cent of all sessions there was a volunteer present. On a time basis they had an even higher proportion (45 per cent) of the total indicating that the sessions attended by volunteers tended to be longer than those worked by professionals.

Often professional and voluntary workers would work with the same group at the same time, but as the project progressed and the experience and confidence of the voluntary workers increased, they came to take sole charge of more and more sessions. Thus, during 1966 35 per cent of all voluntary worker sessions were run by voluntary workers alone, and during 1967 this figure increased to 55 per cent, and to 57 per cent in 1968. Over the whole evaluation period exactly one-half of all sessions attended by voluntary workers were carried out in the absence of professional workers.

(e) The changing pattern of work

Several changes in the work over the evaluation period have already been noted. The volume of work increased, and voluntary workers came to play an increasing and more individual role. There was also a slight decrease in the proportion of time worked with non-participants, and this was paralleled with a slightly larger decrease in the actual number of sessions without participants. These changes have to be linked to the needs of the clients, which were constantly changing throughout the project. If these changing needs were to be met then the service offered had to be flexible.

First, the type of work, whether casework, group work, or casual contact work, will be examined, then the change in specific services offered and used will be reviewed.

Group work and casework   It was intended from the outset that the main method to be used in the project would be group work (although a caseworker was employed as a member of the team on a part-time basis), and the fact that three of the four professional workers were employed to work with groups illustrates the emphasis placed on this method in the planning. The terms 'group work' and 'casework' mean various things to various people, and pages could be expended in definitions of these two terms. In order to classify sessions for the purpose of analysis a practical and meaningful definition is necessary. From a fieldworker's reports it was often difficult to see the depths at which the worker was operating, since comments on what the worker was actually trying to do seldom occurred. Thus, in some instances the group work may not have been very much more than an adult taking a group for an activity. The important point for the following analysis is that when the sessions are classified according to whether they were group work, casework, or street work (i.e. casual contact), it is not intended to imply that all sessions in a particular category would meet a rigorous test of intensive group work or casework. A minimal definition of the categories employed would be 'work with groups' and 'work with individuals', but this is likely to underestimate the nature and quality of the work.

Because of the informal nature of the work it was often very hard to classify particular sessions. Three different types of fieldwork report forms were used, group work, casework, and streetwork, but the heading on the top of the form did not always correspond with what was reported to have taken place during the session; many sessions had elements of all three types of work in them. The fieldwork reports, from which this analysis is made, were classified by the research worker thus helping to ensure uniformity of judgement throughout.

The casework category has been divided up into 'individual' and 'family' (by which is meant work with the client's immediate family). The figures for January 1966 include eleven reports from the Bridge Café which have been classified as group work. The analysis is for all sessions, irrespective of whether participants were present or not. The 31-month evaluation period is grouped into 3-month intervals (see *Table 9*).

Table 9 Percentage distribution of sessions by type (casual, casework, group work) January 1966 to July 1968 by 3-month intervals

	Casual work	Casework		All case	Group work	Total
		Individual	Family			
1966						
Jan–March	23	13	4	17	60	100 (185)*
April–June	39	12	2	14	47	100 (244)
July–Sept	18	9	5	14	68	100 (178)
Oct–Dec	17	22	6	28	55	100 (358)
1967						
Jan–March	12	25	7	32	56	100 (459)
April–June	15	29	11	40	44	99 (331)
July–Sept	11	35	13	48	40	99 (416)
Oct–Dec	8	29	9	38	54	100 (435)
1968						
Jan–March	7	38	10	48	44	99 (538)
April–June	5	41	12	52	43	100 (323)
July	3	47	11	59	39	100 (103)
All 1966	24	15	5	20	56	100 (965)
All 1967	12	30	10	40	49	101 (1641)
All 1968	6	40	11	51	43	100 (964)
1966-7-8	14 (487)	28 (1003)	9 (306)	37 (1309)	50 (1775)	101 (3570)

* Numbers in brackets are actual figures.

Over the whole period 50 per cent of the sessions were group work, 37 per cent casework, and the remainder street (casual contact) work. The proportion of both individual and family casework increased considerably over time. This type of work doubled in 1967 as against 1966, and in 1968 casework actually exceeded group work. The decrease in casual work (halved in 1967 as against 1966) is explained by the fact that this was a technique mainly used at the start of the evaluation period to re-establish contacts, and the need for it soon ended. At a later stage such contacts tended to occur when workers were looking for individuals who had been particularly elusive. The increase in casework has important implications for social-work practice and will be taken up later. It is accounted for by work with a number of adolescents who had few, if any, friends, and could not, because of the severity of their maladjustment, function adequately in a group situation. The work with these young people escalated as the severity of their problems was realized, and, in some cases, as they became more demanding of the worker and his time. It had been hoped that the period of casework would be succeeded by one of group work, but in six cases this development did not take place. The increase in individual

Table 10   Distribution of participants according to type of
         work received

Group work	20
Mainly group work, with some casework	7
Mainly group work, with some casual contact	1
Casework	2
Mainly casework, with some group work	3
Casework and group work in equal proportions	3
Mainly casual contact	4
Little or no work	14
	—
Total	54

CATEGORIES: *Group work* 90 per cent of the session received by the client were in this category; *mainly group work with some casework* 60—85 per cent of the work was group work, the remainder casework; *mainly group work with some casual contact* as for above except remainder was casual contact; *casework* 90 per cent or more casework; *Little or no work* less than one contact a month. The remainder of the categories were worked out on the above principles.

casework in 1968 (38 per cent to 47 per cent from January to July) occurred partly because of the policy adopted in the termination programme.

It is difficult to categorize work with any one client, since it often changed over time in response to changing needs. But a breakdown on the assessment of workers would suggest the following distribution in the case of participants (*Table 10*).

In addition to the above figures, 3 non-participants were worked with intensively over a long period of time on a casework basis. These results are to be contrasted with the data presented earlier which showed that 37 per cent of the total number of sessions during the evaluation period were casework sessions.

The service provided by the project has been classified so far by the method of work adopted, but it is also possible to classify it by the needs of the clients. For the purpose of examining how the pattern of service changed over time, the fieldwork was divided into five categories as follows:

(a) *Work:* Included here are all services in the field of employment. Some will be instances where the worker took an active part in helping the young person to obtain employment; others will be connected with the discussion of problems arising out of the work situation which did not require any further action on the part of the worker.

(b) *Accommodation:* Similar to the above category except that the service is concerned with accommodation.

(c) *Recreation:* This service includes those instances where the worker actually provides facilities for leisure, and where he attempts to improve the satisfaction of the client in his use of leisure.

(d) *Representation:* Services where the worker acts in some way on behalf of the client, such as speaking in court for him or mediating between client and his parents. Also included are services that facilitate contacts between clients and others, for example, probation officers.

(e) *Social development:* This includes a wide range of services not included in the four categories above. The major area is the provision of social and educational experience, for example, experiment in interpersonal relationships, and exploration of attitudes to various subjects such as parents, police, crime, etc.

The method was to analyse the content of fieldwork reports. Many sessions were found to contain work that fell into two or more of the above categories. It was not possible to say what proportion of each session was devoted to each of the two or more categories of service, since the information contained on the reports was rarely sufficient to enable any accurate division. Thus, where two or more categories of services were provided within the one session they are counted separately. The analysis is a frequency count only, and makes no allowance for the amount of time spent on each service.

Over the period January 1966 to July 1968 there were 2,883 instances of service in the social development category, or 43 per cent of the total; employment problems accounted for 14 per cent; accommodation 4 per cent, recreation 27 per cent; and representation 12 per cent. The figures for each year of the period are given in *Table 11*.

Table 11 Analysis of content of social-work programme by clients' needs January 1966 to July 1968 (the figures in brackets are percentages)

	Work	Accommo- dation	Recreation	Represen- tation	Social develop- ment	Total
1966	193 (11)	43 (2)	576 (33)	91 (5)	827 (48)	1730 (99)
1967	462 (15)	126 (4)	814 (26)	398 (13)	1292 (42)	3092 (100)
1968	310 (17)	73 (4)	416 (22)	308 (16)	764 (41)	1871 (100)
Total	965 (14)	242 (4)	1806 (27)	797 (12)	2883 (43)	6693 (100)

As is to be expected from the figures in *Table 11* there is an absolute increase over time in all five types of service. Within the year totals in the period January to March 1966 there were 24 instances of services connected with the field of 'work' and just two years later it had risen to 180, i.e., more than seven times. Similarly 'social development' rises from 178 to 447 during the same periods, an increase of just over two-and-a-half times. The most dramatic rise is in 'representation' which moves from 11 instances to 150, an increase of just under fourteen times. 'Recreation' almost doubles in the period, and the services connected with 'accommodation' increases over seven-fold, and at its peak in the first quarter of 1967 was eleven times greater than in the first three months of 1966.

To allow for the increase in service provided, the percentage of the total service for each category was calculated. Services connected with work increased from 7 per cent of the total in the first quarter of 1966 to 17 per cent two years later; 'representation' from 3 per cent to 14 per cent, accommodation from 1 per cent to 3 per cent, but with a peak of 6 per cent in April to June 1967. Both recreation and social development services decreased in importance, the former from 33 per cent in 1966 to 22 per cent in 1968, the latter from 48 per cent to 41 per cent.

Over the whole 31-month evaluation period (January 1966 to July 1968) the major change was the increase both in relative and absolute terms of those services connected with work, accommodation, and representation. These areas tend to be the ones in which the worker is likely to provide a more tangible individual service and are usually concerned with the solution of an immediate problem. Those services concerned with recreation and social development, which were likely to be less concerned with immediate solutions to problems and direct personal service, increased in absolute terms, but their relative importance as part of the whole service pattern decline over time.

(f) The amount of fieldwork

This section does not present new data but looks at the fieldwork as a whole, irrespective of which type of worker it was done by or which type of client received it. Two measures are used: first, the number of sessions; and second, the number of client-hours of fieldwork (see *Table 12*). The latter does not take into account the number of workers present at any one session but only the length of that session.

Throughout the period work built up into a peak, and then tailed off as the project neared its end. The period January to March 1967 saw something of a crisis in the workload on the professional workers and the figures show this as a peak. In the period January to March 1968 more sessions took place than in January to March 1967, but the amount of time spent on them was some 20 per cent less. This arose because of the policy adopted in the termination phase of having shorter sessions, thus allowing the workers to make more contacts with those participants who were relatively under serviced. The average length of each session varied from a little under two-and-a-half hours (2.4) to just over two-and-a-half hours (2.6) in 1967 to exactly two hours in 1968. In terms of sessions, there was an average of 3.8 per day, and over

Table 12　The amount of fieldwork (number of separate
sessions and number of hours worked) by
3-month intervals January 1966 to July 1968

	No. of sessions	*Client-hours*
1966		
Jan—March	185	393
April—June	244	617
July—Sept	178	434
Oct—Dec	358	964
1966 total	965	2408
1967		
Jan—March	459	1242
April—June	331	1030
July—Sept	416	1077
Oct—Dec	435	943
1967 total	1641	4292
1968		
Jan—March	538	1057
April—June	323	678
July	103	175
1968 total	964	1910
1966, 1967, and 1968	3570	8610

nine hours fieldwork per day, every day, throughout the thirty-one
months of the evaluation period.

In this long chapter the essence of the Wincroft Project can be
found. It has described the changing pattern of relationships between
workers and participants, from the initial uneasy encounters through
the period of testing and exploitation to the strong and confident
understandings of 1967, and, finally, to the parting of the ways in
1968. The routes followed by each individual worker and each young
person differed considerably. For some the work was a series of crises
with little in between, for others progress was steady and relatively
smooth, but for most the pattern was that normal for all adolescents — it had its ups and downs.

NOTES AND REFERENCES

1 G. Goetschius and J. Tash, *Working with Unattached Youth* (Routledge and Kegan Paul, London, 1967), p. 68.

2 Gisela Konopka, *Social Group Work: A Helping Process* (Prentice-Hall, New York, 1963).

3 For example, Howard Jones, *Reluctant Rebels* (Tavistock Publications, London, 1961).

4 See Chapter 1, n. 25.

5 A 'session' is taken to mean a morning, an afternoon, or an evening in the official conditions of service for youth leaders.

6 M. Davies, *Probationers in their Social Environment* (HMSO, London, 1969) is the first published report of this research.

7 One professional worker was replaced, thus making an overall total of 156 workers over the whole period.

PART TWO

Research

5 · The research design

The emphasis so far has been on the description and analysis of the social-work programme, and the implication underlying much of this discussion has been that the project, at least to some degree, achieved its objectives successfully. Any doubts raised about its effectiveness have been left as they were expressed by the social workers. The time has now come, however, when a different test of effectiveness has to be applied, the test of scientific evaluation. It was for this purpose that a research worker had been employed and the participant group was matched with a control group so that the behaviour of both could be carefully measured and compared. The intention was to establish that the difference, if any, in the behaviour of the two groups at the end of the project could be legitimately attributed to the efforts of the social workers. The problems of finding a control group (p. 184) and measuring the changes in the behaviour of both groups will be the main concern of this chapter, but first it may be worth saying something about the use of evaluation in social work.

The absence of evaluation in social-work practice in Britain is remarkable. [1] Even in America, with its much more massive tradition in applied social science, there can be found relatively few examples of its use. Fortunately, most of the examples have been generated from delinquency control and prevention programmes, and therefore a more detailed comparison with the present project may be justified. [2] The lack of interest in evaluation by most practitioners is likely to be a function of the priorities that they assign to the use of their resources. In a situation where social agencies are made continually aware of the gap between needs and services, it may seem a luxury to indulge in a kind of research that may only go to show that the scarce resources are producing little effect. Indeed, since this is the conclusion of most evaluation studies to date, this kind of research would be a form of suicide in situations where social workers have tenuous control over their resources. But clearly there are other reasons for the lack of interest. One is the lack of a scientific tradition in British social work; very few social workers are made competent in research methods by their training. Another is that research-oriented social workers are often overwhelmed by the technical difficulties of evaluation research, and

179

prefer to investigate more manageable problems. In addition, it is not unusual for people who show great dedication in their work to believe that the latter must be effective, and therefore to feel it unnecessary that it should be subjected to the sceptical scrutiny of research workers. Nor can the ethical doubts about the wisdom of giving one group a service, while offering nothing to a group in comparable need, be easily passed over. However, whatever the reasons for the absence of evaluation, this paucity of experience is the background against which the present attempt must be judged.

A brief review of the form of other evaluation studies may be useful, bearing in mind the objectives that social workers set themselves, the subjects of their efforts, the methods by which they operated, the design of the research evaluation of their programmes, the data used in this evaluation, and the consequences of the findings of the research. Seven studies will be considered, some for their similarity of method, others because of their research design. All had delinquency control as one of their objectives, and all are American.

One of the earliest and best-known studies in the field of delinquency prevention is the Cambridge—Somerville Study started in the late 1930s. [3] The target group was drawn randomly from names, suggested mainly by teachers, arranged in pairs matched for age, class, intelligence, and delinquency potential. The method was to offer something more comprehensive and more routine than social workers are usually able to offer – a 'big brother'. Help was extended over a four-year period to 255 boys who were eleven years old at the commencement of the work. Each boy received about a year's service. Delinquency records of the two groups have been continually analysed since the end of the study, and in 1959 it was reported that the treated group had just as many convictions as the untreated group, and that both the numbers and types of crimes were similar in the two groups. [4] One interesting finding was that a dozen boys who had received really intensive service did better than a comparable group of controls. [5]

Another more recent study, much closer in method to the Wincroft Project, was the Mid-City Project which has been reported on by Miller. [6] Here again the primary objective was delinquency prevention and control, and the method a combination of detached group work, family casework, and community organization. Seven detached workers worked with one group each in four neighbourhoods for periods ranging from ten to thirty-four months; from 30 to 50 boys received a service each month. These boys were compared with a control group and it was found that on 'All major measures of violative behaviour, disapproved actions, illegal actions, during-contact Court appearances, before-during-after appearances, and Project-Control appearances' there was a negligible impact. Reports on this project are especially interesting for what they have to say about the difficulties in obtaining cooperation between agencies working with the same boys in the same area. [7]

A third study, which is very close to the Wincroft Project in terms of research design, is the Seattle Atlantic Street Center Project. [8] A number of high risk boys (126, all negroes) were selected from junior high schools in Seattle, and 108 were randomly assigned to the treatment and control groups, 54 to the one and 54 to the other. They were offered a programme beginning with a weekly club and widening out into social work with the family. With few exceptions all boys in the experiment received a standard two years of intensive treatment from early 1965 to early 1967, and during this time averaged over 14.5 contacts per month. It is claimed that this reduced the degree of school acting-out behaviour. The interesting thing about this project is the sophistication of the research design and the care with which the treatment group was selected and the treatment measured. [9]

Little would be gained in listing all the relevant evaluation studies, but perhaps mention ought to be made of three others. The Maximum Benefits Project was also concerned mainly with negro boys, and the chief service they received was from social caseworkers with whom each child had about a dozen interviews, as did their mothers. Followed up eight years later, 69 per cent of the treated children and 63 per cent of the untreated children had become official delinquents. [10] The Youth Counselling Service described by Meyer, Borgatta, and Jones in *Girls at Vocational High* did no better. [11] About four hundred girls were identified as potential problems and one-half of these were offered counselling service. Of the 200 offered counselling service 125 girls were offered individual therapy. On none of the criteria, social adjustment in school and delinquency, did the treated group do better. A similar experience was recorded by the New York City Youth Board when they offered the services of a child guidance clinic to 22 boys; ten years later exactly the same number of delinquents could be found in both the treatment and the control groups. [12]

This brief review of related studies should lead us to expect no dramatic changes in the delinquency or social adjustment of the participant group as a result of the influence of the Wincroft Project. It would appear that the level of contact compared favourably with that offered in other projects, but it is of course impossible to say whether the quality of the service was better or worse. Most of the American projects relied mainly on professional social workers. It is possible, though difficult to establish, that the boys dealt with in the American projects were living in less favourable social conditions than those in Wincroft. It has certainly been the practice in both countries to offer a service to the 'hard-to-reach', or in England, the 'unattached', adolescent, although these young people are not likely to be responsive to programmes of social work. At best it would appear that any positive results seem short term and at worst that these programmes of social work have no measurable impact on teenage boys living in slum conditions.

The basic requirements of an evaluation study would seem to be: an operational definition of what is to be achieved through the programme; the establishment of a baseline from which the programme starts; a record of the input of effort; an account of the movement from the baseline, if any, with varying levels of input, and a follow-up to see if that change is maintained. A completely satisfactory scientific design requires a control group and the assignment of clients at random to the experimental and control groups. [13] This aim was not achieved in the Wincroft Project, although a considerable effort was made to find a group of boys like the participant group in an area like Wincroft.

The Wincroft Project was intended to help a group of boys reach a 'dynamic adjustment', and thereby to control their delinquency. It proved much easier to measure progress towards the second objective than towards the first, although it must be admitted that there are considerable difficulties in using recorded delinquency as a measure, and in treating the many different ways of looking at delinquency. No satisfactory measure of 'dynamic adjustment' exists, and the most that could be hoped is that the measure used would have some objective meaning to other research workers. To this end a baseline was achieved by having teachers complete the Bristol Social Adjustment Guides, the only suitable test available in England at that time. It would have been clearly advantageous if the same test could have been used at the end of the programme as at the beginning, but it is not only unsuitable for the post-school situation (except for the few for whom the youth club edition could be used), it would also have been impracticable to have it completed for the control group with whom there had been no contact. It was therefore necessary to use a test that could be done in an interview with a boy. After consultation with the Home Office Research Unit it was decided to use the recently developed Jesness Inventory in its anglicized version. [14]

Stott's Bristol Social Adjustment Guides have been discussed in Chapter 1 but a word of explanation about the Jesness Inventory is required here. It consists of 155 statements to which the respondent is asked to reply 'true' or 'false'. Three examples are 'My feelings get hurt easily when I am scolded or criticised' (question 8); 'I never lie' (question 19); 'If I could only have a car at home things would be alright' (question 77). A global score, termed the Asocial Index, is produced as well as a number of separate scale scores. The Inventory is claimed to measure 'a generalized tendency to behave in ways which transgress established rules', with the Asocial Index being a 'a single best general solution . . . where . . . comparison of groups was the prime consideration'.

The Jesness Inventory was, however, only one part of the interview carried out with each member of both the control and the participant groups at the end of the project. This interview also covered areas of the boy's adjustment in the home, at work, in leisure, in relation to his peers of both sexes, and a self-report on his own past delinquency. These interviews took place after the completion of fieldwork on the projects, and they were completed in the months of September and October 1968.

A team of nine experienced interviewers, all married women, were carefully recruited for the full survey. They were not told about the real purpose of the interview, that it was a comparison of the two groups, until after the interviewing had been completed; the research was presented to them as a general survey of attitudes among working-class adolescents who might possibly be delinquent. This was to avoid any interviewer bias that might otherwise arise. As a further precaution respondents were randomly assigned to interviewers. A pilot study had already taken place outside the two areas and from this it had been found that use of a vehicle for the interview and a payment of ten shillings to respondents helped to solve the problem of lack of privacy in the home and the possible non-cooperation of the respondent. Nine respondents, eight of them members of the control group, were in residential training at the time of the interviews, and since some of the institutions could not agree to the visit of a female interviewer, two of the authors and a student (on the Diploma in Youth Work Course at the University of Manchester) with some experience of interviewing visited these boys.

The response rate of 90 per cent was felt to be very satisfactory, although it proved not possible to interview three participants (6 per cent) and ten controls (14 per cent). Of the total, one had emigrated, one had died, two refused to cooperate (both controls), and one was being sought by the police. The remaining eight had left their previous addresses and could not be traced despite repeated efforts. The relatively high response-rate was undoubtedly a product of the instructions to the interviewers to call back until they found the respondent at home – this often necessitated five or more visits. However, the result also says much for the persistence of the interviewers who were initially faced with what was for them a completely new interviewing situation. All reported good cooperation from most respondents.

Before examining the critical matter of the control group in the research design it might be worth reminding the reader that the statistical analysis of the social work (in Chapter 4) has already shown the way in which the input of worker-effort was measured in the project; by worker-sessions or client-hours. In the next chapter it will be possible to relate different levels of success within the participant group to different levels of service received. Nothing, however, can be said about the differences in the quality of the service rendered.

The rest of this chapter will be concerned with finding a control group for the participant group. The obvious choice would have been to list all of the boys in Wincroft who were in need of the services of social workers and then to assign randomly one-half to the treatment group. This solution to the problem of research design was although attractive technically never a practical possibility in the context of the style of social-work programme being offered. It would have been impossible to segregate one-half of the Wincroft social network from the other without justifying why the first half should be receiving the attention of the workers. Any explanation of the research would have immediately affected the programme of work and introduced the possibility of bias into the research results. The control group had therefore to be found from a different area of the city, and it was clearly sensible to choose it from an area as like Wincroft as possible.

The first move in the search was to consult the housing department of the local authority which suggested three possible areas and these were compared with Wincroft on the available statistics. The closest comparison was taken as the control area. There was a good deal of superficial similarity in the housing of the two areas: both were situated on arterial roads leading from the city centre which was a little over a mile away in each case; the houses in each area were of a uniform, terraced cottage variety, and demolition under the corporation redevelopment plan was being carried on in both locations. The control area was, however, larger and less overcrowded than Wincroft; it had more illegitimate births, a lower infant mortality rate, and a higher birth rate. But on none of these criteria were the differences very large, as the figures below indicate. Using the Wincroft figure as a baseline of 100 (to help conceal the precise location of the area) the control area showed an acreage of 153 per cent, a population of 90 per cent, and a density per acre of 59 per cent of Wincroft. Both areas had lost approximately 80 per cent of their population between 1951 and 1963. [15] The birth rate in the control area was 115 per cent, the illegitimacy rate 122 per cent, and the infant mortality rate 78 per cent of the Wincroft rate. Death rates were about the same. On over-crowding the control area had only 62 per cent of the Wincroft percentage of persons more than 1.5 per room. [16]

As a further check on the choice of the control area the delinquency figures for the two areas were compared. The calculation of crime rates for small areas is very time-consuming and in the present instance it was necessary to consult crime reports for those police beats that corresponded to the geographical boundaries of the two areas. The offenders were then checked for age and residence. Three measures of delinquency were obtained and only indictable offences were included in the analysis. Overall there was a higher proportion of delinquents in the control area: in 1965, 5.49 per cent (males 9.94 per cent) of all juveniles (10-16 years) were convicted by the courts in the control area and 4.62 per cent (males 8.45 per cent) in Wincroft. However, when the number of *offences* committed by juveniles is investigated and compared with the population at risk it was found that the rates were almost identical, 6.35 per cent and 6.20 per cent, for Wincroft and the control area respectively. The first set of figures relating to offenders counts the same adolescent twice if he is convicted a second time within the period. This is evened out by the second set of figures, but this indicates that the number of offences per offender was higher in Wincroft.

Offences committed by juveniles in the two areas were broken down

Table 13   Type of indictable offences committed by juveniles in 1965

Type of offence	Wincroft	Control area	Manchester
Against the person	2.3	6.8	1.2
Against property (mainly theft)	97.0	92.0	96.9
Other	0.7	1.1	1.9
Total	100.0	99.9	100.0

into two broad categories: those against the person, and those against property. These figures are given in *Table 13* with a comparison for those of the city as a whole. In both areas the majority of indictable offences committed by juveniles were against property, involving some form of theft.

Only the social statistics referred to earlier and the delinquency figures were used in the choice of the control area, since the decision had to be made speedily. Nevertheless, a great deal of other information was collected subsequently which confirmed the wisdom of the choice. Some of this information had been collected by the Education Committee for administrative purposes and some of it was collected in the schools survey mentioned in Chapter 1. We shall now consider comparisons on the basis of this other information.

One of the few indications of the comparative social status of the two areas came from answers to a question in the schools survey. The measure used was to ask respondents which of twelve possessions [17] they had in their home. Obviously in status-enhancing questions of this nature there will be some exaggeration by respondents, but it was felt that the same effect would appear in each area and it was the relative measure rather than the absolute value that was required. Wincroft averaged 6.6 possessions per respondent family and the control area was slightly higher at 7.1. The difference however, was not significant, $t = 1.43$, $P > .10$. A similar question, this time directed to respondents' personal possessions was asked. In this instance the direction of the difference was reversed with Wincroft respondents claiming an average of 4.0 and the control area 3.7. Again the difference was not significant, $t = 1.43$, $P > .10$.

Both areas were served by four secondary modern schools. [18] Although the number of pupils on the roll varied from year to year in each of the eight schools, those in Wincroft were on average only about three-fifths the size of those in the control area. During the period of the project there were two types of secondary modern school in Manchester — selective and ordinary. In the former pupils could stay beyond their fourth year, while in the latter they could not. If they wished to continue in school in the latter case then pupils had to transfer to another school. Only one of the above eight schools was selective, the single-sex local authority school in the control area, but this only became so in 1967. Three of the schools in Wincroft were closed under the authority's secondary schools reorganization plan in 1968, and one in the control area changed its function from a mixed secondary modern to a comprehensive. Staff establishment was related to number of pupils in each school, but it was not possible to ascertain the actual against the theoretical staff-size for the schools. The average class-size for each school and for each area was calculated together with the attendance figures, and these are given in *Table 14*.

Table 14 A comparison of average class-size 1964-65 and average attendance rates 1964-66 (percentages in brackets)

	Average class-size	Range	Average daily attendance*	Range
Wincroft	29.1	26.8-35.1	(85.6)	(82.0-89.1)
Control	29.1	25.3-33.2	(85.6)	(84.3-89.0)

* Average daily attendance represents attendance as a percentage of average class-size.

School sizes may have differed but the class-size and average attendance rates were identical. In both cases, however, Wincroft had a wider range than the control area.

Although both areas came under the same local education authority, it was decided to investigate in each area whether the proportion of pupils receiving selective education differed. The primary schools, seven in each case, that served each area were examined and the number of pupils going on to different types of schools in 1966 is given in *Table 15*.

Both areas have similar percentages of children receiving grammar school education (9 per cent in each case) but a larger proportion of children in the control area received technical education. If all selective schools are considered, then almost identical proportions of pupils in each area received this form of education. Thus, the figure for Wincroft is 39 per cent and for the control area 40 per cent.

Table 15 Comparison of type of selective schooling received by children leaving primary schools in 1966 (percentages in brackets)

Area	Grammar	Technical	Selective Secondary Modern*	Ordinary	Total
Wincroft	22 (9)	42 (18)	27 (12)	142 (61)	233 (100)
Control	17 (9)	48 (24)	13 (7)	121 (60)	199 (100)

* See text, p. 187 for an explanation of this distinction.

Two of the schools in the control area, but only one in Wincroft, were denominational. Two of the schools in Wincroft, but three in the control area, were coeducational. Proportionally more in the control area received their education in coeducational schools than in Wincroft, 63 per cent compared with only 15 per cent. A sizable minority of those in the control area (40 per cent) attended a denominational school, whereas the figure for Wincroft was only 6 per cent. However, the proportion in each group receiving secondary modern schooling was very similar, 93 per cent and 89 per cent. The number attending technical schools was very small, less than 5 per cent of the total subjects, although there were slightly more participants than controls in this category. Few in either group attended a special school.

Attitudes to school and education were examined by five questions in our schools survey (see Chap. 1), but only one question differentiated significantly between the two areas. On four out of five questions the control area respondents showed a more positive attitude to school and education. Thus, fewer Wincroft respondents planned further education on leaving school (75 per cent as against 79 per cent), and a greater proportion wished to leave school before they reached the age of 15 (20 per cent as against 13 per cent) and fewer to stay on after 15 (33 per cent as against 43 per cent). On a five-point scale [19] of attitudes to the importance of school and education there was no difference between the two areas in terms of overall positive, either medium or high, attitudes expressed towards education. In Wincroft 71 per cent of answers fell on this side of the scale and in the control area 73 per cent. But there was a difference, and it was statistically significantly ($P < 0.2$), in the degree of positive attitude expressed, 45 per cent of control area respondents scoring in 'the high positive' category and 26 per cent of those in Wincroft.

The research worker visited all of the eight schools on a number of occasions in connection with the completion of the Bristol Social Adjustment Guides and the schools survey. His subjective impressions were that the quality of the educational service was better in the control area. This was based partly on the quality of the buildings, three of the schools in the control area occupied new (post-1950) premises, while none in Wincroft did. Furthermore the attitude expressed by headmasters in the control area towards their pupils seemed to be more sympathetic and understanding. However, with the exception of the data in *Table 16*, this impression is not confirmed statistically by the objective measures.

Neither area contained a full-time youth club but in both cases there were clubs, within half-a-mile of the Municipal Ward Boundary (3 near the control area and 4 near Wincroft). Measurement of youth club membership is difficult, since the concept of what actually constitutes membership will vary. However, it would not seem unreasonable to suppose a 'subjective' concept will be equally applicable in each area. In Wincroft 52 per cent of respondents claimed 'membership' of one or more clubs while the figure for the control area was higher at 62 per cent.

A second kind of information which may have its bearing on delinquency and social adjustment in the two areas is the job situation. The type of job obtained in the two areas will of course be related to the quality of education received. The jobs open to them are not limited to the job opportunities available in each area since boys in both areas were free to seek jobs in areas other than that of their residence. The City of Manchester Careers Advisory Service (Youth Employment Service) kindly prepared a list of the jobs obtained by pupils leaving the eight schools in 1966 (at summer and Easter). They classified the jobs into 'good apprenticeships', 'jobs with some training',

Table 16 Comparison of types of jobs obtained by school-leavers in the two areas in 1966 (figures in brackets are percentages)

	No. of leavers	A	B	C
Wincroft	172 (100)	85 (49)	50 (29)	37 (22)
Control	177 (100)	99 (56)	44 (25)	34 (19)

A: good apprenticeship
B: jobs with some training
C: jobs with little or no training

and 'jobs with little or no training'. The original figures contained some fifth-year leavers at one of the schools and those were removed to make the comparison more valid.

The greatest difference between the two areas is in the percentage of pupils obtaining type A (good apprenticeships) jobs, with the control area having 7 per cent more in this category. Much of this difference is accounted for by the high contribution to this category of one school which made up almost a half (45 out of 99) of the total leavers obtaining this type of job. The differences are however not significant, $\chi^2 = 1.514, P > .30$.

A further source of information about the importance given to work in the two areas came from our schools survey, though 29 of the respondents (approximately equal proportions in both areas) failed to answer this question. Of Wincroft respondents 94 per cent replied that type of job of leaving school was 'very important' as against 83 per cent of the control area respondents. This difference was not significant, however. On factors influencing the choice of job respondents from Wincroft schools stressed those concerned with immediate reward, such as high wages and shorter hours. In contrast, control area respondents put relatively more stress on those factors associated with long-term rewards. The difference was not however, statistically significant ($\chi^2 = 3.71, P > .30$).

It would appear that the two areas corresponded on certain major variables that might appear to be relevant to the experimental programme, but it is interesting to pursue some of the subtler differences that may have occurred. Among these are the attitudes of youth in both areas to adults in general, to their parents in particular, and especially where it concerns discipline. It could be that attitudes towards adults were crucial to the success of the social-work programme since all the workers were adults. If the general attitude of adolescents to adults in Wincroft was one of acceptance and in the control area one of rejection and hostility, then it could be said that there was a built-in bias towards the success of the programme. In fact the reverse was the case, with a higher proportion of respondents in Wincroft seeing 'most' or 'some' adults as 'against young people' (67 per cent against 58 per cent). The direction of this attitude, i.e. adults seen as hostile or not hostile, did not differ significantly, but the proportion of control area respondents answering that 'most' adults were seen as hostile, did differ significantly at the 10 per cent level. However, this finding was only partly confirmed by a second question. A larger proportion of control area respondents felt that 'grown-ups are usually against me' (12 per cent compared with 9 per cent), but more Wincroft respondents felt that their relationships with adults was better than that of their peers, 'get on with adults better than others of my own age' (29 per cent as against 14 per cent).

Unfortunately, questions about attitudes and behaviour directly relevant to delinquency in the two areas had to be omitted from the schools survey at the request of the local education committee. Nevertheless, something remained in the form of an attempt to explore attitudes towards what Miller calls 'focal concerns'. [20] Miller has suggested that the lower-class culture is a generating milieu for gang delinquency and he has identified a number of preoccupations or 'focal concerns' to which members of working-class society adhere, and which are conducive to the adoption of delinquent behaviour patterns. These focal concerns were used as an indication of the degrees of commitment to a delinquent set of values. They were included in the present survey in the form:

You should try to keep out of trouble at all costs.

It's the cute ones who get the most out of life.

People who do what they're told all the time never learn to stand on their own two feet.

There's always a chance that you won't get caught for stealing little things so you might as well try.

To be worth living life must be exciting.

Unless you show how tough you are people don't admire (respect) you.

How much you get out of life depends mainly on your luck.

Although the difference was not statistically significant, it was found here that the respondents in Wincroft shared a higher number of focal concerns, 2.97 against 2.60. Moreover, Wincroft had a higher proportion of respondents agreeing with five or more of the concerns, 16 per cent as against 9 per cent, and a smaller percentage in agreement with two or less, 42 per cent compared with 52 per cent.

Any claim in this study for a successful outcome to the social-work programme would be jeopardized if it were shown that the two groups to be compared were exposed to radically different social environments. Fortunately, however, an examination of the available official statistics about the two areas, together with the material from the survey, reveals in the majority of instances differences between the two areas that were not statistically significant. However, where differences did exist, it was almost always Wincroft that was the less socially advantaged area. Thus Wincroft was more overcrowded, had a higher infant mortality rate, and more indictable criminal offences per head of the juvenile population at risk. Data from our schools survey produced evidence of larger families, expectation of more immediate rewards from jobs, fewer household possessions, a less positive attitude to education, and a higher degree of commitment to delinquent preoccupations. Of 44 comparisons between the two areas Wincroft was more socially disadvantaged in 30 cases, the control area in 10 cases, with the rest being exactly equal, although in only a small number of the 40 cases was the difference statistically significant. Thus, the chances of success for the social-work programme were not in Wincroft's favour.

Having chosen the control area it was necessary to find a control group. Because of the method of selection it cannot be claimed that either the control or the participant group is representative of the adolescents in the two areas just examined. Nevertheless, 82 per cent of the total membership of these two groups did attend the eight schools in which the schools survey took place. Whenever possible in the following comparison data on the two groups will be related to that obtained from respondents to the schools survey.

It will be remembered from Chapter 1 (p. 21) that the selection criteria for the treatment group were for boys to be aged between 14 and 17 at the beginning of 1966 and for them to have had convictions for two or more offences, or a score of above five on the Bristol Social Adjustment Guides Maladjustment (or Delinquency Prediction) Score. The control group was to be matched on these criteria. The idea of matching assumes that all variables are to be held constant except the single experimental one, in this case the treatment programme, but clearly, matching for type of area, age, delinquency, or maladjustment score does not account for all of the possible variables relevant to the outcome. Since, as has been explained earlier, it was not possible to allocate boys randomly to the treatment and control groups the unmatched differences between the treatment and control groups may well account for the differences that were found in the evaluation at the end of the Wincroft Project. Moreover, as Wilkins points out, the effect of matching certain factors may be to conceal the influence of their unknown correlates. [21] The matching procedure used in the present study is open to criticism in that it proved impossible with the available research resources to carry out individual matching. This would have required starting with a very large population on the factors to be matched in order to find individuals with the required combination of factors. Instead the groups were matched with respect to the frequency of the main variables in each group. [22] Whether the control group can qualify for this title in the scientific sense may be disputed, but it still is useful to offer it as a group comparable to the participants, and by the current standard of evaluation in social research the comparisons are relatively rigorous.

Convictions were measured from police records. A 'caution' was counted as a conviction, although this is not strictly accurate since the offender has not been found guilty by a court. However, since the young person has committed an offence detected by the police and has presumably admitted committing it, this cannot be ignored. Where a young person is remanded several times by the court on the same offence or offences this is counted as one court appearance only. The commission of certain offences often means that the young person will almost automatically be charged with several related offences. One example is a charge of taking and driving away a vehicle which is often accompanied by charges of driving without insurance and driving without a licence. After some deliberation it was decided that these should be counted as separate offences, since it is conceivable that the offender would have a driving licence and could be insured. When charged with specific offences members of the control and participant group would sometimes ask for certain other offences to be 'taken into consideration' (usually abbreviated to TICs.). Since evidence from the social-work team suggested that pressure was brought to bear on young people charged with offences to admit others of a similar nature, it was decided to use a separate measure for this type of charge rather than include them under the main offences. Sometimes there was a gap between the date of arrest for a specific offence and the subsequent court appearance. Since the evaluation period had a definite beginning and end a matter of a few weeks could be crucial and so the date of actual commission of the offence was counted rather than the date of court appearance. Where a charge was dismissed this was not, of course, counted.

The distribution of offences for those participants and controls who had appeared in court before 1966 are given in *Table 17*.

Table 17   Distribution of number of convictions for separate offences in the two groups prior to 1 January 1966 (not including offences taken into consideration)

No. of offences	Participants	Controls
1	7	4
2	6	15
3	4	5
4	2	5
5	3	5
6	1	1
7 or more	2	3
Total	25	38

Those participants convicted have an average of 3.0 offences each, and the mean for the whole group of 54 is 1.6. The figures for the control group are 3.2 and 1.6 respectively. Neither difference is significant, $t = 0.577, P > .50$ and $t = 1.234, P > .20$ respectively.

Those who had not committed the requisite number of offences were included by their score on the Bristol Social Adjustment Guides, the scores for which are given below. Excluded from the table are the 7 unconvicted individuals for whom it was not possible to have a school guide completed but who were included in the study on the basis of the club edition of the Bristol Guides. It would not be correct to include the scores obtained on a different form of the guide. Some of the 18 boys with two or more convictions also had guides completed, but these are also excluded from *Table 18*.

The average maladjustment score for participants is 16.45 and 17.70 for controls. On the delinquency prediction score the difference is in the same direction but slightly smaller, participants scoring 17.24 and controls 17.87. In neither case is the difference significant.

The final criteria for selection was age. The average age of participants was 14 years 10.8 months and of the controls 14 years 7.8 months. Some 92 per cent of controls and 86 per cent of participants

Table 18 Comparison of Bristol Social Adjustment Guides scores (maladjustment and delinquency prediction) for the two groups

	Participants		Controls	
Score	Maladjustment	Delinquency prediction	Maladjustment	Delinquency prediction
0−5	2	11	3	15
6−10	9	4	11	6
11−15	6	5	5	5
16−20	4	1	6	3
21−25	3	3	3	0
26−30	2	1	6	0
31−35	0	1	4	4
36−40	2	0	1	2
41 plus	1	3	1	5
Total	29	29	40	40

fell within the range 14 to 16 years. The difference is not significant at the 5 per cent level ($t = 1.230, P > .20$).

Thus on the three main matching variables (age, two or more convictions, and delinquency or maladjustment score) participants have slightly fewer offences, are slightly older, slightly less maladjusted and slightly less likely to become delinquent, but in no case is this difference statistically significant. The purpose in examining the remainder of the data is to see if the groups differ on other variables in any significant ways that could affect the outcome of the treatment programme.

As has been shown in the first chapter, families in Wincroft and the control area were large. Participants' and controls' families were no exception to the general pattern of the neighbourhood; the average number of children per family was 4.4 for the former and 4.6 for the latter. The largest family was fourteen children and six families had nine or more children. It is perhaps of interest to present these figures in more detail.

In both groups average family-size (number of children per family) approximates to that revealed by the schools survey reported earlier, the exception being that participants tend to come from families somewhat smaller than the average for Wincroft given by the schools

Table 19 Family-size of participant and control
groups at the start of evaluation period, 1
January 1966

No. of children	Participants	Controls
1	4	6
2 & 3	21	26
4 & 5	16	20
6 & 7	5	8
8 & 9	4	11
Over 9	3	3
Unknown	1	0
Total	54	74

survey with the converse true for controls. However, the differences are not significant nor is that between the two groups.

A 'broken home' is often held to be a cause of delinquency and it was therefore important to match the groups on this variable. The figures given in *Table 20* are what was known of the family situation of subjects at the beginning of 1966.

A slightly higher proportion of controls came from families with the natural mother and father present, but not significantly so. There is some variation between the groups in the type of parental situation other than this, most noticeably in the numbers coming from homes with one or no parents. Thus, more controls (26 per cent compared to 20 per cent of participants) come into this category, but again this difference is not statistically significant ($\chi^2 = 0.472, P > .30$).

The matching of the participant and control group on convictions for separate offences (*Table 17*) relies upon one kind of measurement of delinquency and this could produce different results from delinquency measured in other ways. Some of these other measures will now be examined in *Table 21*.

The average number of court appearances was 2.2 for participants and 2.3 for the controls; for the two groups as a whole 1.0 and 1.2 respectively. Differences are not significant in either case ($t = 1.194$, $P > .20$, and $t = 0.782, P > .40$). These figures are similar to those for number of offences in which the control group average also slightly exceeded that of the participants.

Table 20 Parental situation of the two groups at the start of the evaluation period, 1 January 1966 (figures in brackets are percentages)

	Participants			Controls		
Mother & father	37	(70)		53	(72)	
Mother only	6	(11)		13	(18)	
Father only	4	(7)	'Broken'	5	(7)	'Broken'
Step-father & own mother	3	(6)	(30)	0	(0)	(28)
Step-mother only	0	(0)		1	(1)	
Parents cohabit	2	(4)		2	(3)	
Relatives	1*	(2)		0	(0)	
Unknown	1			0		
Total	54	100		74	100	

* This boy's parents were alive and living together but he lived with relatives.

Table 21 Number of court appearances resulting in a finding of guilt prior to 1 January 1966

No. of court appearances	Participants	Controls
1	12	13
2	6	10
3	1	8
4	3	5
5	3	2
Total	25	38

To examine the type of offence committed by members of each group, crimes were classified into 'serious' and 'minor', using a modified and anglicized form of the classification system devised by Sellin & Wolfgang. [23] The details of how each type of crime is classified is given in Appendix II.

A number of separate points arise out of *Table 22*. Of the total number of offences in each group, 74 in the participant and 123 in the

Table 22 Number of serious and minor crimes committed by the
control and participant groups prior to 1 January 1966

No. of offences	25 participants		38 controls	
	serious	minor	serious	minor
1	8	7	7	13
2	6	4	14	1
3	4	0	6	1
4	1	0	6	0
5	4	0	1	0
6	0	0	0	0
7 or more	1	0	3	0
Total offences per category	63	11	105	18

control, an equal percentage of the total offences in each group (85 per cent) are classified as serious by the method used. The average number of serious offences per offender was 2.52 for the participants and 2.76 for the control offences ($t = 1.651, P < .10$). Minor offences showed a smaller difference but in the same direction, participants averaging .044 per offender and controls .047. The small size of the numbers in the latter case and their distribution make a statistical test inapplicable. Thus, although the ratio of serious to minor offences for the two groups was equal the average number of both serious and minor offences committed by the control group was higher. But from the data presented in *Table 21*, where it was found that the mean total number of offences was slightly higher this difference was to be expected. Of the 25 participant offenders all but one had committed at least one serious offence, although some had committed both serious and minor offences. In the control group the proportions were the same with only one offender not committing one or more serious offences. Thus in both groups the proportion of minor offenders was very small and roughly equal, 3 per cent and 4 per cent.

Earlier in this Chapter (p. 193) the process whereby offenders came to have 'offences taken into consideration' at a court appearance was briefly examined. For the reasons outlined these have been used as a separate measure and are presented in *Table 23*. The very large numbers of cases that are asked to be considered, the maximum

Table 23 Number of offences taken into consideration, control and participant groups, prior
to 1 January 1966

No. of offences	Participants	Controls
No offences admitted	11	20
1–2	2	5
3–5	2	5
6–10	3	3
11–20	2	2
21–30	2	1
31–40	2	1
41 plus	1	1
Total	25	38

number at any one court appearance of an offender in this study was 63, seem to confirm the validity of the decision to treat them separately in the analysis.

Fourteen of the 25 participants who had appeared in court prior to January 1966 asked for a total of 251 offences to be 'taken into consideration', an average of 17.9 per offender. The figures for the 18 controls were 197 and 10.9. A larger proportion of all participant offenders (56 per cent cf. controls 47 per cent) asked for offences to be considered when they appeared in court; the difference was not statistically significant ($\chi^2 = 0.170$, $P > .50$). The difference in mean number of offences taken into consideration is similarly not significant, but the non-normal distribution of offences makes the 't' test of doubtful validity here.

How subjects were dealt with by the court is of some importance to the study since it is possible that it was the treatment ordered that brought about any subsequent differences between the groups. In Chapter 6 it will be necessary to examine in close detail the other forms of treatment experienced by the two groups. Here the sentences received by both groups prior to 1966 are examined but not in as close detail as is done later. Prior to January 1966, 8 subjects in the control group had experienced some form of residential penal training; 5 of these had been, or were currently, in an approved school; the remainder had experienced a period of three months in a detention centre. By the time the evaluation started, 6 of these 8 boys had spent three months or less in one of these two types of residential institution, 1 less than six months and 1 less than twelve months. The total period of time spent in an institution by these 8 boys was 23 months. The proportion of participants in the convicted group that had received some period of residential training was slightly higher (24 per cent cf. controls 21 per cent); this involved 6 boys, 4 of whom had been, or were currently, in an approved school and 1 in a detention centre; the other had experienced a one-month period in a remand home while awaiting sentence. The total period of time spent by participants in these types of institutions was 40 months, and an average of 6.7 months per boy which was more than that for controls who averaged 2.9. The smallness of the numbers involved does not allow for a test of significance, but this difference will be noted in the following chapter when the total periods (to July 1968) of residential training are examined.

The number of court appearances and the number of convictions for offences committed by an individual are not necessarily related to the number of sentences received. Thus, some court appearances could result in two or more separate sentences yet several offences might result in one sentence. Therefore the figures in *Table 24* will not match up with those of either *Table 22* or *Table 23*.

Some subjects will have received more than one of the same type of sentence (e.g., two separate probation orders). This accounts for the differences between the figures in the timetable for residential training and those discussed in the text. In the case of the 4 participants who

Table 24 Comparison of participant and control groups by type of sentences prior to 1 January 1966 (figures in brackets are percentages)

Type of sentence	25 participants		38 controls	
Caution	1	(2)	3	(3)
Conditional/absolute discharge	8	(13)	16	(19)
Fine	17	(27)	13	(15)
Attendance centre	11	(17)	19	(22)
Probational/supervision orders*	17	(27)	24	(28)
Residential training	8	(13)	10	(12)
Other	0	(–)	1	(1)
Total sentences	62	(100)	86	(100)

* Not including after-care

had attended an approved school, 2 had previously spent one month in a remand home. Thus the figures in *Table 24* do not tell us how many of the subjects had ever received each type of sentence, but how offenders were dealt with. Some offenders had received all forms of sentence, some only one. The proportion of sentences falling into either the probation or residential category was similar, in both cases 40 per cent. But fining was proportionately more common for offences committed by participants, and attendance centres less so. Proportionately more control offences received milder sentences ('discharge'

Figure 1   Diagrammatic representation of the research design

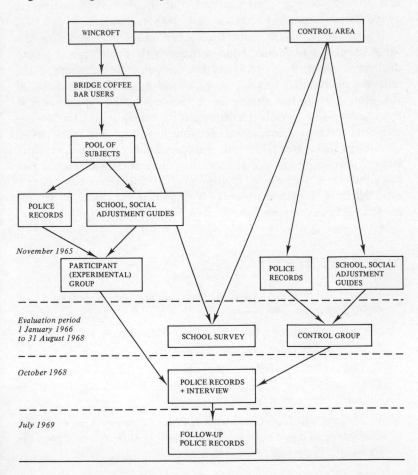

or 'caution'), 22 per cent as against 15 per cent. Overall the differences in sentences were not significantly different ($\chi^2 = 4.108\ P > .30$).

Ten (40 per cent) of the offending participants had committed their first offence by the age of 12 years. By this age somewhat less (32 per cent) of the offending controls had appeared in court. However, the average age of first offence was similar in both cases, participants 13 years, controls 12 years 11 months. The length of time between first offence and the start of the evaluation period was calculated: 15 (60 per cent) of the participants and 26 (68 per cent) of the controls committed their first detected offence between one and twelve months prior to 1 January 1966. On average the participants committed their first offence one year eight months before the start of the evaluation period. For controls the period was one year seven months.

It may be useful in summarizing this chapter to underline the variables taken into consideration in choosing the control group, and to distinguish them from the variables that may be relevant to the outcome of the study but were only known about after the choice of the control group had already been made. Only the type of area as measured by certain social statistics and by delinquency rates, the age and sex of the subjects, their delinquent history and their social adjustment score were taken into consideration in choosing the control group. However, the choice of area, using crude social indices, was seen subsequently as a wise one, corroborated by social and cultural data gathered from the schools survey. It may help the reader to see the research design in diagrammatic form in *Figure 1* on p. 201.

NOTES AND REFERENCES

1 See D. E. G. Plowman, What are the Outcomes of Casework?, *Social Work* **26** (1), January 1969.

2 See Stanton Wheeler (ed.), *Controlling Delinquents* (John Wiley, New York, 1968) for a review of this work.

3 E. Powers and H. Witmer, *An Experiment in the Prevention of Delinquency: The Cambridge–Somerville Youth Study* (Columbia University Press, New York, 1951).

4 W. McCord and J. McCord, with I. Zola, *Origins of Crime: A New Evaluation of the Cambridge–Somerville Youth Study* (Columbia University Press, New York, 1969).

5 R. E. Stanfield and B. Maher, Clinical and Actuarial Predictions of Juvenile Delinquency, in Stanton Wheeler (ed.), *Controlling Delinquents.*

6 W. B. Miller, The Impact of a Community Group Work Program on Delinquent Corner Groups, *Social Service Review* 21 (4), December 1957; also, The Impact of a 'Total Community' Delinquency Control Project, *Social Problems* 10, 1962.

7 W. B. Miller, Delinquency Prevention and Organizational Relations, in Stanton Wheeler (ed.), *Controlling Delinquents.*

8 See *Reports of the Seattle Atlantic Street Center* (April 1968) especially T. Ikeda, Effectiveness of Social Work with Acting-out Youth (obtainable from the Centre).

9 See *Reports of the Seattle Atlantic Street Center* (June 1968), W. C. Berleman and T. W. Steinburn, Delinquency Prevention Experiments: A Reappraisal.

10. C. D. Tait and E. F. Hodges, *Delinquents, their Families and the Community* (Springfield, Ill., Charles Thomas, 1962).

11. H. J. Meyer, E. F. Borgatta, and W. C. Jones, *Girls at Vocational High* (Russell Sage Foundation, New York, 1965).

12 M. Craig and P. W. Furst, What happens after Treatment? *Social Service Review* 39, June 1965.

13 See L. T. Wilkins, *Social Policy, Action, and Research* (Tavistock Publications, London, 1967), Appendix 2.

14 C. F. Jesness, *The Jesness Inventory: Manual* (Consulting Psychologists Press, Palo Alto, Calif., 1966).

15 Reports of the Medical Officer of Health, the City of Manchester.

16 Ibid.

17 List of 12 possessions: telephone; car; bath; refrigerator; vacuum-cleaner; television; spin-dryer; tape-recorder; motor-cycle; radio; record-player; washing-machine.

18 Olive Banks, *The Sociology of Education* (Batsford, London, 1958).

19 Eight statements were listed, four expressing pro-school values, for example, "a good school report or leaving certificate is a help when getting a job", and four expressing anti-school values, for example, "success in school hardly matters as it has little to do with success

in life". Respondents either 'disagreed' or 'agreed' with each statement and were scored overall from −8 to +8, the latter indicating a high value placed on school and education.

20 W. B. Miller, Lower-class Culture as a Generating Milieu of Gang Delinquency, *Journal of Social Issues* 14 (3), 1958.

21 Wilkins, *Social Policy, Action, and Research.*

22 The justification for group matching was found at the time in the Friedman Two-Way Analysis by Ranks. See S. Siegel, *Non-Parametric Statistics in the Behavioural Sciences*, pp. 166–73. This analysis has, however, not been used because of its complexity.

23 J. T. Sellin and M. E. Wolfgang, *The Measurement of Delinquency* (John Wiley, New York, 1964).

6 · The results

The logic underlying the first part of this chapter is that at the start of the evaluation period two groups, experimental and control, have been shown to be comparable with reference to certain factors, in particular, those factors that were seen as a potential influence on the outcome of the treatment programme. The factors on which the groups differed were noted. Therefore, in theory any difference that can be shown to exist at the end of the project might be attributed to the treatment programme. But, since the experiment did not take place under ideal laboratory conditions, results will have to be interpreted carefully to ensure that the difference was not the cause of some extraneous variable rather than the project. For example, it is a possibility that any success in terms of delinquency prevention could be accounted for by the efforts of other intervening social work agencies; although the two groups were matched at the start of the project, obviously it was not possible to control for such intervening variables as the effects of a probation order. All that can be done is to try to separate out for such variables; this involves some sub-group analysis.

Obviously the time-span over which success is measured is important; thus it could be that an absence of significant positive results at the end of the treatment programme occurred not because of the failure of that programme, but because its effects take time to appear. The converse could also occur, short-term success being matched by long-term failure. This is a strong possibility, since withdrawal of fieldwork support from participants could mean a return to former behaviour patterns. Ideally, a number of follow-up studies should take place at various intervals. The financing and time schedule of this present study made it possible to have only one major follow-up at the end of the fieldwork, and a follow-up on delinquency alone about one year later.

The chapter is divided into two major parts: the first considers the question of overall success by comparing the two groups; the second (p. 227) examines the differential success within the participant groups by relating it to variable amounts of exposure to the treatment process, utilizing the type of data presented in Chapter 5.

Although the aims of the social-work programme were laid down, it was necessary to translate these into measurable concepts.

The Cambridge—Somerville Study, in its evaluation, considered three points: the behaviour of the boy; the amount of change that had taken place; and the boy's own opinions on how (or if) the counselling had helped him. As the authors state (p. 345), 'The method, of course, does call for the making of many subjective judgements, including the primary one concerning the effectiveness of the work in individual cases'.

In the present study it was decided to avoid subjective measures as far as possible, because of their unreliability. To have asked the workers to present case material on their clients in order to allow others to rate their success was certain to have led to bias, and to have asked the workers themselves to rate their clients' success would have produced even more bias. Nor would it seem any more reliable to ask the clients themselves whether they felt they had derived any benefit from the programme. Indeed, as was made clear in the last chapter, in order to avoid bias great care was taken in the final interview to ensure that the interviewees were unaware of the real purposes of the survey.

Evaluation in the present project consisted of data from two sources: police records and interviews with the boys. The interview comprised the Jesness Inventory (see Chapter 5), a self-report on delinquency and seven questions on personal adjustment such as relationship with peers, leisure patterns, and relationship to the opposite sex. The final part of the evaluation consisted of a further check on detected delinquency eleven months after the social work had ceased (see Appendix III).

Police records had been used at the end of each year to assess trends in delinquency and for the final evaluation it was decided to supplement police records with a self-report of delinquency from all subjects; so consideration must be given to the results of these two measures of delinquency, taking the official statistics first.

INTER-GROUP COMPARISONS

(i) In Chapter 5 detected delinquency prior to 1 January 1966 in both groups was examined along several separate measures. This will be reported in respect of the period January 1966 to July 1968 [1] using the following hypotheses:

(a) A greater proportion of control group members will appear in court.

(b) Control group members who appear before the court will have more convictions.

(c) Those convicted in the control group will have committed more offences.

(d) Those convicted in the control group will have more offences taken into consideration.

(e) Those convicted in the control group will have committed more serious offences.

(a) A greater proportion of control group members will appear in court

This measure is concerned with the number of subjects in each group who have appeared in court *after* the onset of the treatment programme. The number of such appearances during this period is not taken into account, nor is the seriousness of the crime. Thus, a subject who has appeared in court five times is only counted once. During the period January 1966 to July 1968, 20 of the participants (37.0 per cent) and 41 of the controls (55.4 per cent) appeared before a court on at least one occasion for a criminal offence. Thus, the difference is statistically significant at the .05 level [2] and hypothesis (a) is confirmed. [3]

This was the cumulative appearance rate. *Figure 2* plots the rate for the end of 1965, the end of 1966, the end of 1967, the end of the evaluation period, and one year later.

It will be remembered that both controls and participants started the evaluation period with roughly the same proportion of subjects in each group who had ever been convicted: 46.3 per cent (participants) and 48.6 per cent (controls). Looking at the curves on the graph, both rates of appearance by July 1968 have begun to flatten out, but the distance between them has still continued to increase (5.8 per cent in 1966, 18.1 per cent in 1967 and 18.4 per cent in 1968), even if only marginally, at the end. Thus, at the end of the project there was a significant difference in the appearance rate in court of the participant group in comparison with that of the control group. By July 1969, however, this was no longer significant (see Appendix III) though still in the desired direction.

Figure 2   Comparison of the appearance rates for the two groups, by
years, 1 January 1966 to 31 July 1969

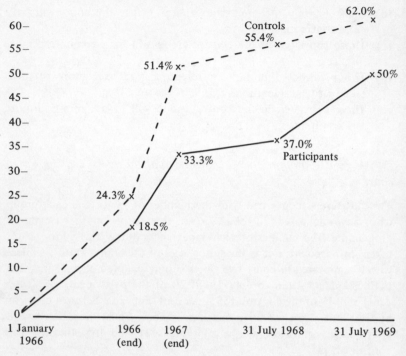

An important intervening variable, the effect of which will be
discussed later, is that once a boy receives some form of residential
training he is no longer, at least theoretically, at risk. This is not so
relevant here where only the first conviction counts, but it is more so in
the remaining comparisons.

*(b) Control group members who appear before the court will have
more convictions*

It will be remembered from Chapter 5 that remands were not counted
under the heading of court appearances. The number of court
appearances made by members of the two groups is in *Table 25*.

Convicted (here referring to convictions during the evaluation
period, irrespective of those before) participants had a total of some 38
court appearances, an average of 1.80 per offender, and the convicted
controls 105 appearances, an average of 2.56 (averages for the groups as

Table 25 Number of court appearances (excluding remands)
January 1966 to July 1968

Number of appearances	Participants	Controls
1	10	13
2	5	11
3	3	5
4	1	7
5	1	3
6	0	2
Total	20	41

a whole are participants 0.72, controls 1.42). This difference was
statistically significant at the .05 level ($t = 1.997$, $P < .05$). The figures
for the period prior to January 1966 were participants 2.16 and
controls 2.29, the difference not being significant.

The second hypothesis, that convicted controls were convicted more
frequently, is confirmed.

*(c) Those convicted in the control group will have committed more
offences*

Offences which are 'taken into consideration' at a court appearance are
not included here for the reasons given in Chapter 5, but are dealt with
separately later.

Table 26 Number of offences committed January 1966 to
July 1968 (excluding offences 'taken into consideration')

	Participants	Controls
1 & 2	12	15
3 & 4	4	9
5 & 6	1	7
7 & 8	2	6
9 & 10	1	2
11 and more	0	2
Total no. of boys	20	41
Total no. of offences	63	179

The 20 'convicted' participants committed 63 offences in all, an average of 3.2 and the figures for the control group were 179 and 4.4. This difference just fails to be significant at the .05 level ($t = 1.425$, $.10 > P > .05$). The figures for the pre-evaluation period were participants 3.0 and controls 3.2, the difference being not significant (see page 194). Thus on statistical grounds the hypothesis must be rejected, but the trend was for participants to commit fewer offences than control group members.

(d) Those convicted in the control group will have more offences taken into consideration

It will be remembered that the two groups differed, but not significantly, on this measure when the period prior to 1966 was considered, with the participant group exceeding the control. The figures for the evaluation period are given in *Table 27*.

Table 27 Number of offenders with offences 'taken into consideration' January 1966 to July 1968

Number of offences	Participants	Controls
0	12	29
1−2	2	4
3−5	3	2
5−10	0	2
11−20	1	2
21+	2	2
	20	41

The 20 convicted participants had 128 offences taken into consideration (an average per offender, excluding those with no cases considered, of 16). The 41 convicted controls had 133 offences taken into consideration with a comparable average of 11.1.

The difference is in the reverse direction to that predicted by the hypothesis above and a statistical test is therefore not applicable. As in the period prior to January 1966 a greater proportion of convicted participants, 8 out of 20, or 40 per cent, had offences taken into consideration than was the case for controls, 12 out of 41, or 29 per cent. However, in the pre-evaluation period two subjects in the participant group accounted for four-fifths of the total TICs in the group.

The three previous measures have shown differences in the opposite direction and it is rather puzzling that there has been no similar movement here. The reasons for the apparent failure of the programme to have an effect on this item are not at all clear. Possible reasons will be discussed later.

(e) Those convicted in the control group will have committed more serious offences

In Chapter 5 the method of dividing offences into two categories, 'serious' and 'minor', using a modification of the classification developed by Sellin and Wolfgang, was indicated. Here the same system of classification is used. The category into which any particular offence falls is given in Appendix II. The distribution of the 'serious' and 'minor' offences committed by each group is given in *Table 28*.

Table 28 Distribution of offenders by the number of 'serious' and 'minor' offences committed January 1966 to July 1968

| | Participants n = 63 offences | | Controls n = 179 offences | |
	serious	minor	serious	minor
0	6	5	5	15
1	6	8	11	5
2	3	4	9	11
3	1	2	8	3
4	1	1	3	1
5	2	0	1	2
6	0	0	3	0
7 and more	1	0	1	4
Total	20	20	41	41

Of the 63 offences committed by participants, 37 (59 per cent) were classified as serious. The proportion for the 179 control offences was 53 per cent. (The figure for the pre-evaluation period was 85 per cent for both groups.) This difference is the reverse of that predicted. The mean number of serious (and minor) offences per convicted group is a reflection of the difference between the means of total offences for the two groups. It is not such a valid comparison as the one made above. For the two groups as a whole, participants committed an average of 1.85 serious crimes and 1.30 minor. The control figures were 2.32 and 2.05. If only those members of each group who committed serious offences (i.e. if the 6 participants and 5 controls who did not commit serious offences are excluded) are considered there is an identical 2.64 per group.

To avoid the influence of the total number of offences it is possible to examine the data, not by offences, but by offenders. Offenders are divided into three categories: those committing serious offences only (serious); those committing both serious and minor offences (serious and minor); and those committing minor offences only (minor). The results of this classification are given in *Table 29*.

Of control offenders 88 per cent committed at least one serious crime, but the percentage for participants was 70 per cent. However, the overall difference, though in the expected direction, is not significant ($\chi^2 = 1.80$, $P > .10$). The proportions for the pre-evaluation period were 96 per cent (serious, and serious and minor) and 97 per cent.

In addition to the information from the official records the subjects in the final survey (see Chapter 5, p. 183) were asked to complete a self-report on delinquency. Respondents were asked to indicate which of sixteen delinquent acts they had committed. These were as follows:

(1) assault
(2) carried an offensive weapon
(3) taken drugs
(4) breaking and entering
(5) shoplifting
(6) larceny from unoccupied dwellings
(7) receiving
(8) consumed alcohol on licensed premises under age
(9) driven under-age
(10) embezzled from work
(11) larceny from slot machines
(12) take and drive away
(13) malicious damage
(14) neglected to pay fare on public transport
(15) slept out
(16) larceny from unattended vehicles.

The choice of individual items for the self-report was determined partly by previous research, partly by knowledge of what were common crimes amongst juveniles, and partly by how easily the crimes could be described in simple language. Answers were divided into three categories: never; once or twice; three or more times. This self-report

Table 29 Classification of offenders by type of offences (figures in brackets are percentages)

	Participants	*Controls*
Serious only	(25) 5	(37) 15
Serious and minor	(45) 9	(51) 21
Minor only	(30) 6	(12) 5
Total	(100) 20	(100) 41

formed the final part of the interview schedule, by which time it was hoped that the interviewer would have established a good rapport with the respondent. The interviewer was instructed that the respondent must complete this section himself. During the time he was doing this the interviewer was asked to check over the answers on the rest of the schedule and not to watch the respondent. It will be remembered that the interview took place in the relative privacy of the interviewer's car. The self-report had a very simple design and the questions were very carefully worded to ensure that the poor reader would not be at too great a disadvantage. The questions were so ordered that the less serious were placed first 'Have you ever travelled on a bus or train and deliberately not paid your fare?' and the more serious later.

The major difficulty with self-reporting of delinquency is under- and over-reporting, but this should equal itself out between the groups. The number of offences admitted by each group is given in *Table 30*. All respondents admitted to at least two offences and none to all sixteen.

Table 30 Number reporting delinquent acts and number of delinquent acts admitted

	Participants	*Controls*
2–3	12	3
4–6	12	19
7–9	15	19
10–12	7	14
13–15	5	8
Incomplete answer	0	1
No answer	3	10
Total	54	74

It will be seen that delinquency was almost universal in both groups according to their own admission.

The mean number of crimes admitted by participants was 6.90 which was less than the figure for the controls, 8.40. This difference was significant at the .025 level ($t = 2.21$).

Strictly speaking this is a measure of the range of crime, that is, the number of different types of delinquent acts committed. Some subjects may have committed the individual crimes more than once and this needs to be examined.

A more valid comparison with the police records of delinquency is obtained by analysing the three categories of response to each question. From this it will be possible to discover whether controls claim to have committed the crimes more frequently than participants, in addition to having committed a wider range. This information is obtained by scoring 1 for a 'once or twice' answer and 2 for 'three or more times'. This provides a total of frequency commission score for each group. The higher the score obtained by the group, the more frequently will its members have committed the delinquent acts. The score for the participants was an average of 9.61 and for the controls 11.87. The difference was significant at the .025 level ($t = 1.993$) as it was for the range of offences committed . Although the police records had not revealed a statistical difference between the two groups on number of offences committed, the difference was in the same direction as the two above measures. The trend from the source of the official statistics is thus confirmed by the two significant differences on this separate measure of offences committed by members of the two groups. There is thus strong evidence for the acceptance of the hypothesis that the control group committed proportionately more offences than the participants in the evaluation period.

As in the analysis of police records the self-reported crimes can be categorized as 'serious' and 'minor'; 11 types of crime were classified as serious, 5 as minor. Of the total number of acts admitted by participants, exactly 50 per cent were classified as serious and the same percentage for the controls: participants reported 245 serious crimes out of 491 crimes, controls reported 376 out of 748. This is in line with the findings from police records. The distribution of self-reported crime divided into the 'serious' and 'minor' categories is given in *Table 31*.

From the evidence in *Table 31* on the mean number of (total) acts admitted and the proportions falling into the 'serious' and 'minor' categories it is to be expected that there will be significant differences

Table 31 Gravity of delinquent acts admitted

	Participants		Controls	
	serious	minor	serious	minor
0 & 1	8	17	1	14
2 & 3	8	25	9	36
4 & 5	15	9	19	13
6 & 7	12	–	13	–
8 & 9	3	–	14	–
10 & 11	5	–	7	–
No answer	3	3	11	11
Total 'offenders'	54	54	74*	74*
Total 'offences'	245	246	376	372

* One control failed to complete this section of the interview.

in the mean numbers of serious and minor acts admitted, with the controls scoring higher in each instance. This was found to be the case for the serious acts (means: participants 4.80; controls 5.97), $t = 2.196$, $P < .25$, but not for the minor acts (means: participants 2.14; controls 2.43), $t = 1.248$, $P > .10$. When these two categories are scored for frequency of commission a similar pattern is found. Controls come out higher in each case being significant for the serious category (the figures are participants 6.49, controls 8.14; $t = 1.92$, $P < .05$) but not for the minor (the figures are participants 3.11, controls 3.73; $t = 0.84$, $P > .20$).

All subjects in both groups admitted at least one serious crime, so it is not possible to divide each group into serious and minor offenders as was done previously.

The self-report substantiated the findings from the police records concerning delinquency in the two groups, but revealed proportionately more significant differences. Although none of the possible intervening variables have been examined, and this difference in behaviour cannot yet be attributed to the treatment programme, it would appear that there was a statistically significant difference between the two groups at the end of the evaluation period with respect to certain measures of delinquency. Five different aspects of delinquency were investigated using the official records and the self-report. In three of the areas (proportions of each group convicted, number of court appearances, and number of offences) there was strong statistical evidence of a significant difference between the two groups. There was some evidence, though not conclusive, for a higher proportion of minor offenders in the participant group. But this was counterbalanced by the proportion of offences that were 'serious'. When number of offences taken into consideration was examined the difference was not in the expected direction.

(ii) The second part of this inter-group evaluation is concerned with the success of the 'adjustment' aims of the project. This was measured by the Jesness Inventory and a number of factual indicators of adjustment.

Although the Jesness Inventory provided an overall measure of adjustment, it was decided to include in the final interview a number of questions about those areas of the clients' behaviour with which the social-work programme has been specifically concerned. This was a, direct attempt to measure to what extent participants had made a 'dynamic adjustment' to work, parents, leisure, and peers. The questions in the final interview that dealt with these topics were phrased as far as possible in terms of behaviour rather than attitudes, since it was felt that questions about behaviour would be meaningful to respondents and would produce more valid answers. For example, on the question of adjustment to work, subjects were not asked how they liked their work but how many jobs they had had and how many times they had been unemployed. Attitudes may determine behaviour, but measurement of the behaviour is seen as being the more valid method of evaluating differences in adjustment. This is particularly relevant to this part of the evaluation since it would have been necessary to develop new attitude measures had greater importance been placed on attitudes.

An important area of the social-work programme was that of employment. Two measures of adjustment to the world of work were included in the final interview: the number of jobs held and periods of unemployment.

To use the number of jobs held by a subject as an index of adjustment can be misleading, since it makes the assumption that to change jobs is a sign of maladjustment. It is to be expected that the adolescent will make a number of changes of employment, especially at the onset of his working career, as he tries to find the job that suits him best. The fact that a boy remains in the same job for a number of years could indeed be a sign of maladjustment rather than adjustment. The problem then becomes one of where to draw the dividing line; how many jobs in what period of time must a young person have before he can be adjudged to have failed to adjust to the demands of the work role?

Apart from the above theoretical discussion two technical points must be mentioned. First, in the interview itself it was necessary to try and allow for memory bias, especially amongst those respondents who had held large numbers of jobs. To this end interviewers were instructed to take respondents through each year of his life since leaving school and to note the number of jobs held in each year. Second, since not all subjects were available for employment for the same period of time it was necessary to make allowances for this. Thus, time spent in residential training and unemployed was subtracted from the total time since leaving school. The question of unemployment is dealt with later.

At the time of the interview two participants were still in full-time education. Three controls had never been employed: two had had a continuous period of residential training since they had reached the age of 15; and one, although he had completed his education, had not subsequently obtained a job. These five subjects are excluded from the following analysis. The 61 remaining controls had a total of 339 jobs, a mean of 5.6 per boy; and the 49 participants a total of 252 jobs and a mean of 5.1. But as suggested earlier it is necessary to make certain adjustments for the period of time available for employment. Originally it was felt that subjects who had been 'available' for less than twelve months should be excluded from the comparison. Two respondents, both controls, were found to have been 'available' for less than twelve months. Both of these boys had spent time in residential training and one had been unemployed for a considerable period of time. But during their 'availability' (one month and five months) both had more than five jobs. Despite the theoretical point made earlier, that job changes in the early part of a working career might not be a good indication of subsequent adjustment, it was fact that both these boys had made a poor adjustment to work and should therefore be included in the analysis.

Table 32 gives the average period of time spent in each job for each subject. This is calculated by dividing the total time available for employment for each subject by the number of jobs reported. The average length of time spent in each job was 9.0 months for participants and 8.3 for controls. Although controls keep their jobs on average for

Table 32 Mean period of time (in months) spent in each job

	Participants	Controls
Less than 3 months	5	15
3 but less than 7	16	20
7 but less than 12	11	10
12 but less than 18	8	8
18 but less than 24	7	2
24 or more	2	6
Never employed	2	3
Not known	3	10
Total	54	74

shorter periods of time the difference was not significant, $t = 0.478, P > .30$.

To equate for the total period of time available for employment, which will differ from subject to subject, a similar calculation was made as for the number of jobs. *Table 33* gives the percentage of time available for employment that was spent actually in unemployment. Thus, if a subject had been available for work for twenty-five months but had been unemployed for ten he would have spent 40 per cent of this time unemployed. Because, for the reasons given above, the interviewer only asked for the three longest periods of unemployment, the figures given will not refer to the total time unemployed but only a proportion of it in the case of certain subjects. In *Table 33* these

Table 33 Percentage of time spent in unemployment

%	Participants	Controls
1—5	7	15
6—10	9	7
11—15	5	2
16—20	3	6
21 and above	1	5
Not known	7	13
Total	32	48
Mean	9.1	14.7

subjects in both groups who had never been unemployed are excluded.

When the period of time unemployed was calculated as above, it was found that on average controls had spent a greater percentage of the time available for employment actually unemployed. The mean percentages were 9.1 per cent and 14.7 per cent, the latter being the figure for controls. However, this difference failed to be significant ($t = 1.263, P > .10$).

There appears to be, by the measures chosen, no statistically significant impact by the social-work programme on the participants' adjustment to work, although there would seem to be a tendency for fewer of them to have been unemployed and for these to have been unemployed for shorter periods.

The adjustment of subjects to parents was measured by two questions in the final interview. The first attempted a fairly direct evaluation of relationships with parents. But in order to elicit a more truthful answer to the direct question the schedule led up to it with two preliminary questions. It was felt that a direct question without previous probing would produce answers of a non-committal nature. The second question was concerned with the frequency and length of time for which subjects had left home 'after a quarrel'. As an indirect measure of relationship with parents it is possibly a more valid indication than the first question, since it is not so likely to receive a guarded answer.

The answers to the direct question on relationship with parents were coded into a five-point scale and this is given in *Table 34*.

The proportions of subjects answering in each category are practically the same for each group, and by this superficial measure it must be

Table 34 Reported relationship with parents (figures in brackets are percentages)

	Participants	*Controls*
Very good	11 (22)	14 (23)
Good	23 (45)	27 (42)
Neutral	12 (24)	16 (25)
Poor	5 (10)	4 (6)
Very poor	0 (0)	3 (5)
Not known	3	10
Total	54	74

Table 35   Number of times left home (those who had
left home only)

	Participants	Controls
1	9	6
2	4	4
3 or more	2	5
Not known	3	10
Total	18	25
Mean	2.3	2.8

concluded that the social-work programme was ineffective in securing a better relationship with parents. The indirect measures showed, however, more promising outcomes, for although a higher proportion of participants had left home 'after a quarrel' with parents, 77 per cent as against 71 per cent, the controls who had left home had done so on more occasions.

Table 35 shows that those controls who had left home had done so an average of 2.8 occasions; the figure for participants was 2.3. The difference was not, however, significant, $t = 0.536, P > .25$.

The longest period spent away from home 'after a quarrel' varied considerably from one night to 40 weeks, but it was noticeable that more of the participants returned home after a relatively short period, one week or less as *Table 36* shows. Two-thirds of the participants were back home within a week or less of leaving, but in the case of controls, over two-thirds spent more than a week away before returning. This difference, using the Fisher test, was significant at the .05 level.

Table 36   Longest period spent away from home 'after a
quarrel'

	Participants	Controls
One week or less	10	4
2–4 weeks	2	2
5–8 weeks	0	2
More than 8 weeks	3	7
Not known	3	10
Total	18	25

On the first measure of adjustment to the home situation there was no difference between the two groups on reported relationships to parents. But when leaving home 'after a quarrel' was considered as an indication of this relationship, some tentative evidence was found for participants who had 'ever' left home left less repeatedly than controls. Although this difference was not significant, when the length of time spent away from home was considered (i.e. the longest period away from home), it was found that participants returned home significantly more quickly than controls. From this evidence it is suggested that although the social-work programme did not prevent tensions arising in the family for the participant, in cases where such tensions led to the boy leaving home he was helped to return home more quickly.

The final area considered by these indicators of adjustment is leisure and peer relationships. The difficulty from the research point of view was how to measure adjustment in this area. The questions included on the schedule used in the final interview were all of a direct nature. Thus respondents were asked if they had a group of friends they 'regularly went around with', if they had a 'steady girl-friend', and if they 'attended any form of clubs or organizations'. Certainly the first two are biased in favour of positive responses, since to admit a negative answer can mean loss of status to the respondent. The third, although it was intended to take a wide range of formal organizations, not merely youth clubs, is not necessarily a valid measure of adjustment to leisure. However, these weaknesses were realized when the questions were formulated, but in the context of the form of the final interview no suitable alternatives were found. *Table 37* indicates that the proportion of subjects in each group claiming to attend some form of club in their leisure time was approximately equal.

It was mentioned in Chapter 4 that many of the participants had no

Table 37   Leisure: attendance at clubs (figures in brackets are percentages of known figure)

| | All ages | |
	participants	controls
Attenders	14 (27)	16 (25)
Non-attenders	37 (73)	48 (75)
Not known	3	10
Total	54 (100)	74 (100)

stable relationships with peers. It was also noted that many had difficulty in making relationships with the opposite sex. In the final survey proportionately more controls (77 per cent) claimed to have a regular group of friends, the figure for participants being 63 per cent. The direction of the difference was reversed for those claiming a steady relationship with a member of the opposite sex, participants 53 per cent, controls 45 per cent. This difference was not significant, $\chi^2 = 0.391$, $P > .25$. There are reasons for believing that, especially in working-class youth culture, close relations with friends of the same sex are mutually exclusive of close relations with the opposite sex, and that in terms of maturation the boy who has advanced to courtship will have left his regular group of mates behind him. If this is so the above figures are indicative of movement in the right direction.

The final set of comparisons to be made between the two groups is on the Jesness Inventory. The Inventory provides an overall score, the Asocial Index, and ten sub-scales which measure personality characteristics. Although the Asocial Index is derived from the sub-scales, it is possible to compare the two groups on each scale. The Inventory is relatively new to this country and although considerable work with it has taken place in the United States, its country of origin, less has occurred here. From the work of Mott (1969) [4] it was decided to compare the two groups on the Asocial Index and three of the sub-scales (those demonstrated as distinguishing between English samples in approved school and borstal training). On all of the scales used here the higher the score obtained the greater the degree of maladjustment, but on other of the sub-scales the score is in the reverse direction.

From the mean scores on the Asocial Index, which measures 'a generalized tendency to behave in ways which transgress established rules', it was found that controls were more 'asocial'. The mean score for participants was 19.88 and 20.63 for controls, but this difference was not significant, $t = 0.783$, $P > .20$.

None of the scores on the three sub-scales produced a significant difference in the expected direction. The social maladjustment subscale, which measures 'the extent to which the individual shares attitudes expressed by persons who show an inability to meet in socially approved ways, the demands of living', gave a score of 26.70 for controls and 26.71 for participants. On the alienation sub-scale ('the presence of distrust and estrangement in relationships with others, especially with authority figures'), the controls (11.98) scored slightly lower than the participants (12.08). Scores on the manifest aggression sub-scale (a measure of 'the perception of unpleasant feelings, especially feelings of anger, and discomfort concerning their presence and control') were in the reverse to that expected with the mean for participants (17.04), exceeding that for the controls (16.16).

In view of the experience of Mott and others in their use of the Jesness Inventory it is disappointing that the scores used here should fail to discriminate between the two groups. This lack of difference is even more difficult to explain since data on delinquency in the two groups given earlier did show a significant difference on certain measures. The means on the Asocial Index did differ in the expected direction, but this was not significant. Two possible reasons for this are suggested: first, a technical point − it may be that although the Inventory can discriminate between delinquents and non-delinquents, and various degrees of delinquency such as probationers and borstal and approved school inmates, it is not sensitive enough to do so between the two groups compared here; a second point, and this will be developed further at the end of this chapter, is that the Inventory is basically a measure of attitudes. Measures previously used in this chapter have concentrated on behaviour. It may be that changes in behaviour precede those in attitude and that the major short·term influence of the social-work programme has been to influence the former with little or no effect on the latter.

INTERVENING VARIABLES

As suggested earlier, it is possible that any improvements that may have occurred in the participant group may have arisen not because of the treatment programme but because of some unexpected difference between the two groups that occurred after the start of that programme. The example given was of the efforts of other treatment agencies working with subjects. Obviously an approved school or probation order made during the evaluation period was something that could not be controlled. It has been seen in Chapter 5 that the two groups were fairly comparable with respect to the type of sentence they received prior to January 1966, but what happened after this date was a matter of chance so far as the research was concerned.

Before investigating this topic it is necessary to take into account another factor that is potentially more important to the results of this study. Early in 1969 it was discovered in a public discussion of the project that during the first eleven months of the evaluation period the Police Research and Development Branch of the Home Office conducted an experiment in Wincroft and the surrounding area. The Chairman of the Youth Development Trust and the project director had discussions with a number of police officers in 1963 and 1964 and intermittently thereafter, but the confidential nature of the experiment presumably meant that its existence could not be revealed to them until after its completion.

The experiment attempted 'to discover any relationship which may occur between the level of foot patrolling' and the level of criminal activity 'measured in terms of crimes prevented, arrests made, traffic offences detected and traffic accidents prevented'. The method was to vary the number of men per beat from zero to four. A control area was used. Manchester was only one of four cities which took part in the study and it is thus difficult to say how far the results as a whole are applicable to Manchester. In general, increasing the manpower above one man per beat did not result in a reduction in crime, although there was some tentative evidence that increasing the level of patrol directly from one to three men per beat did result in a reduction in crime. Abstracting from the results for Manchester alone it was found that whereas the number of crimes reported in the control area rose by 14 per cent during the year of the police experiment (December 1965 – November 1966) compared to the previous twelve months, those in Wincroft rose by 33 per cent. This was the only measure from Manchester that could be extracted from the total results and it does not suggest that the experiment prevented crime in Wincroft. The experiment was concerned with offenders of all ages, not only juveniles, and no breakdown of age of offenders detected in Wincroft is available.

Originally the study had been planned to carry out two sets of experiments simultaneously. To this end three areas were chosen, matched by beat size and population. The area that was not used was the same as that chosen for the control area in the present project. This provides further confirmation of the similarity between Wincroft and the control area. The area used as a control in the beat-patrol experiment, although perhaps suitable for its purposes, was not considered suitable to compare with Wincroft because of the presence of an immigrant community.

It was fortunate that with the results of the above experiment demonstrated that crime level was insensitive to increased level of foot patrol. If the opposite had been found to be the case then it could have been claimed that it was this rather than the social-work programme that produced the changes observed in delinquency amongst participants.

The second possible area of uncontrolled influence on the two groups is in the intervention of other social-work agencies. The break-down of sentences for the two groups in the period prior to January is given in *Table 24* (p. 200). During the evaluation period, the 20 convicted participants received a total of 41 sentences and the 41 controls 105. Here the interest is not in the sentences themselves, but in the offenders receiving them. It is possible to compare the two groups by the proportion of subjects with sentences that involved social work (probation orders, detention centres, [5] approved school, and borstal) during the course of the experiment and those not receiving such treatment. *Table 38* gives this information. Boys who received more than one form of social work are only counted once.

Table 38   The experience of social work in the participant and control groups (percentages in brackets)

	Participants		Controls	
	at Jan 1966	by July 1968	at Jan 1966	by July 1968
Social work	15 (28)	21 (39)	19 (26)	30 (41)
No social work	39 (72)	33 (61)	55 (74)	44 (59)
Totals	54 (100)	54 (100)	74 (100)	74 (100)

By the end of July 1968, the end of the evaluation period, 39 per cent of participants and 41 per cent of controls had received some form of social work. The proportions are almost identical but with slightly more of the controls being recipients. It cannot, therefore, be argued that the changes observed in delinquency between the two groups was the result of a greater proportion of participants being in receipt of social work from other agencies.

It is possible to divide the social work into three types, probation, detention centre, and approved school/borstal. The difficulty here is that some boys will have received two or three types of treatment.

Where this occurs the boy is classified by that treatment involving the greatest amount of contact. The amount of contact involved in each form of treatment is ranked as follows: probation; detention centre; approved school/borstal; with the latter providing the maximum.

Table 39   Types of social work received during the evaluation period

	Participants	*Controls*
Probation*	14 (67)	13 (43)
Detention Centre	2 (9)	5 (17)
Approved School/Borstal	5 (24)	12 (40)
Total	21 100	30 100

* The Principal Probation Officer of Manchester has kindly supplied the following information. The 2 supervised for one year received an average of 26 contacts, those 8 supervised for two years an average of 51.6 contacts, and the 3 supervised for three years on average of 55.6 contacts. There is no information on the remaining person.

A greater proportion of controls are found in the approved school/borstal and detention centre categories, although the overall difference is not significant ($\chi^2 = 3.183$, $P > .20$. The type of social work received is often linked to number of court appearances, the more of the latter the further along 'the sentencing tariff' the boy will go.

The figures in *Table 39* are thus not independent of those for delinquency examined earlier in the chapter. On the basis of these, proportionately more controls would be expected to have reached the maximum stage in 'the sentencing tariff'.

Arising out of type of sentence is the amount of time spent by members of each group in residential training, that is 'not at risk'. Although the period in which subjects have the opportunity to commit crimes is theoretically the same for both groups, this is modified in practice by the total amount of time spent by each group in residential training where they are not at risk. Measurement was somewhat complicated here by the fact that some boys committed offences while absconding from approved schools and the period at liberty has to be offset against the total period of training. Fourteen controls spent a total of 174 months in residential training during the evaluation, an average of 2.4 months per (total) group member. Six participants had a total of 79 months residential training, the mean per (total) group member being 1.5 months. Thus it cannot be claimed that the lesser amount of delinquency in the participant group can be accounted for by a lesser period at risk.

Intra-group comparisons

So far the analysis has compared differences between the two groups at the end of the evaluation period. It is now proposed to examine some of the differences within the participant group. The previous analysis regarded the participant group as homogeneous in terms of the treatment variables but, as has been shown in Chapter 4, there was considerable variation among clients in the amount of treatment received, the type of treatment (case, group, etc.) and the type of worker (professional or voluntary).

The questions that it is hoped to answer here, which are perhaps most relevant to the practising social worker, are as follows. Do clients who had different levels of contact have different outcomes on the 'success' variables? In terms of the selection criteria which participants appeared to respond better to the treatment programme? It may be helpful to cast these questions, in terms of hypotheses, as follows:

(a) The greater the amount of contact received the more 'successful' would a client be in terms of the outcome variables.

(b) The treatment programme was more successful with those participants who (i) had a low maladjustment score, (ii) had not previously been convicted, (iii) were youngest at the start of the programme.

These hypotheses are cast in a simple form, but the analysis needed to test them is more complex. Chapter 5 showed that there was a wide variation amongst participants in the number of offences they had committed prior to the start of the evaluation period and in their scores on the Bristol Social Adjustment Guides. Now it is to be expected that the outcome of any particular subject will be at least partly dependent on this prognosis at the start of the evaluation period. Thus it may not be meaningful to compare the outcome of two subjects who have, say, equal amounts of contact but differ widely in their Bristol Social Adjustment Guide score or criminal record at the start of the period. Therefore it will be necessary in the analysis to take into account the differences in prognosis at the start of the project. The difficulty from a practical point of view is that the total number of subjects is only 54 and anything but a two- or three-fold break-down of any variable, that is more than a 2 x 3 table, will produce very small numbers in each of the cells. Because of this the two criteria used for selection of the participants, criminal record and BSAG score (maladjustment), were simply dichotomized as high and low in the attempt to equate for prognosis of 'success'. The cutting-point used in the former measure is no appearances before a court (low) and one or more appearances (high); and in the latter a score of 15 or below (low) and 16 or above (high). The analysis starts using previous delinquency as the prognosis for success and this is then repeated using the maladjustment score of the BSAG.

If the treatment variables were compared with every measure of success this would result in far more data than it is possible to accommodate in this book. Therefore it was decided to use seven of the variables only. Selection was determined by those variables that seemed most relevant to the objectives of the project. The use of convicted delinquency and the Jesness Asocial Index scores need little justification since these measure the delinquency prevention and adjustment aims of the project. The measures of peer-group membership and courtship were included because of the large social development component of the services given (see Chapter 4, p. 172). Problems with employment were included because they also occupied a considerable proportion of the workers' time. It was felt that the best of the three measures available here was the period of time spent in unemployment. This, rather than the frequency of changing jobs or whether or not the participant had 'ever' been unemployed, seemed a more valid index of adjustment to work. The relationship of the adolescent to his parents is included as an increasing area of concern for the workers. Although the family casework sessions (see Chapter 4, p. 168) were not the only occasions when this relationship would be discussed, the increase of this type of session from 5 per cent in 1966 to 11 per cent in 1968 clearly indicates the growth of work in this area. Of the three measures of the subject's relationship with his parents, two are used here: first, the client's own assessment of the relationship; second, the period of time spent away from home after a quarrel. It will be remembered that this measure, rather than the fact that a subject had or had not left home, significantly differentiated between the control and participant group.

The effect of contact

The measure of client-hours (see Chapter 4) was used rather than the frequency of contact, since it was felt that the former gave a better indicator of the total amount of work with clients. Contact was divided into three categories, designated below as high, medium, and low. The following cutting points were used: high equals more than 7 hours of contact per month; medium equals from two hours up to and including 6 hours per month; and low equals less than 2 hours per month.

(a) Previous criminal record   The 54 participants were divided, using the cutting-points given above, into those convicted before 1966 (25 cases) and those who were not (29 cases). Dividing amount of contact into three groups and previous criminal record into two, six sub-groups of participants were formed (*Table 40*). Overall there was no significant

Table 40 An analysis by previous conviction and amount of contact received

	Those convicted before 1 January 1966		Those not convicted before 1 January 1966	
	n	Mean number of hours	n	Mean number of hours
High contact	6	416.2	9	388.4
Medium contact	13	142.3	9	143.7
Low contact	6	11.9	11	14.8
Total	25	176.5	29	170.8

difference between the proportions to be found in each sub-group ($\chi^2 = 2.504$, $P < .25$) nor the mean amount of contact given to (previous) non-delinquents as against delinquents ($t = 0.116$).

Subjects in each of the six sub-groups were divided into those convicted during the evaluation period and those not convicted. (Because of the smallness of numbers in the sub-groups the actual number of persons is shown after every percentage in the following analysis.) Although in the case of both those who had been convicted prior to 1 January 1966 and those who had not, the percentage convicted subsequently rose as contact decreased from high to medium (those previously convicted, high 50 per cent (3), medium 62 per cent (8); those not previously convicted, high 22 per cent (2), medium 44 per cent (4)), the percentage convicted decreased as contact decreased from medium to low (previously convicted equals 33 per cent

(2), not previously convicted equals 9 per cent (1)). None of the differences were significant (Fisher Test) except that proportionately more of those convicted prior to 1 January 1966 were convicted after, compared with the total group not convicted before (previously convicted equals 52 per cent subsequently convicted; previously not convicted equals 24 per cent; $\chi^2 = 3.35, P$ (1-tailed) $< .05$).

This measure distinguished significantly between the control and participant group but not between sub-groups receiving various levels of contact. The tendency for the low contact group to have a low reconviction rate yet for the medium contact group to have a higher rate is puzzling and will be examined later.

Mean scores on the Asocial Index of the Jesness Inventory failed to show any significant difference between the two groups, control and participant. Similarly when scores were dichotomized, using a score of 20 as on the cutting-point, the relationship between high Jesness AI score and level of contact was not in the expected direction in the case of those who had previously been convicted. Thus the following proportions fall in the high Jesness score category for high, medium, and low contact respectively, 67 per cent (4), 67 per cent (8), and 40 per cent (2). The figures for those who had not been convicted previously conform more to the expected pattern, but with the reversal in the low contact group: high equals 22 per cent (2), medium equals 56 per cent (5), low equals 20 per cent (2). As is to be expected from these figures there is a significant difference between previous criminal record and Jesness score (high or low), $\chi^2 = 3.12$, P (1-tailed) $= < .05$.

The inter-group analysis and the measure of friendship and courtship failed to reveal a significant difference, but in the latter measure participants reported more stable relationships with members of the opposite sex than did controls. This transfer from friendships with members of the same sex to ones with the opposite sex, which could well preclude the former, was felt to be an important step in maturation.

Examining the intra-group relationships between friendship and amount of contact received, the proportion in the category who claimed to be without friends increased in the previously convicted group as contact decreased. 33 per cent (2), 43 per cent (6), 80 per cent (6), but the difference failed to be significant on the Fisher Test. For the group who had not previously been convicted, the proportion without friends increased as contact decreased but not so dramatically

(22 per cent, 44 per cent, 30 per cent) and again the difference was not significant. (Unlike the three measures above, this measure was not significantly related to whether or not the subject has been previously convicted.) Thus 48 per cent of the previously convicted group (11) and 32 per cent of the not previously convicted group (9) claim to be without friends, $\chi^2 = 0.728$, P (1-tailed) < .25. Since previous conviction (or non-conviction) did not influence the outcome of this measure the two groups were combined, but although the proportion without friends increased from 27 per cent (4), to 43 per cent (9), to 47 per cent (7) as contact level decreased, the difference was not significant at the .05 level.

Among those who had previously been convicted, the proportion claiming a stable relationship with the opposite sex decreased as level of contact decreased, the proportions being 83 per cent (5), 50 per cent (6), and 40 per cent (2), but this is not statistically significant. A similar decrease is noted for those not previously convicted when contact decreases from high to medium, 78 per cent (6) to 22 per cent (2), but this was not significant (Fisher Test) at the .05 level. But in the low contact group there is a similar reversal of the trend found on the first three measures considered, with the proportion claiming a stable relationship with a member of the opposite sex being 60 per cent (6), although in this instance this is below the proportion for the high contact group. The difference between this measure and whether or not the subject had previously been convicted was very small and not significant. When previous criminal record is ignored the percentages claiming a stable relationship are 80 per cent (12), 38 per cent (8), and 53 per cent (8) as contact decreases. The difference between high and medium levels of contact is significant $\chi^2 = 4.950$, P (1-tailed) < .025, but the reversal of the trend occurs in the low contact group, as can be seen from the above figures.

Of the three measures of relationship with parents only one, period of time away from home after a quarrel, was found to distinguish significantly between the participant and control group. (The answers to the direct question on relationship with parents were combined into two groups, those claiming a good relationship (good) and those claiming a neutral or poor relationship (neutral or poor). For the previously convicted group the proportion claiming a 'good' relationship decreased as level of contact decreased, 67 per cent (4), to 58 per cent (7), to 40 per cent (2), but the differences were not significant. Similarly, for those who were not previously convicted the proportion with a 'good' relationship did not vary markedly with level of contact, though those with high contact had better relationships; the figures were, in decreasing order of contact 88 per cent (8), 70 per cent (7), 67 per cent (6).

A good relationship with parents was not associated with previous conviction/non-conviction ($\chi^2 = 1.2077, P < .15$), but the trend was in the expected direction with 75 per cent (21) of those who had not previously been convicted, against 57 per cent (13) of those convicted, claiming a 'good relationship'. Comparing level of contact with relationship with parents, that is, ignoring whether or not the subject was previously convicted, the percentage claiming a 'good relationship' decreased with contact 80 per cent (12) to 62 per cent (13) to 60 per cent (9), but the overall difference was not significant, $\chi^2 = 1.514$, $P > .25$. Only 4 participants had spent a period longer than 1 week away from home after a quarrel and although this differed significantly from the situation in the control group, there was, if anything, a reverse to the expected relationship with contact. With numbers being so small, previous criminal record was ignored (the difference was not in fact significant on the Fisher Test). As contact decreased so did the proportions staying away from home for longer than one week, from 50 per cent (1) to 25 per cent (2) to 20 per cent (1), which was, as is stated above, the reverse of the predicted direction.

None of the three measures of work-adjustment were significant when the differences between the control and participant group were considered. The measure of adjustment to employment used in the sub-group analysis is length of time spent in unemployment. This is calculated by relating the time spent in unemployment to the length of time available for employment. This is then dichotomized as high and low. In the previously convicted group there is no relationship between level of contact and unemployment rate, the proportions in the high unemployment category are 67 per cent (2), 67 per cent (6), and 50 per cent (1) as contact decreases. For the not previously convicted group the figures are 40 per cent (2), 75 per cent (3), and 33 per cent (1) with contact decreasing. Again the reversal of trend in the low contact group is observed. None of the differences were significant, nor was that between the convicted and non-convicted as a whole.

(b) Previous maladjustment (BSAG) score The second possible method of distinguishing between the prognosis of subjects in the treatment programme is the Bristol Social Adjustment Guide Score.

A maladjustment score was obtained for 48 of the 54 participants during the selection of the treatment group phase of the project, although only 36 were selected as participants because of it. Using a cutting-point of 16 and above, two groups, high and low, are formed. As for the previous analysis each of the two groups were divided into three categories of contact, using the same cutting-points. Six sub-groups were thus formed (*Table 41*).

Table 41　An analysis of maladjustment score at 1 January 1966 and amount of contact received

	High maladjustment score			Low maladjustment score		
	n	*Mean number of hours*	*Mean maladjusted score*	*n*	*Mean number of hours*	*Mean maladjusted score*
High contact	8	394	27.9	6	401	9.8
Medium contact	10	145	27.0	10	146	10.1
Low contact	7	20	21.1	7	12	9.1
Total	25	190	24.4	23	172	9.7

There was no significant difference between the proportions of subjects falling in each group or in the mean number of hours of contact.

In the high prediction (maladjustment score) group, the proportions of subjects convicted during the evaluation period rose from 25 per cent (2) to 50 per cent (5) as contact decreased from high to medium levels and then dropped to 29 per cent (2) at the low level of contact. This is similar to the pattern found when previous convicted/non-convicted was considered. For the low prediction (maladjustment score) group the proportions reconvicted were 33 per cent (2), 60 per cent (6), and 0 per cent (0) with contact decreasing. Again the reversal of the expected trend in the low contact group appeared. Previous prediction on the maladjustment score was not related to subsequent conviction, 36 per cent (9) of the high prediction group being reconvicted and 35 per cent (8) of the low prediction group. In the earlier part of this section contact was compared with most of the variables, ignoring whether or not subjects had been previously convicted, and to repeat this here (i.e. ignoring maladjustment score) would be basically to repeat this earlier exercise, the only difference being that here the maximum size of the group is 6 less than in the former instance.

The effect of using maladjustment score rather than previous conviction is, on the subsequent reconviction measure, to increase the difference between high and medium levels of contact. For previous conviction the figures were 50 per cent (3) and 62 per cent (8) and for maladjusted 25 per cent (2) and 50 per cent (5). This could be produced by the fact that for three of the subjects reconvicted no maladjustment score could be obtained.

On the Asocial Index of the Jesness Inventory which it will be remembered did not differentiate significantly on the inter-group comparison, the scores for both the high and low prediction groups followed a similar pattern. As contact decreased from high to medium, the proportions in both groups (high and low prediction) having a high Asocial Index score rose but then fell again as level of contact decreased further. Thus, the figures for the low prediction group were 33 per. cent (2), 50 per cent (5), and 43 per cent (3) and for the high prediction group 38 per cent (3), 67 per cent (6), and 0 per cent (0). No significant differences in the expected direction were found, nor was there any association between the outcome on the Jesness score and previous prediction; high prediction and high Jesness score equals 39 per cent (9), low prediction and high Jesness score equals 43 per cent (10).

In the high maladjusted group those claiming to be a member of a same sex peer-group declines from 75 per cent (6) to 44 per cent (4) to 33 per cent (2) as contact declines, but in the low prediction group there is no clear association, the figures being 67 per cent (4), 70 per cent (7), and 57 per cent (4). Again none of the differences are significant, nor is the association between previous prediction and having friends ($\chi^2 = 0.359$, $P > .25$) although a greater proportion of the high maladjusted group claim to be without friends, as is to be expected 48 per cent (11) as against 35 per cent (8).

For those with a low prediction the proportion that claimed a steady relationship with a member of the opposite sex declined from 67 per cent (4) to 40 per cent (4) to 29 per cent (2) as level of contact decreased. But, although a similar pattern was found for the high prediction group when contact decreased from high to medium, 75 per cent (6) to 33 per cent (3), there was a rise in the low contact group to 83 per cent (5). None of these results differed significantly. More of the high prediction group claimed to have a stable relationship, 61 per cent (14) as against 43 per cent (10), but again the difference was not significant ($\chi^2 = 0.784, P < .20$).

To discover if any participants seemed to be completely isolated from friends, those who had neither a girl-friend nor a stable group of friends were compared with those who had either or both. For the low prediction group those who had neither type of friend increased as contact decreased, from zero to 20 per cent (2) to 41 per cent (3). In the high prediction group there was no clear pattern with decreasing contact, from zero to 33 per cent (3) to 17 per cent (1). For both the high and low prediction groups as a whole the proportion of isolates was similar, high = 17 per cent (4), low 22 per cent (5) and not significantly different. These two measures were not combined in the previous section and so it is useful here to combine the two prediction categories. When prediction was ignored the percentage of isolates rose from zero to 27 per cent (5) to 31 per cent (4). The difference between high and low contact was significant at the .05 level on the Fisher Test. Similarly, combining medium and low contact levels and comparing the resultant category with the high amount of contact group, the results are significant at the .05 level ($\chi^2 = 3.271$).

In the high prediction group similar proportions of subjects at the high (75 per cent) (6) and medium (78 per cent) (7) levels of contact reported good relationships with parents. However, at the low level of contact the proportion drops to 50 per cent (3) but the differences are not significant. For the low prediction group, the proportion reporting a neutral or poor relationship increases as contact decreases from zero to 50 per cent (5) to 29 per cent (2) but again the difference is not significant, although in the expected direction. Equal proportions (70 per cent) of both the high (16) and low (16) prediction groups report a good relationship with their parents. Only 11 subjects had left home following a quarrel and only 2 of these had left home for longer than one week, and therefore it was not possible to break this down by amount of contact. Therefore, in considering amount of contact and previous maladjustment score the measure of whether or not the subject has left home following a quarrel was used. Amongst the high prediction group the proportion who had left home increased as contact decreased, from 13 per cent (1) to 44 per cent (4) to 50 per cent (3), but the difference was once again not significant on the Fisher Test. In the low prediction group the proportion leaving home increased from zero to 30 per cent (3) as contact level fell from high to medium but rose again to zero when contact fell to the low level. More of the high prediction group (8) left home (35.6 per cent) than in the low prediction group (13 per cent, 3) but the difference, χ^2 = 1.9116, P > .10 (l-tailed) failed to be significant.

Those who had been unemployed were divided into high unemployment and low unemployment groups as described earlier. It was found that contact level in the high prediction group discriminated significantly at the .05 level (Fisher Test) between those who had a high and those who had a low unemployment record. Therefore the proportion in the high contact group with a high unemployment record was zero, medium = 83 per cent (5), low = 50 per cent (1). (High versus medium significant at .05 level, high versus medium combined with low at .05 level). In the low maladjustment score group the trend was in the reverse to the expected direction with proportions having a high unemployment record decreasing as contact decreased 100 per cent (3) to 40 per cent (2) to 33 per cent (1). There was little difference between the two maladjustment groups in the proportions of subjects with a high unemployment record (high maladjustment = 50 per cent (6), low = 55 per cent (6)).

PARTICIPANTS AND SUCCESS

Although, when success variables were considered individually, previous prognosis, whether it was maladjusted score or previous conviction, was only sometimes able to differentiate significantly between subsequent 'success' and 'failure', it is possible to determine which clients were 'overall' more successful. The method of producing this analysis was rather unsophisticated and involved obtaining first of all an overall measure of success by combining the 11 variables used earlier. This was done by counting the number of variables for each participant where 'failure' occurred. A 'failure' was where, for example, a subject had a 'high' score on the Jesness Asocial Index, or was reconvicted, or had a high unemployment record. A total of 11 variables were used giving a total of 'failures' for each subject. In fact, numbers ranged from 0 to 10. The distribution of 'failure scores' was then divided into three groups of clients as follows:

high success participants: 0 to 2 'failures' n = 16
medium success participants: 3 to 5 'failures' n = 19
low success participants: 6 or more 'failures' n = 16

The three participants who did not take part in the after-test were excluded from the groups since an overall score could not be calculated

Table 42 A comparison of the three success groups by previous
conviction/non-conviction (n = 51)

	Previously convicted	*Not previously convicted*
High success	2 (13%)	14 (88%)
Medium success	9 (47%)	10 (53%)
Low success	12 (75%)	4 (25%)
Not known	2	1
Total	25	29

for them. The three success groups were then compared by previous
conviction/non-conviction *(Table 42)* and maladjustment score
(Table 43).

As is to be expected the social-work programme was overall more
successful with participants who had not been convicted before the
start of the evaluation period. The percentage for the high success
group was 13 per cent, medium success 47 per cent, and low success 75
per cent. The overall difference in *Table 42* was significant $\chi^2 = 7.673$
and P (1-tailed) $= < .025$.

Table 43 A comparison of the three success groups by maladjustment score (n = 46)

	n	*Mean maladjustment score*
High success	15	13.73
Medium success	19	19.42
Low success	12	19.58
Total	46	

This analysis was repeated for maladjustment scores with the results
shown in *Table 43*. The mean maladjustment score of those with
medium (19.42) and low (19.58) success was similar but differed from
that of the high success group (13.73). A comparison between the
means of the high and low success groups revealed that the difference
just failed to be significant $t = 1.647$, P (one-tailed) $> .10$. The
comparison between high and medium success is, however, significant
$t = 1.8228$, $P < .05$ (one-tailed). Thus those with higher maladjustment
scores responded less successfully to the treatment programme.

Table 44 A comparison of the three success groups 'combining' for
high maladjustment score plus previous conviction (n = 46)

	High score + previous conviction	Others
High success	0 (0%)	15 (100%)
Medium success	7 (37%)	12 (63%)
Low success	6 (50%)	6 (50%)
Total	13	33

If those participants who have a high maladjustment score *and* who
had been previously convicted are compared with those who *either* had
a high score *or* had been previously convicted (or neither), the results
are those shown in *Table 44*. The proportion of participants who had a
high maladjustment score and who had also been convicted prior to the
evaluation period rose as level of success decreased, from zero to 37 per
cent (7) to 50 per cent (6). To test for significance it was necessary to
combine success groups. Combining the medium and low groups and
comparing them with the high success group the difference was highly
significant, $\chi^2 = 6.822$, $P < .005$ (one-tailed). Combining the high and
medium groups and comparing them with the low group the difference
just failed to be significant, $\chi^2 = 2.322$, $P > .10$ (one-tailed). Thus the
social-work programme was less successful with those previously
convicted who also had a high maladjustment score.

Table 45 A comparison of the three success groups by age at 1
January 1966 (n = 51)

	14 years and less	15 years or older
High success	9 (56%)	7 (44%)
Medium success	7 (37%)	12 (63%)
Low success	5 (31%)	11 (69%)
Total	21	30

The ages of the subjects in the three success groups are compared
in *Table 45*. The proportion of participants who were 14 years old and
under at the start of the evaluation period decreased as level of success
decreased, low 56 per cent (9) to 37 per cent (7) to 31 per cent (5).

However, the overall difference failed to be significant at the .05 level, $\chi^2 = 2.285, P > .10$ (one-tailed). Thus, although the tendency was for a greater success with younger participants the differences were not significant.

CONCLUSION

The difficulty in providing a summary of the research findings, as was stated at the beginning of the chapter, is that generalizations are bound to occur. No doubt some people will wish to use the research evidence of this study to support, or perhaps decry, future projects using the 'detached' social-work method as employed here. However, if the generalizations only are used and the qualifications given in the main body of the text not consulted, such evidence may be misused.

On the basic question of whether or not the project was a success, whether the participant group performed better on the evaluative measures than the control group, the simple answer is cautiously positive. The results do not substantiate any more grandiose a claim. In the area of delinquency prevention the evidence would seem to suggest that the social-work programme did prevent delinquency. In the area of social adjustment, as measured by the Jesness Asocial Index, the project seems to have been only very marginally effective. In the field of employment there was some tentative evidence that the programme reduced the time subjects spent without a job, but little that it prevented them from being unemployed, although there was some tentative evidence that it helped improve stability of employment by reducing the frequency with which participants changed their jobs. Similarly, with regard to participants' relationship with parents, although the workers seemed unable to improve this overall, they were able to help negotiate a speedy return where the participant had left, or was ejected from, the home. However, the workers seemed unable to prevent them actually leaving home. The programme had some success in encouraging the younger participants to make use of clubs and organizations. Some success was noted in enabling participants to form steady relationships with the opposite sex, but not in helping them to develop relationships with their own sex. On this point it was felt that a stable relationship with the opposite sex might preclude one with peers of the same sex.

A possible explanation of the discrepancy between the results on delinquency measures and the Jesness Inventory is that social attitudes change much more slowly than behaviour. Many, if not most, of the participants had to continue to live in the same milieu in which they had previously taken part in criminal behaviour. It may well have been necessary for them to continue to express attitudes that were prevalent in that environment in order to maintain acceptance within their society, even though they had ceased to express these attitudes in behaviour.

A number of extraneous influences that occurred after the selection of the two groups were examined. However, it was found that these intervening variables did not have a biasing effect on the programme in so far as these effects could be measured. This is not to say that there were not other factors that may have had an unequal influence on the two groups and thus on the outcome of the project. But in a study with this type of design it is not possible to control for everything, nor is it possible to be aware of every factor that might have a bearing on the outcome.

It would seem that a relatively high level of contact was required to have a positive effect in terms of the outcome variables on participants. It was found that a level of contact of over seven hours per month produced a greater effect than between two and six hours per month. Since very few of the differences were statistically significant this finding can only be tentatively advanced.

On certain of the outcome variables, for example reconviction, it was found that contact did not have a linear relationship with outcome but was in fact curvilinear. That is, as amount of contact decreased so delinquency, for example, increased. But then as contact decreased further so did delinquency, rather than increasing further as would have been expected. This result was not, however, found on all variables. When this phenomenon was discussed with members of the social-work team they felt that it had arisen because, deliberately, they had had only minimal contact with those participants who, in their opinion, no longer seemed in need of the services the project could offer. Since the team did not have access to the criminal records and social adjustment scores of clients their basis for this assessment was different from those used as a prediction of outcome that appeared earlier in this chapter. The social-work assessments of participants varied over time and it is not possible to assign an overall assessment to individual participants from the records of team assessment meetings.

There is some tentative evidence for the team's explanation in *Tables 44 and 45* above. Certainly a smaller proportion of the low contact sub-groups had been previously convicted although this was not statistically significant. On the maladjustment scores the mean score of the low contact group was at 15.1, less than that for the other two contact groups combined, 19.2. However, again this difference was not statistically significant ($t = 1.264, P < .20$). Although this would seem a logical explanation, perhaps somewhat *post hoc*, the research evidence does not provide statistical confirmation.

When the differential overall success rates of participants were examined it was found that the programme was more successful with those not previously convicted, those with a low maladjustment score, and those who were 14 years of age or less when the evaluation period began. Those who had a high maladjustment score *and* had previously been convicted were even less likely to respond to the treatment programme. All of these results are what might be expected from any social-work programme and, indeed, had they been otherwise might have led to doubts about the validity of the data, especially the outcome variables.

Of necessity this resumé of the results of the research programme has had to leave out some of the important qualifications that appear in the main body of the text. To gain a comprehensive understanding of the research findings it is necessary to read all of the chapter and not merely these conclusions.

NOTES AND REFERENCES

1 The information on delinquency in the following year was available only after the main computing operation was completed in the spring of 1969. A separate note is given in Appendix III.

2 $\chi^2 = 3.52, P < .05$. Since the direction of the difference between the two groups is predicted by the hypotheses, the region of rejection is one-tailed.

3 The lay reader unfamiliar with statistical method will find an explanation of methods used in this chapter in A. R. Ilersic, *Statistics* (MSL Publishers, 1963).

4 J. Mott, the Jesness Inventory: Application to Approved School Boys. *Studies in the Causes of Delinquency and the Treatment of Offenders*. Home Office Report No. 13 (1969).

5 Although detention centres are usually thought of as punitive rather than remedial, some do have social workers, and inmates receive a period of after-care on release. Hence its inclusion in the social-work category.

6 Numbers in the sub-groups may vary with number of respondents, in particular those affected by the absence of two participants in the final interview.

PART THREE

Conclusions

7 · Conclusions

It is difficult to assess how far the particular experience and conclusions of one social-work programme focusing on 54 boys and taking place in one neighbourhood of one large town in the North of England can be seen to have more general implications. However, it can be claimed that this particular programme was carefully evaluated and from the solid foundation of evidence that resulted some generalizations are possible. Moreover there are elements in this particular situation that are typical of the background to the adolescent years of many boys in the central slum areas of other large towns – their social segregation from adults, their position at the base of the social pyramid, and their lack of positive and helpful contact with the middle classes are not unique, neither is the central formative influence of their peers or their exploitation of the opposite sex. Their life-chances have been largely determined by their parents' lack of wealth, their own lack of education, and the poverty of their environment. These are the life-chances that they share with a substantial segment of the urban working class.

The first question might be whether the objectives set out for the project were in fact realized. Were the 54 young people helped 'to reach a dynamic adjustment to society'? Was their delinquency controlled? It will be remembered that the concept of dynamic adjustment was intended to indicate to the workers that the Youth Development Trust was concerned not merely with helping young people to adjust to their environment but also with helping them to change it. Indeed, the very existence of the project brought a radical change to their personal environment by introducing middle-class attitudes into their lives. One aim was to assist the participants to become more conscious of the factors, both personal and social, that shaped their lives and of the ways in which they could exert more control over their own destinies. If they became dissatisfied with the poor range of jobs available in the neighbourhood they could be helped to apply for better jobs elsewhere; if they saw how the social pressures of their peers were forcing them into delinquency or maladjustment they could be helped to develop social ties elsewhere. It might be said, however, with some justification perhaps, that they were not confronted with the political choices that

245

they might have to make to change their environment, and the concept of adjustment usually implied more effective relationships at the personal level rather than more active citizenship. It might be argued that this more modest objective had to take priority with young people so lacking in immediate personal satisfactions and so apathetic towards the wider society, but this would perhaps be *post hoc* reasoning. It is more likely that the emphasis on personal adjustment was a consequence of the methods of casework and group work that were employed.

The interest of the project in maladjustment brought it much closer to the objectives of the Mental Health Services, and also to the preventive objectives of the Children's Department (now within the Personal Social Services Department), than to the objectives of the Youth Service. It was much more concerned with helping the deviant become more acceptable and more accepted than with helping the normal youngster cope with the predictable stresses of growing up; it was much more concerned with reducing misery than increasing pleasure. Maladjustment, however, was not seen just as the consequence of some failure in early family experience but also in terms of the social structure of Wincroft and of the wider society, and the failure of either to provide a satisfactory role for these young people. Membership of the café network gave a personal support not provided by the social structure, but only at the price of bringing its members into conflict with adult society.

Whatever the stated objectives of the project, they were meant to be interpreted in the light of the needs of the young people as they themselves revealed these needs. It is interesting therefore to remember the results (presented in Chapter 4) of the analysis of the service given: of the total fieldwork 43 per cent was classified as helping with social development; 27 per cent in the field of recreation; 14 per cent with problems arising out of employment, or lack of it; 12 per cent in representing the boys' interests to other agencies; and 4 per cent with accommodation problems. Although only 9 per cent of all sessions were seen as family casework, this almost certainly underestimates the extent to which family problems were raised, since the term 'family casework session' was applied strictly to those sessions in which a worker was in face-to-face contact with members of the boy's family. Discussions about parents, but in their absence, occurred fairly often and were classified as 'social development'. It is worth noting that educational matters were given little attention. A steady increase in the demand for casework, reflected in the increasing proportion of this form of service, occurred as the project developed. This demand came almost exclusively from the more disturbed participants and has implications for the selection of clients, since it is a much less economic form of service than group work.

How far was the project successful in achieving the secondary objective of delinquency control? This is easier to comment upon than the primary objective of promoting dynamic adjustment. The research findings indicate that participants had been charged with committing significantly less crime than controls during the evaluation period. This finding, which perhaps should not be undervalued, has not as yet occurred in projects of a similar nature. The evidence on the 'dynamic adjustment' objective is more ambiguous. The main measure of adjustment, the Asocial Index of the Jesness Inventory, showed no statistically significant difference between participants and controls, but the difference that did occur was in the right direction. Employment and unemployment records of participants were only slightly better than those of the control group. Evidence as to the effect of the programme on improving relationships with families seemed to show that although these could be patched up when a rupture in the relationship had occurred there was, overall, no relative improvement.

It would be natural to try and rationalize away what appear to be failures by claiming that the measuring devices were invalid. Though there may be some seeds of truth in such a rationalization, the argument helps us very little. More pertinent is the point made at the end of the preceding chapter that behaviour, especially that likely to result in fairly drastic punishment, is relatively more easily changed than are social attitudes. Also, the suggestion that attitudes can be retained after the behavioural concomitants have ceased seems feasible, especially if these attitudes are upheld by a culture in which the actor is still participating. For a participant to refrain from delinquent behaviour yet subscribe to those cultural values supportive to it, since he still has to function as a member of that culture, is by no means out of the question. It is also suggested that attitudes change (if they changed at all) much more slowly than behaviour. Thus the relatively short evaluation period, only 31 months, may not have been long enough to measure any effect the programme might have had in this respect.

The experience of the Wincroft Project may indicate the value to policy-makers of being clear and specific about the objectives of the social services, whether these are provided by the smallest voluntary organization or the largest national ministry. Given that objectives can be operationally stated it becomes possible to establish whether the organization of services facilitates the achievement of those objectives. Unfortunately, this has not been done either by the individual ministries concerned with youth policy or, as it needs to be, across the whole range of central and local government activity in this field. It would appear from the experience of the Wincroft Project that policies aimed at delinquency prevention or to assist disadvantaged youth in their social adjustment are not well served by the present divisions of responsibility between Education, the Personal Social Services, and the Home Office, especially since this is accompanied by a marked lack of coordination between the individual services.

It would appear that the services are ineffective in other respects. They are often located both geographically and socially too far away from the client, and in this the professional social workers suffer from the same disease as that of the administrators, they are office-bound; workers wait for clients to come to them, on the workers' ground, rather than themselves reaching out to meet clients. As a result, the services often come into operation too late in the day. Instead of being a preventive force with an established base for action in a setting normal to young people, they are a force called into play when a crisis is already upon the client. The method usually chosen at this point, casework, tends to disregard important social pressures upon the boy, such as his peer-group and network, and to concentrate either upon his own internal psycho-dynamics or upon relationships within his family. He may even be removed from his environment and sent for residential training in circumstances bearing little relationship to the challenges he has to face at home. It is not surprising that such large sections of the Wincroft adolescent community see little relevance for them in the services provided and thus fail to use them unless they are compelled to do so.

More detail is required to support these criticisms of the existing services. First, it is useful to list the central and local government departments concerned with the needs of youth: a Youth Service deals with the recreational needs of the 14-20 age-group and is administered as part of the Further Education provision, both nationally and locally; a Youth Employment Service exists for those under the age of 18, provided sometimes by the local education authority (as in Wincroft) and sometimes by the Department of Employment and is controlled by that Department nationally; a Personal Social Services Department has primary responsibility for a preventive service for those under the age of 17 – this is administered locally by the Social Services Committee and nationally by the Department of Health and Social Security; schools show a growing interest in recreation, careers guidance, and counselling; a Probation Service is provided by the Magistrates' Committee and inspected by the Home Office; a Social Security office is provided by the DHSS; numerous other bodies have responsibilities for the special needs of some adolescents, for the mentally and physically handicapped, for those in hospital, and so on. This picture of fragmented state administration is matched by the multiplicity of voluntary organizations, sometimes providing the same service as the local authorities on their behalf, sometimes providing it in competition, and often not providing it at all. The most depressing feature of this situation is that there is little awareness on the part of those concerned, either administrators or fieldworkers, of the need to coordinate their efforts. No machinery exists, to ensure coordination among them over cases locally as in Wincroft or over policy nationally in London. [1]

The most serious consequences of this situation are to be found in the lack of urgency and focus for dealing with the needs of young people with problems. This not only applies to specific problems such as homelessness with which the Youth Service is familiar but can do nothing about, but also to the fact that young people without homes are often the same young people who are without jobs and in trouble with the law. The Children's Departments (now absorbed into the Personal Social Services Departments) which might have offered the focus for urgent action have, however, never paid much attention to those over 16. Four years ago (1968) the Seebohm Committee confessed that they had 'not been able to give adequate attention to the organization of social services for young people, and for that reason make no specific recommendations for their reorganization. . . . Our failure in this respect is not due to any thought that these services are unimportant; plainly they are vital and in need of urgent development.' They excused themselves on the grounds that 'there has been no completely comprehensive enquiry covering all aspects of their needs and such an enquiry is overdue. We recommend that it should be undertaken urgently'. If 'urgent development' and 'urgent enquiry' were needed in 1968 how much more pressing the need must now have become.

Besides being fragmented services for the young are often administered in ways that make them hard to use, especially on two counts;

physical distance and social distance. For example, there was no office of the Youth Employment Service, the Children's Department (as it then was), the Probation Service, or the Further Education Service in Wincroft, the nearest full-time official was a club leader in a club outside of the area. It is probable that boys as socially immature as the participants will find it difficult to use these services, especially as their parents are unlikely to encourage or accompany them in doing so. But the geographical distance was sometimes less important than the social distance involved. Not only were some officials predictably officious in their dealings with aggressive youths, but even sympathetic officials found, as the project workers also found, that there was a cultural chasm between them and some of the youngsters they were trying to help.

These boys' experiences at school had not been happy ones. Neither they nor their parents were closely involved with the process of education, and so those most in need of the civilizing and socializing influences of education benefited least from attendance at school. A point sharply made elsewhere, [2] and endorsed here, is that there is a need for the school to be more closely connected to the community it serves, and the provision of more rather than less service for difficult boys from the teaching profession in close consultation with local youth-serving agencies. Although the project had some contact with the schools in Wincroft it should probably have attempted more actual cooperation with them, but, as was stated in Chapter 4, this liaison was by no means an easy one and plans to enlist cooperation were partly frustrated. It has been demonstrated that the teacher in the school setting is among the first able to identify the potentially troublesome child, and it seems to be of vital importance that any programme aimed at social change and social adjustment should involve schools in the neighbourhoods in which work is undertaken.

Many of the participants who had received the services of social workers, usually from the Probation or the Child Care Services, were likely to be bewildered by the service being offered, ignorant of its purpose, but convinced of its irrelevance. Many were probably not aware that they were clients in a casework relationship (any more perhaps than they were aware that they were clients in group work in the Wincroft Project). Group work did, however, offer something that casework could not – the opportunity for more accurate diagnosis, as a result of workers being able to see the way that a boy reacted to his peers, and thus the possibility of his receiving support from friends who were part of his social milieu, which may well have meant more to him than the efforts of adult social workers who were not. There would clearly be some advantage if group work were seen more widely as a complementary method to casework, and more will be said about this later (p. 263).

If, for many of the participants, the help the social services offered seemed irrelevant to their problems, the very mention of the police brought forth in practically all cases a response of violent antipathy. Tales of beatings in the cells and forced false confessions abounded. No doubt many of these were exaggerations and some pure fantasy, made up to justify a confession especially if accomplices had been implicated. There was never any evidence to substantiate the claims of brutality.

Court procedure, even to those who frequently experienced it, remained a mystery to many of the participants and certainly it baffled, on occasions, the workers accompanying them. A great deal of time was wasted in waiting around to appear. If the cultural chasm between some of the officers of the social services and the participants was wide, then that between them and most of the magistrates was a virtual rift valley. Many magistrates seemed totally unaware of the culture and environment inhabited by the accused young persons brought before them, even though they had the benefit of a probation officer's written report.

Much of the comment this far has been about social-work services and since the Wincroft Project was generated from the Youth Service it is important to explore the latter's relevance. The use made of professional effort in the Youth Service is determined by two central features of its organization: its location in educational administration, both nationally and locally, which leads to its dependence upon the objectives and skills of further education, and now, increasingly, of the schools; and its reliance upon the mixed youth club as its major method. Despite the brief and sporadic flirtations of the Youth Service with work with the 'unattached' no serious efforts have been made to use the social-work method within its structures. Moreover, despite the fashionable talk of relating the work of clubs to the communities in which they are located, clubs are still very isolated from communities. [3] The club that has a parents' association or involves many parents in its functioning is exceptional. Club leaders spend relatively little of their professional time in their locality outside of the club walls, and their work is shaped by which young people present themselves for membership, and, usually, how long they choose to stay.

Little effort is made to meet them before they join or to follow them up after they leave. It is likely that the more socially deprived youngster does not join clubs as frequently as other ordinary working-class young people, and when he does join he does not sustain his membership for as long.

The detached youth-work method described in this report shows that it is possible to work with very difficult boys, to develop work with them to a level not unlike that of a good youth club, and to sustain this work over a much longer period. Detached youth work is of course much more expensive in terms of manpower but much less expensive in capital and maintenance cost of buildings. The lasting changes it achieves are not visible in terms of bricks and mortar but in social attitudes and behaviour — the foundations of a civilized community. There is now some sign that the DES will encourage local education authorities to expand work in socially deprived areas, and to shift its priorities from buildings to professional expertise.

The Youth Employment Service has until the recent past shown even less concern for the socially deprived than the Youth Service, and its professional practitioners have been trying to change its image from an Employment (and therefore placement) Service that has traditionally concerned itself with those who are unemployed or difficult to employ towards a Careers Advisory Service that has particular relevance to those young people interested in making a career. In any case it has been seriously understaffed and the officers find it difficult to justify the extra effort that needs to be devoted to boys who keep changing their jobs, or who are work-shy. Furthermore, the professional skills of the careers officer do not include casework, and the officer may soon find himself out of his depth when the specific problem of employment reveals associated problems of family conflict, homelessness, and delinquency. [4] It has become clear from the Wincroft Project and from other reports that the detached worker who tries to help the socially deprived will very often need to help settle them into employment and for this purpose he can often act as a link to the Youth Employment Service.

Perhaps the most profound implications of the Wincroft Project's work are those for the social services for young people rather than those for provision of formal or informal education. The findings expand the possibilities raised, but not always realized, by the 1963 Children and Young Persons Act for the prevention and treatment of maladjustment and delinquency within the community. Although very few of the participants would have been brought into the care of the local authority it is likely that with their delinquent histories more would have appeared before the courts and eventually been taken into residential training without the support they received from project workers. How heavy the cost of this training would have been to the community and what would have been the personal consequences for the boys concerned do not need stressing. The 1969 Children and Young Persons Act is also relevant here in that it is likely that some of the work of this project could have been recognized as 'intermediate treatment' had the Act been in operation.

One specific gap in the social services has become clear from this work and is now being uncovered in other parts of the country also: the need for short-stay accommodation for adolescent boys. A substantial number of the participants (18 out of the 54) had at some time during the four-and-a-half years of the project left or had been forced to leave their homes. During their absence from home many had slept 'rough' in old cars or derelict houses, or had slept on the floors of the commercial cafés in the neighbourhood. Others were more fortunate, staying with friends, or in lodgings until the trouble blew over. The nearest accommodation provided by the Ministry of Social Security was some nine miles away, and completely unsuited to their needs. Homelessness considerably increases the chances of adolescents getting into trouble with the law and adequate short-stay accommodation is a key service in the prevention of delinquency.

A second specific gap noticed many times before and confirmed by this project is the absence of any psychological guidance services after school-leaving age. There is no specialized service which can be called upon officially for testing young workers or for the provision of skilled psychiatric support for youth workers. Not that the child guidance services are all that effective for the children while they are still at school, for although 34 of the 54 boys had been rated on the Stott BSAG maladjustment score as having scores over 10 only one had ever been to a child guidance clinic. In any case the clinic that served this area was without a psychiatrist for long periods and often had long waiting lists for psychological testing.

The concern of the project with maladjustment has implications for other services concerned with mental health. Adolescence represents perhaps the last opportunity for any fundamental change in the structure of personality and sometimes it is the first occasion on which certain mental disorders reveal themselves. It might be thought therefore that any policy of community mental health (such as that embodied in the Mental Health Act of 1959) would have regard to the preventive possibilities of work with adolescents. In fact no such initiative has been taken. Nor have the institutional services been any more advanced than this in their treatment of the adolescent. There was (at the time of the project) no adolescent unit in the mental hospitals in the region in which the project was located. [5] Probably at least four participants could have benefited from treatment had it been available and had it been possible to get them to the place where it was being offered.

The criticisms that have been made of the structure of existing youth welfare services may be challenged on the grounds that it is easy to carry out an experimental project whereas it is another matter to organize an efficient routine service. It will be said too that special projects attract resources out of all proportion to what might be expected in routine provision because of the way they dramatise, or even glamourize, social problems. The same results, it will be claimed, could be expected with the same level of resources employing conventional methods. Further, such projects exercise no continuing responsibility to the community, they enjoy the luxury of pointing out other people's shortcomings without staying to support them, and even experiment with young people and having proved their point leave them. It has been said that they are a way of distracting attention at relatively little cost from the real and expensive problems of changing the society, and that research has become one of the most useful weapons in the armoury of the politician who wishes to take no action. [6] All these criticisms have been levelled against other projects, and are likely to be made about the present one, and they therefore need to be answered.

The total cost of the Wincroft Project from its start in 1964 was £29,673 of which £9,447 was spent on research. Included in this figure for research is the expenditure for the year following the completion of the fieldwork programme. During the currency of the programme something like 600 young people were given service, but since the quality of that service varied and cannot be assessed except during the evaluation period, our comments will be confined to that 31-month period, for which the cost was £15,200, excluding the research. No charge has been made for the services given by the Director of the Department of Youth Work of the University of Manchester. For this sum 11,878 hours of fieldwork were carried out. Thus the cost per hour of fieldwork was approximately 25/6. This figure for the face-to-face work includes all costs of such things as renting of premises, office equipment, volunteer expenses, and time spent in discussing the work and clients away from the fieldwork situation. It does not take into account the expenditure prior to January 1966. Unfortunately, there are no known comparable figures for the Children's and Probation Departments on the cost per hour of service to clients.

There is a saying common in the Youth Service that if one youth worker keeps two boys from going to approved school he has saved the cost of his salary. The difficulty is of course in proving that he was instrumental in preventing them going there. In the present project it is possible to calculate the amount of time that participants would be expected to spend in residential training from the actual amount of time thus spent by controls. This figure can then be compared with the actual amount of time participants spent in residential institutions. The calculations would only take into account those sentences which occurred after the start of the evaluation period and not those before, even though the young person might still be receiving such training during the evaluation period. From January 1966 to July 1969, one year after the end of the social-work programme, controls had been sentenced to and received a total of 909 weeks of residential training. Seven boys were still undergoing training and, calculating on the basis of an average length of borstal training of 18 months, were expected to receive a further 153 weeks during the following twelve months giving an overall total of 1,062 weeks. By July 1969 participants had spent 169 weeks in such training and were expected to receive a further 13 weeks giving a total of 182 weeks. Correcting for the differences in size of the two groups we would have expected the participants to have spent an extra 593 weeks in training had they followed the pattern of the control group. The cost of residential training given by the Home Office (1967, mid-term for the project) was £17 5s for a borstal and £17 14s for a detention centre. Using a figure approximately midway between these two sums we get a hypothetical saving for participants of 593 x £17 10s = £10,378. Making similar calculations for offenders not receiving institutional training it would have been expected that a further 7 participants would be convicted and an extra 38 court appearances made for a further 69 offences by July 1969. Also it would be expected that they would have received another 8 years of Probation Orders (see Appendix III). It is not possible to cost out these expected extra court appearances, offences, or

Probation Orders but these would all add to the above figure of costs for residential training. The figure for 'saving' on residential training, is only just over two-thirds of the cost of the project social work during the evaluation period. However, these calculations are only for savings in the short-run period. If the trend in the control group of more residential training continues then there will be a cumulative saving in the years to come with the full cost of the social-work programme in the evaluation period being met in perhaps the next three or four years. [7]

The value of the present project was in any case never intended to be seen wholly in terms of delinquency prevention and indeed this objective was secondary to that of the promotion of positive social attitudes. In the field of social adjustment there is some apparent contradiction between the evaluation provided by the social workers in Chapter 4 and the evidence of the research in Chapter 6. In the former chapter the social workers point in their case studies to specific changes they have witnessed while in the latter chapter the research found little statistically significant difference between the control and the participant group on the measures of the after-test. Comparing the two sets of evidence it may be that the instruments selected to measure the change were not sufficiently sensitive and a reply to a questionnaire may be less reliable evidence than the observation of a social worker. On the other hand the social workers had a direct interest in believing their work to be successful, and may not have been objective about it. Although the research evidence was not statistically conclusive the differences that occurred were in the expected direction and this gives weight to the doubts about the sensitivity of the after-test.

A further criticism of experimental projects is that of exercising no continuing responsibility within the community, and this is more easily answered. Although no work continues now in Wincroft this is because in the planning of the project it was anticipated that the participants would be old enough to stand on their own feet by the end of the project. In any case Wincroft is fast disappearing under slum clearance schemes. The work of the Youth Development Trust continues in the Manchester conurbation, for it was always intended that it should be a permanent part of the scene there. Indeed it now operates three projects like the Wincroft Project. It should be remembered, too, that the way in which experimental projects are financed makes it very difficult for anybody wishing to undertake a long-term commitment to do so. The Department of Education and Science places a three-year limit upon their grants and they are careful to avoid taking on the normal financial responsibilities of local authorities. With one or two notable exceptions (ILEA in particular) the local authorities have shown little enthusiasm to date for incorporating work with the 'unattached' as part of the routine Youth Service provision. Nor are the traditional voluntary youth organizations any more enthusiastic about sharing what little money there is available with such a noisy and challenging newcomer. The experience of the Wincroft Project seems to show that not only is it extraordinarily difficult to generate this kind of social action, but it is equally difficult to sustain it financially after the initial experimental phase. Money may be made available for a short-term experiment but rarely is it provided to maintain an ongoing detached work service.

The Wincroft Project was unusual compared with other British projects (the American situation is very different) in the emphasis it placed upon research. This was facilitated by the good working relationship between the Youth Development Trust and the University of Manchester, which avoided some of the difficulties experienced by the university in Bristol where the Bristol Social Project involved the university in conflict with the local community. [8] This good working relationship also ensured that the level of research met the standards of a university rather than those of a voluntary youth organization.

It could be argued that the research design used in the present study was not the most useful. The use of random allocation might appear to have many advantages over a study of the present type, for instance if participants had been allocated randomly to different treatment sub-groups, for example voluntary or professional workers, this would have made possible a reliable analysis of the effectiveness of different approaches. Also, having a group of subjects and randomly allocating them to the treatment or control group would have eliminated the necessity of choosing a control area. However, on the technical level, a large number of subjects would have been necessary in order to use this design. On a more practical level, and this is far more important for the present study, given the fact that the treatment took place in the subjects' own milieu contamination of controls and participants by contact with the workers would have been impossible to prevent, had all young people been drawn from the same area. If the social work had taken place away from the area in which the subjects lived and played, as occurred in both the Seattle Atlantic Street Center and the

Cambridge—Somerville Projects, such a design would have been possible. Given the form of the social-work programme in Wincroft little alternative to the present research design was possible.

It was disappointing that the resources for research (one research fellow) in the Wincroft Project were such that it was impossible to develop a theoretical basis for the treatment programme. It is not possible therefore in theoretical terms to say what it was about the programme which led to the reduction in delinquency. Given the same conditions with the same kind of boys and the same resources, it would be feasible to repeat the previous success for the records of the present project are sufficiently detailed to make this kind of operation possible. But until one can spell out a theory that accounts for delinquency and maladjustment in Wincroft, and another theory that accounts for the success of treatment of this delinquency and maladjustment, it will not be possible to see how to repeat the operation with only those elements of action needed for its success. Considerably greater resources would be needed for this kind of research and although there can be no more guarantee of success than there can be in any investment in scientific research, the chances are that in the long run it would be cheaper than repeating the kind of small-scale evaluative research possible in the present project.

Whether or not there is a role for experimental projects, and what that role should be, there are clearly aspects of the present experience that could be incorporated into the practice of youth work. Services could be more selective in line with the emerging principle of 'positive discrimination' and directed towards those who are predictably at risk, and likely to respond to treatment. The use of buildings could be more flexible. Workers could work more effectively in teams and volunteers could be used more extensively. Group work could be used to complement casework and permissiveness could be seen as a technique rather than an ideology.

One concept central to the Wincroft Project was that of the participant. It was intended to convey to the workers that special attention should be directed to his needs, and that the workers should be guided by objective criteria of selection rather than solely by their own judgement or by the demands that young people made on them. It was certainly a valuable guide to the workers in establishing priorities for their own action. As was noticed in Chapter 4 only one of the judgements made by workers was not borne out by inquiries made in the schools or from police records, and only two of the participants included because of their BSAG scores seemed not to warrant special effort by the team. This would appear to be the first time this kind of concept has been employed in detached youth work in this country.

It has often been recommended that the schools should identify the children at risk in the community and the Bristol Social Adjustment Guide has proved a practical way of achieving this. As a method of identifying the most maladjusted members of the school community it appears to be effective (those boys who were known to the workers as category one in the termination programme had all been given high maladjustment scores by their teachers). It is less reliable in differentiating the minor degrees of maladjustment. One of the major advantages of the BSAG is that it does not involve the potential client in completing a questionnaire or a test and thus avoids the danger that the potential client, having completed a test or battery of tests and subsequently being included in a treatment programme, will be led to identify himself as 'bad', 'special', or 'delinquent' with subsequent effects on the success of the treatment programme.

It would appear that the most maladjusted youths responded least well to the services of the detached youth workers, but this might mean that there would be some advantage in their identification in order to avoid wasting limited resources upon them or allowing a longer period of work to achieve any modification of the behaviour of these hard-core clients. This may appear rather callous but it is difficult to see what is to be gained by trying to do work seen from the outset as unlikely to be a success. Although a lower cut-off point was used on the BSAG scores no upper one was used. By including only those boys in the treatment programme who scored 15 or less on the pre-project delinquency-prediction score the percentage of those who were subsequently reconvicted could have been reduced from 36 per cent to 22 per cent. This includes only those for whom a delinquency-prediction score is available. Similarly if a cut-off point on the pre-project maladjustment score of 22 had been used, then by excluding those who scored above this figure, the percentage of those who scored 25 or above on the post-project Asocial Index could have been reduced from 17 per cent to 10 per cent. It would appear from the results in Chapter 6 that the programme was more effective with those with lesser degrees of maladjustment, but the lower the bottom cut-off point used, the more are subjects not in need of treatment included and the greater the numbers included in the treatment group. Also, the lower the upper cut-off point is the more people who would have benefited are excluded from the programme. There would seem to be very valid reasons for having both an upper and lower limit of degrees of maladjustment in selecting clients for inclusion in detached-work programmes. The fixing of these limits must depend very much on the resources of the project concerned and the number of clients it can include in its programme.

On the question of number of clients, the figure of 54 in the present project was a rough estimate made before the project began with the intention that the workers should not be over-burdened. An identical figure was arrived at by the Seattle Atlantic Center Project with similar resources. [9] Although in that instance the group work sessions did not take place within the boys' own milieu, and thus the group size was always static. In the present project, although the number of participants was 54 their associates swelled the size of the total load. The norm of frequency of contact aimed at in the present project, one contact per week per participant, was not in fact reached, the average being one contact every ten days, but this was partly because subsequently workers discovered that some participants did not need this level of contact. With the achieved number of contacts during the 134-week evaluation period (4,837) and the aim of one per week the theoretical maximum number of participants would have been 36 (4,837/134).

The experience of the Wincroft Project suggests a basis for selecting clients and also offers a commentary on several contentious issues concerning the use of resources in youth work, particularly the use of buildings and volunteers. Buildings were used in several ways: the Bridge Café served as a point of contact and also provided a useful introductory role for the workers; the rented house was a place where small groups could be taken to work at some activity in relative peace and quiet; the office was somewhere where the workers could be contacted on a drop-in basis. Other rooms in the neighbourhood, in church halls and clubs, were used on occasions for activity groups. There is no question that the work would have been less effective if no premises had been available, but premises were always regarded as expendable. Once they had served their purpose they were discarded. In the case of the Bridge Café particularly it was important not to let concern for protecting the property come between the young person and the worker. Premises should not be thought of as fortresses into which the workers retire to protect themselves but rather as somewhere for clients to pursue their needs for privacy and relationship.

A special word ought perhaps to be said about the use of the café within the context of the whole project. Although cafés are still being used in work with the 'unattached' there is much less interest among professional workers in their possibilities. Where they are used, as in Wincroft, they are now part of a much wider and more flexible strategy and not the sole location for social-work activity. It would be regarded by the present authors as an open question whether or not the project could have proceeded as quickly and effectively without the use of the Bridge Café. On the other hand the emotional wear and tear in coping with the testing behaviour there was considerable, and might not have been as intense if contact had been established on neutral ground.

One of the more unusual features of the Wincroft Project was the extensive use of volunteer help: 151 volunteers assisted during the four-and-a-half years. Since it has sometimes been suggested that detached youth work requires special skills, and also that the clients are especially difficult to work with, it is a matter of some importance to know how volunteers made out. Moreover, additional volunteers were never a clear net gain to the project for they demanded some of the professionals' valuable time. It would appear that the volunteer is no less effective in detached youth work but it must be remembered that in the Wincroft Project the very difficult boys were serviced almost entirely by professional workers.

If volunteers are to be used, they must be used properly, and this means adequate selection and training arrangements. Most volunteers in the Wincroft Project were recruited on personal recommendation and this ensured some reliable judgement of their capabilities. It also meant that they knew what they were taking on. Little can therefore be said about the way to make formal selection effective. It is in the nature of this kind of programme that the individual worker sees little of other workers and training provides an opportunity for them to get together and exchange their experiences. The training programme must be directly geared to the problems felt to be important by the volunteer and not planned to suit the logic of an academic discipline. Therefore it will usually be most appropriate to use the discussion method, but the Wincroft experience suggests that role-playing, as long as it enacts situations close to reality, may also be useful. Personal supervision, as used by the professional workers, would be an advantage but this is an expensive method of training and suitable supervisors are hard to find.

One disappointment in Wincroft was that almost none of the volunteers were recruited locally. This was partly a function of the ease with which they were recruited from elsewhere in the city and of the difficulty in recruiting them locally. A much more concentrated effort would have been needed to involve local people and this would have had to be justified by a clearer idea of the special contribution local recruits could have made to the project. It must be remembered that many of the participants were ostracized locally by respectable residents and it would have needed very good reasons for them to reverse these attitudes. This would have required changes in their role and status which were not required of outsiders.

Volunteers have been shown to play a useful role in this programme but the role of the professional workers was altogether more crucial: they were responsible for making contact in the first place and initiating the relationships; the volunteers were then introduced by them and supported until they had established themselves. Volunteers relied upon professional workers for their assessments, their plans, and their evaluation. They expected the professional workers to produce the resources when they were needed. But it is perhaps dangerous to overdo the word 'professional' and important to remember that their role was largely a function of their being available as full-time workers. A substantial number of the voluntary workers were after all professional teachers and social workers. Three of the Wincroft team had been trained in youth work but perhaps more important than training was the fact of their previous experience, not in detached work it is true but it had been with the same kind of youngster they met in Wincroft. Not unimportant also was that they were a team whose abilities and temperaments complemented each others and they could derive a mutual support from this that was not open to the volunteer worker. It has often been said that because of the special stresses to which he is subjected the detached worker should never work alone and it would seem that the experience of having a team of four considerably aided the workers in meeting these stresses.

It is difficult to generalize from the present experience as to what a committee employing this type of worker should look for. There is no doubt that this field attracts a great many people who share the adolescent conflict with respectable adult society, or who are so individualist that they find it difficult to cooperate with other workers. It would seem to be important that the workers are secure in themselves, able to stand a high level of stress over a long period, resourceful enough to exploit situations to the advantage of their clients, and capable of explaining their client's needs to unsympathetic officials. Two of the five workers employed were already known to the Committee before they applied to join the team; three (including the two above) already had proven records of success in club work; the least successful worker had no background or experience of similar work.

Although it is important to get the setting for the work right, to ensure that the clients likely to succeed are selected, to choose competent workers, whether voluntary or professional, and see that they have the resources they need, in the end it all comes down to what happens in the relationship between client and worker. This is not to imply that the client-worker relationship should be a casework relationship, for the Wincroft Project has shown how social group work can be used and indeed the client may well be a group rather than an individual. Social group work is still not established as part of the average social worker's equipment and it may be that the level of skill that could be achieved in Wincroft was limited by the general ignorance of group work in Britain. There is no doubt that much of the work took place in groups but this would not establish that it was social group work. On most occasions the project worker's role was limited to one of support rather than interpretation. The present report may do something to advance the cause of social group work and provide materials for teaching that method.

One of the more interesting developments for the professional social worker in the Wincroft Project was the shift from group work to casework as relationships developed. It suggests that caseworkers might find some advantage in associating with young people who might be their future clients before they become so — not just for the obvious preventive purpose but because in the event of a failure they already have a solid foundation of understanding from which to carry out their casework. If this is so, it implies that social workers should be much more accepted figures in local communities and not appear on the scene for the first time when there is a crisis.

One central sociological fact about the adolescent society in Wincroft was the café network and it might well be asked how this fact can be acknowledged by the method of social group work when the network may include over a hundred young people and its influence on their behaviour may be considerable. The project was never able to provide a direct answer to this question. The workers could do very little in the cafés except establish and maintain contact with participants, their actual work had to be done elsewhere and this sometimes meant inducing young people away from the café network. Certain members of the network were seen to have a high status within the network and were able to influence values and behaviour of other boys. A few highly disturbed boys would repeatedly be charged with crimes but along with a different group of adolescents each time. Frequently, the members of these 'groups' would have none or only minor previous convictions. It may be that by concentrating on these 'leaders' a programme of detached youth work could have greater influence. However, it would be necessary to investigate this structural component of the network more fully before implementing such a scheme. Although very few sociologists have ever directly reported on the functioning of these cafés, it is likely that they will be found in most central slum areas. To suggest as some youth workers have done that these café operators could be enlisted as social workers gravely misunderstands their situation.

One further aspect of the method of working in Wincroft deserves some comment, since it has been widely misunderstood, this is the use of permissiveness as a technique and must be distinguished from permissiveness as an ideology. Permissiveness is a technique to keep open a relationship where the client can and will break it off if he is subjected to the disciplines that normal adolescents would accept. It has a particular value to the withdrawn child who may need to be encouraged to act out some of the aggressive feelings that he normally conceals because he is fearful of the consequences, and also to the child who tests adults out in order to prove that they will punish him and do not love him. It is not a technique to be used indiscriminately with all children and it must always be seen as a transitory strategy used until a normal basis of social functioning can be restored. It cannot be truthfully said that all workers on the Wincroft Project understood what they were doing when they allowed wide degrees of licence to the young people. Sometimes it was because they had shared in the unspoken compact that surrounds work of this nature: that in some way it challenges existing structures and methods and therefore challenges authority. Much clearer guidance ought to have been given to the voluntary workers, for some, having abandoned the common-sense convictions of adult-adolescent relationships, found themselves utterly at sea when the new basis for communication they expected to happen did not materialize.

The approach of preventing and treating the social disorder of delinquency within the community is not unique to this project. It is part of a gathering confluence of thought and policy in many personal social services, that proposes that the patient or the client, whether an individual or belonging to a group or network, should be helped to function adequately within his normal circumstances, rather than being taken away into the new and strange situation of an institution in a different community. Assistance needs to be directed not only towards the client but also towards the groups or communities of which he is a member. A great deal has been spoken and written about community policies, but they are only slowly being applied in practice. [10]

In the course of implementing a policy of preventive social action considerable ethical problems of the kind experienced by workers in this project will arise. It seems common sense to prevent social problems rather than cure them, but what right does that give anybody to intrude upon the private lives of citizens who have not yet committed any offence nor have shown any signs of deviancy that might disturb their neighbours? The young people who shared in this project did not ask the workers to enter their lives, although they were free at any time to break the contacts. In the end these young people were glad to have had this experience and they demanded more attention than the workers could give, but in the beginning they were not so certain. The workers too were not sure of themselves and were not always able to work entirely free of a guilty feeling that they may be doing something wrong by intruding.

The ethical problems were made more difficult by the decision to build research evaluation into the work. The group of participants had been matched with a number of similar young men in another area who were to act as a control group. It would not have been possible to inform the participants of this method of evaluation without the possibility of their influencing the results in some way. Moreover, in order to match the two groups in terms of criminal records and to compare their subsequent offences it was necessary to have access to police records, and this would have been difficult for the police to justify for a normal social-work programme. Although research has an important role to play in social-work practice, and it contributed greatly to the present project, its role is not limited to the particular research design of this experimental project. Indeed it is hoped that a function of this book will be to promote research of different kinds.

Another difficult ethical problem for the workers was the one of confidentiality. On the broader issues of revealing information about clients this is a problem common to all social workers, but in detached work the special feature of confidentiality is knowledge of criminal activities. To the non-practitioner this may not seem an issue since he may feel that the duty of the worker is to inform the police about any criminal behaviour that comes to his notice. In practice, matters are seldom so simple as this. Many stories of criminal exploits told to workers have little or no basis in fact. Tales of 'jobs' are told to workers to test them, impress them, and are sometimes merely part of the fantasy life of the disturbed adolescent. To give the police information about crimes picked up in this manner is not likely to be very helpful. Where the worker has knowledge of crimes before they take place the situation is somewhat different, although again it must be remembered that fantasy planning also occurs. The policy adopted in the present project was to attempt to point out the consequences of the planned illegal behaviour and to inform the adolescents concerned that the worker could have no part in the exploit and would have to leave if they continued with their plans. Again workers were sometimes offered what was said to be stolen property and here the policy was not to accept or buy anything that was known or thought to be stolen. Thus the general policy on illegal behaviour was for the worker to position himself so that he would not share any knowledge of this behaviour and thus would avoid being obliged to reveal information to the police. A situation may arise, though this did not occur on the present project, where the worker feels compelled to inform the police, and it is important for the worker to make a careful assessment before acting. Informing the police of every alleged crime would be helpful neither to the police nor the worker's relationship with his clients. This may seem like a doctrine of expediency but it is suggested that a policy on this matter that is drawn up outside the fieldwork situation may well need to be modified in the light of experience gained within it.

After five years of close involvement in the Wincroft Project it is difficult for the authors to stand back and examine the exact function the project served in the wider society. It was not just an attempt to devise new methods of dealing with delinquency within the rubric of social work; nor was it intended to assist the middle classes in manipulating the working classes more successfully or to help those with authority preserve that authority. It was a response to an awareness that the conformity of modern society generates deviance, and those who succeed have their counterparts in those who fail. It was a response to an awareness that the welfare state was a facade behind which the middle classes could take comfort but one that did not match the realities of need and distress among poor people. It was a response to an awareness that added to the traditional burdens of the poor there is now the weight of a bureaucracy that, ironically, is employed to serve them. More hopefully the Wincroft Project was directed toward creating a society where being young and being older could be more important than being of different social classes.

NOTES AND REFERENCES

1 The reorganization of social services following the recommendations of the Seebohm Committee will not help since that Report explicitly avoided consideration of services for youth. See also the recommendation 6(g), p. 3, in the recent report of the Youth Service Development Council, *Youth and Community Work in the 70s* (HMSO, London, 1969).

2 Op. cit., Chapter 5.

3 Op. cit., Chapter 4.

4 But see the Report of the National Youth Employment Council, *Socially Disadvantaged Youth*, Department of Employment, London, 1970.

5 See Youth Development Trust, *Young and Sick in Mind* (privately printed 1970). Obtainable from 22 Cromwell Buildings, 11 Blackfriars Street, Manchester M3 5BJ.

6 See, for example, the attack on the EPA Projects made by Professor J. B. Mays, The Research Smokescreen, *Guardian*, April 1968.

7 See Appendix III, p. 273.

8 J. Spencer, *Stress and Release in an Urban Estate* (Tavistock Publications, London, 1964), p. 314.

9 T. Ikeda, Effectiveness of Social Work with Acting-out Youth, *Reports of the Seattle Atlantic Street Center* (April 1968).

10 For one account of the lack of progress see Anne Lapping, Community Careless, *New Society*, 9 April 1970.

Appendices

Appendix I. Classification of voluntary workers by occupation n = 151

	M	F
Students on university postgraduate youth-work course	13	18
Students on other youth-work courses	2	1
Other students	16	16
Total no. of students	31	35
Professional occupations (lecturers, teachers, social workers, clergy)	19	23
Housewives	–	9
Skilled manual	10	1
Semi-skilled manual	8	5
Others/occupation not known	7	3
Overall total	75	76

Appendix II. Classification of serious and minor crimes

A modified form of the scheme suggested by Sellin and Wolfgang (*The Measurement of Delinquency*, 1964, pp. 154-6) was used. Here the offences committed by the two groups were divided into seven categories as follows:

(a) Any offence that results in bodily injury to the victim regardless of seriousness.

(b) Any offence that does not result in bodily injury but involves the loss of property through theft, regardless of the amount involved or whether the property is recovered.

(c) Any offence not included under (a) and (b) that results in damage to property regardless of the amount of money involved.

(d) Any offence not included under (a), (b), and (c), which involves some form of intimidation. This may involve a direct threat to a personalized victim or to the public in general.

(e) Any offence not included under (a), (b), (c), and (d) that involves the threatened loss of property.

(f) Any offence not included under (a), (b), (c), (d), and (e) that involves the violation of administrative rules of government, public order, or social harmony.

(g) Any offence not included above which if committed by an adult would not be considered an offence. Sellin and Wolfgang term these 'juvenile status' offences.

It was sometimes difficult to classify an individual offence as details were often lacking. Thus an offence such as attempted house-breaking with intent may have involved actual damage to property, but this may not be reported on the criminal record. However, since both groups of subjects are classified according to the same criteria, mis-classifications of certain specific offences will not be so important.

Appendix III. The control and participant groups one year later

The research evaluation that was built into the present project has concentrated on the actual period of the operation of the social-work programme. It was hoped, however, that the short-term effects that were demonstrated to have occurred (see Chapter 6) would be increased with time, that is, the programme would not only be effective while operating but would have a preventive effect after it had ceased. To be a truly effective programme, short-term benefits must be maintained in the long term.

It was not possible with the limited research resources available to repeat the after-test that was conducted in 1968. However, it was possible to examine police records to compare the two groups on convicted delinquency from July 1968 to July 1969.

During this twelve-month period a further 7 participants and 5 controls appeared before a court for the first time since the start of the evaluation period in January 1966. This brings the cumulative reconviction rate in the participants group to 50 per cent, an increase of 13 per cent, and in the case of the controls to 62 per cent, an increase of only 7 per cent. Although the proportions of each group that had been reconvicted at July 1968 differed significantly (see Chapter 6, p. 209) by July 1969 this difference was no longer significant ($\chi^2 = 1.431$, P (one-tailed) $> .10$), but is still in the expected direction.

Participants appeared in court a further 21 times during this period, giving a total of 59 and a mean of 2.19 per offender, or 1.09 for the group of 54. Controls appeared in court on a further 28 occasions, giving a total of 133 appearances and a mean of 2.89 per offender, or 1.80 for the group of 74 as a whole. The difference between the mean number of appearances per offender was just significant at the .05 level ($t = 1.677$).

The additional 21 court appearances by participants represented a further 29 offences, giving an overall total of 92 and a mean of 3.41 per offender, or 1.70 for the whole group. Controls committed a further 42 offences making a total of 221 and a mean of 4.80 per offender, or 2.99 for the group as a whole. The difference between the mean

273

number of offences per offender was significant, $t = 1.727$, P (one-tailed) $< .05$.

There has been a relatively greater increase in the number of 'new' offenders in the participant group, compared with the controls, but when the number of subjects who were convicted in this 12-month period are examined, rather than the number of 'new' offenders, the proportions in each group are more equal. Fifteen participants, 7 of them 'new' offenders, were convicted at least once between July 1968 and July 1969. In the control group during the same period 17 subjects were convicted, 5 of them being new offenders. During this year 1 participant and 6 controls spent all the twelve months in residential training. Two controls spent 6 months and a further three controls were given sentences totalling in excess of twelve months. Thus, calculating the proportion of each group convicted during this period against the numbers at risk, 53 in the case of participants and 66 for controls, 28 per cent of the former and 26 per cent of the latter appeared in court on at least one occasion in the year following the end of the treatment programme. The tendency was for a larger proportion of those offending in July 1968–July 1969, in the case of the participant group to be 'new' offenders, 7/15 (47 per cent) as against 5/17 (29 per cent) for controls. However, this difference was not statistically significant ($\chi^2 = 0.410, P > .50$).

Using the classification of offences developed in Chapter 6 (see p. 197) 19 (66 per cent) of the 29 offences committed by participants were of a 'serious' nature while the proportion for controls was 52 per cent. Although this difference was not statistically significant ($\chi^2 = 0.735, P > .30$), it is in the opposite direction to that expected. This difference follows the trend found at the end of the treatment programme when 59 per cent of participant offences and 53 per cent of controls were classified as 'serious'.

The results on delinquency, so far as court appearances and number of offences committed are concerned, bear out the expected pattern with both measures now distinguishing statistically between the two groups. The relatively larger percentage of 'new' offenders in the participant group during the period and the tendency for members of that group to commit more offences of a serious nature is against the expected trend. This might suggest that with certain clients the project acted as a holding operation and there was a deterioration in behaviour after the end of the social-work programme.

In terms of returns from the programme, the results for 1968-69 are very encouraging. During this period 11 subjects in the control group spent a total of 425 weeks in residential training while the figure for participants was 52 weeks (one boy in borstal). Thus in this 12-month period alone there was a hypothetical saving (see Chapter 7, p. 255) of 258 weeks of institutional training, based on the calculated expected rate and the actual rate for the participant group. Using the sum of £17.25 per week (p. 255) as the cost of such training this represents a 'saving' of £4,450 in this year alone, a year in which there was no expenditure on the social-work programme, which we must add to 'savings' for the evaluation period of £10,378: together almost the total cost of the project.

Author Index

Subject Index